IMAGES OF THE
MODERN VAMPIRE

IMAGES OF THE MODERN VAMPIRE
The Hip and the Atavistic

Edited by Barbara Brodman and James E. Doan

Fairleigh Dickinson University Press
Madison · Teaneck

Published by Fairleigh Dickinson University Press
Co-published with The Rowman & Littlefield Publishing Group, Inc.
4501 Forbes Boulevard, Suite 200, Lanham, Maryland 20706
www.rowman.com

10 Thornbury Road, Plymouth PL6 7PP, United Kingdom

British Library Cataloguing in Publication Information Available

Library of Congress Cataloging-in-Publication Data

Images of the modern vampire : the hip and the atavistic / edited by Barbara Brodman and James E. Doan.
    pages cm
  Includes bibliographical references and index.
  ISBN 978-1-61147-582-1 (cloth : alk. paper) — ISBN 978-1-61147-583-8 (electronic)
1. Vampires. I. Brodman, Barbara, editor of compilation. II. Doan, James E., editor of compilation.
  GR830.V3I58 2013
  398'.45—dc23   2013025471

♾™ The paper used in this publication meets the minimum requirements of American National Standard for Information Sciences—Permanence of Paper for Printed Library Materials, ANSI/NISO Z39.48-1992.

Printed in the United States of America

Contents

Acknowledgments

THIS BOOK, AND ITS PREDECESSOR *The Universal Vampire: Origins and Evolution of a Legend*, is the product of a vampires-in-the-mist experience that began in July 2006, when we both presented papers at the Conference on Icons and Iconoclasts at the University of Aberdeen, Scotland. Neither paper we presented then—Brodman's on the evolution of the 17th-century Don Juan legend and Doan's on Shakespeare's use of history in his plays—dealt specifically with the vampire. Over a few pints of stout, we began discussing parallels between Don Juan and the Byronic vampire anti-hero, which led to a paper, "From the Sensual to the Damned: Legends of Don Juan and the Vampire," that we subsequently presented at the 2008 National Popular Culture & American Culture Associations Conference in San Francisco. The topic stuck and led us to develop a book project that would explore in detail the origins and evolution of the legend.

We took our proposal to the International Conference on Vampires: Myths of the Past and the Future at the University of London in November 2011, gave out calls for papers, and were overwhelmed by the quality and quantity of the essays we received. We circulated additional calls for papers with equally impressive results, leading to the production of two impressive volumes on the Universal Vampire theme.

We would like to thank those friends and colleagues whose assistance made these books possible. Harry Keyishian, director of Fairleigh Dickinson University Press, and Brooke Bures, associate editor for the Rowman & Littlefield Publishing Group, made the challenges of turning an idea into a book easy and enjoyable. Ruth Nemire set us on the right course. At Nova Southeastern University, Dean Don Rosenblum and Director of Humanities Marlisa Santos gave us institutional support without which completion of this project would have been impossible. And our dear friend and colleague Suzanne Ferriss helped us in more ways than we can express, sharing her vast publishing experience with us unreservedly.

Introduction

Barbara Brodman and James E. Doan

IN *THE UNIVERSAL VAMPIRE: Origins and Evolution of a Legend*, we discussed the development of the vampire in the West from the early Norse *draugr* figure to the medieval European revenant and ultimately to Dracula, who first appeared as a vampire in Anglo-Irish Bram Stoker's novel *Dracula*, published in 1897. We also looked at the non-Western vampire in Native American and Mesoamerican traditions, Asian and Russian vampires in popular culture, and the vampire in contemporary novels, film and television. We continue the multicultural and multigeneric discussion in this volume, which traces the development of the postmodern vampire in films ranging from *Shadow of a Doubt* to *Blade*, *The Wisdom of Crocodiles* and *Interview with the Vampire*; the male and female vampires in the *Twilight* films, Sookie Stackhouse novels and *True Blood* television series; the vampire in African American women's fiction, Anne Rice's novels and the post-apocalyptic *I Am Legend*; and the vampires in Japanese anime. Finally, we present a new Irish Dracula play, adapted from the novel and set in 1888.

Part 1, "The Vampire in Modern Film," traces the development of the film vampire from its earliest depiction in Murnau's 1922 *Nosferatu* to the iconic *Shadow of a Doubt* (1943), though in the latter case more figurative than literal. One theme that links the two is the "perverse sexuality" revealed in Count Orlock's (and in the novel Dracula's) relationship with Mina, and Uncle Charlie's with his niece Charlie in the Hitchcock film, as explored in Victoria Williams's essay "Reflecting *Dracula*: The Un-dead in Alfred Hitchcock's *Shadow of a Doubt*." Similarly, we see this perversity in the "degenerate" Bulgarian vampire, Steven Grlscz, in relation to his victim, Anne

Levels, in *The Wisdom of Crocodiles* (1998). In this film and others from its era, such as *The Hunger* (1983), we note that the 19th-century vampire has a difficult time adapting to its un-dead life in the 20th century. As Murray Leeder suggests in the conclusion to his essay "'A Species of One': The Atavistic Vampire from *Dracula* to *The Wisdom of Crocodiles*," "Perhaps we can ultimately understand Steven Grlscz as being what the atavistic vampire becomes when sapped of that broader fin-de-siècle context: a sickly creature out of his proper time, a pathetic and anachronistic 'species of one.'" Melissa Olson's essay "Dracula the Anti-Christ: New Resurrection of an Immortal Prejudice" explores the inherent anti-Semitism found in *Dracula*, where the count is described with "hooked nose," "shifty eyes," "massive eyebrows" and "bushy hair." She sees this transferred to the film *Dracula 2000*, where he is portrayed as a reincarnation of Judas Iscariot and thus the ultimate anti-Christ, paving the way for new interpretations of the vampire. This section concludes with Simon Bacon's "Eat Me! The Morality of Hunger in Vampiric Cuisine," which demonstrates that we are not so much what we eat, but what we are eaten by. By using Emmanuel Levinas's notion of the possibility of transcendence through the ethical encounter with the hungry other, he shows that our relationship with the vampire becomes of vital importance. The un-dead are no longer our dark reflections from hell but are inextricably linked to our aspirations to enter heaven. Referring to film vampires such as *Twilight*'s Cullen Family, who disavow human spiritual ascendance, he calls for a return to old-fashioned bloodsuckers that will allow humans to exceed the limits of their earthbound flesh.

Part 2, "Race, Gender and the Vampire," delves into the theme of social protest in vampire arts and letters. In Donna Mitchell's "The Madonna and Child: Reevaluating Social Conventions through Anne Rice's Forgotten Females," feminist theory is applied to two leading female characters of Rice's *Vampire Chronicles*, Gabrielle and Claudia. "Following her rejection of the social expectations on the expectant mother, Gabrielle confesses that her greatest desire is to reject the many sexual inhibitions placed upon women," Mitchell tells us. And when Gabrielle goes on to state that "in this moment . . . I belong to no-one," Mitchell interprets this declaration as clearly indicating that Gabrielle feels trapped within the constraints that society has put on her life as an upper-class woman and that she has become "the aporetic embodiment of de Beauvoir's feminine and emancipated woman." A similar theme is pursued in Karin Hirmer's "Female Empowerment: Buffy and Her Heiresses in Control," though in this essay the author brings into question the degree of control exercised by any of the female protagonists of the most popular modern television vampire series, including *Buffy*.

The remaining three essays in this part of the collection focus on how the various manifestations of the vampire in film, literature and lore reflect the class struggles of particular historical eras. In "Lightening 'The White Man's Burden': Evolution of the Vampire from the Victorian Racialism of *Dracula* to the New World Order of *I Am Legend*," Cheyenne Mathews suggests that the vampire, who once held an inconsequential role in arcane pagan beliefs, later emerged as an explication for the discrepancy between old and new, superstition and science, and fiction and fact; while Zélie Asava, in "'You're Nothing to Me But Another . . . [White] Vampire': A Study of the Representation of the Black Vampire in American Mainstream Cinema," highlights filmic representations of the black vampire as signposts of certain cultural assumptions about race and gender that continue to endure today.

Last in this part of the collection is Marie-Luise Loeffler's "'She Would Be No Man's Property Ever Again': Vampirism, Slavery, and Black Female Heroism in Contemporary African American Women's Fiction," in which Loeffler analyzes black women authors' utilization of the trope of the vampire as a transgressive narrative strategy for the recovery of things (racial and cultural) forgotten and the tragedy of forgetfulness.

The third and final section of the collection, "New Readings of the Vampire," is a mélange of essays that examine what one might describe as the anti-vampire: a New Age vampire that shares little in appearance or action with its pre-21st-century predecessors. The focus of the first five of these essays is *Twilight*, with its vampires who abstain from human blood, sparkle like diamonds and display a controlled demeanor that stands in stark contrast to the obsessive behavior of a human heroine who strives to be like them. In "Blood-Abstinent Vampires and the Women Who Consume Them," Alaina Christensen applies the theories of Jean Baudrillard which examine the importance of "sign value" in a consumer society, and how the human body serves as "the finest consumer object": in *Twilight*, Bella and the readers' relationships to vampires are driven by the need to appropriate the signified value of their bodies for themselves. In his essay, "'*Exactly* My Brand of Heroin': Contexts and the Creation of the *Twilight* Phenomenon," Ben Murnane examines two identifying factors of a literary phenomenon: sales and a book's or series' impact on the broader culture, to both of which he attributes *Twilight*'s status as a literary-cultural phenomenon. Hope Jennings and Christine Wilson, in "Disciplinary Lessons: Myth, Female Desire, and the Monstrous Maternal in Stephenie Meyer's *Twilight* Series," go on to analyze one of "the most popular teen-girl novels of all time"—and potentially one of the largest cultural influences on young women coming of age during the early 21st century—in terms of its potential to glorify an anachronistic female role more at place in the 19th century than as a positive or realistic role model for 21st-century girls. Sarah Heaton's essay "Vampire Vogue and Female Fashion: Dressing Skin and Dressing-Up in the Sookie Stackhouse and *Twilight* Series" explores the complex relationship between clothing and the skin for both the human and the vampire in the two series. Bella's and Sookie's denial that they dress well feeds into anxieties about their bodies, skin and femininity, yet they have nothing to hide but themselves, whilst the vampires who have everything to hide all dress well. Batia Boe Stolar, in "The Politics of Reproduction in Stephanie Meyer's *Twilight* Saga," reveals that though the saga seems to reinforce conservative notions of family and procreation, allusions to biological advancements in the fields of cryogenics and cloning destabilize the saga's essentialist valorization of sex. It is this tension that further challenges and redefines the function of the vampire in an age that continues to strive for prolonging and enhancing the quality of life.

From the world of *Twilight* we move into the world of human-vampire chiropterans, chevaliers and Queens that is *Blood+*. In her essay "The Vampire from an Evolutionary Perspective in Japanese Animation: *Blood+*," Burcu Genç observes that "use of the scientific discourse of their day by *Blood+* creators domesticates the vampire in its own unique way with a passage from world of fantasy to that of science-fiction." We then bring the collection to a close not with a journey into the future but with a return to the roots of the Western European vampire legend. The last essay, "Adapting *Dracula* to an Irish Context: Reconfiguring the Universal Vampire," by James E. Doan and Barbara Brodman, incorporates a play written by Doan (*The Irish Dracula: A Melodrama in Five Acts*). And in this way, we bring our two-volume collection full circle to the beginnings of the European literary vampire in the 19th century.

I
THE VAMPIRE IN MODERN FILM

1

Reflecting *Dracula*: The Undead in Alfred Hitchcock's *Shadow of a Doubt*

Victoria Williams

THE UNDEAD APPEAR IN A NUMBER OF Alfred Hitchcock's films and fall into two main types. First, there is the undead love, including the ever-present Rebecca who haunts the living in the 1940 film of the same name and Madeleine who seems to return from the dead in *Vertigo* (1958). Then there are the undead killers, such as Mother in *Psycho* (1960), given a life of sorts by her murderous son's impersonation of her as he kills. It is, though, *Shadow of a Doubt* (1943) which sees Hitchcock present the ultimate undead character, the vampire, particularly the iconic vampire Count Dracula as depicted in Bram Stoker's novel, *Dracula*, through both visual imagery and narrative in the form of Uncle Charlie, played with brilliant, understated menace by Joseph Cotten. An uneasy interplay of ancient folklore and age-old concerns about violence and sexuality surrounds the figure of the vampire, a haunting presence from ancient legends and literature, and, from the first, *Shadow of a Doubt* presents Uncle Charlie as a monstrous, vampiric male, resting on his bed in Philadelphia with his hands resting across his stomach, as Jonathan Harker finds Dracula lying in his coffin in the graveyard of the Count's castle near the beginning of Stoker's tale. It is Uncle Charlie's habit to rest during the day, something his landlady encourages by pulling down the blind in his room so that he is free of sunlight. However, the blocking out of the daylight does not induce sleep in Uncle Charlie: rather he becomes alert, rising from his bed stiffly in the manner of Count Orlok rising from his coffin in the 1922 film *Nosferatu*, directed by F. W. Murnau, a director Hitchcock frequently cited as an influence on his own work as he admired Murnau's ability to conjure "a menacing atmosphere to provoke archaic fears."[1] In

Shadow of a Doubt Hitchcock investigates the ancient fears inherent in all vampire stories, yet he also recognizes the disturbing ambivalence of the vampire, who is at once terrifying yet sexually attractive, and he presents Uncle Charlie as dashing, yet terrible.

Apart from resting on his bed, the only other time that Uncle Charlie is shown to be stationary in Philadelphia is when he is hovering vampire-like over the city streets on a rooftop perch, surveying the detectives who would hunt him. By showing Uncle Charlie lying still in the darkness, Hitchcock establishes his villain as a daylight-dwelling monster and also directs the viewer to recognize the connection between Uncle Charlie and his niece, also known as Charlie, which will come to the fore later in the film, for Charlie is also shown prostrate on her bed the first time we see her. Indeed, as Maria Tatar and James McLaughlin have both pointed out, it seems that here Hitchcock is slyly suggesting the incestuous nature of the Uncle Charlie/Charlie relationship that becomes evident later in the film, for as the camera tracks from shots of the respective towns in which Uncle Charlie and his niece live, through windows and into their bedrooms to observe voyeuristically both recumbent in their beds, it is hinted that the two Charlies are lying abed thinking of each other in bed, or more precisely, they are thinking of being *in* bed with each other.[2] Incest is a barely concealed undertone of *Shadow of a Doubt* and acts as a metaphor to convey the transgressive power of Charlie's fierce attachment to desires which are personified by her uncle.[3]

Uncle Charlie may lie prostrate in the manner of, say Count Orlok, but he lies not in a cobweb-covered coffin but upon a particularly non-Gothic crocheted floral blanket. This is apt, for Uncle Charlie is a mundane vampire, an urban serial killer known as the Merry Widow Murderer as he feeds off the wealth of the rich widows he kills by strangulation, a method of killing which requires strong hands, such as those Dracula employs to force Mina Harker's lips to his breast, and a form of murder that focuses upon the neck as does a vampire's bite. Uncle Charlie gains his sustenance from his victims, whom he manages to ensnare by making himself attractive to them, a modus operandi he demonstrates when he charms his sister's widowed friend Mrs. Potter. Interestingly, Uncle Charlie is never shown eating despite his frequent appearances at his sister's dinner table, recalling the many times Dracula joins Jonathan Harker for supper yet does not eat. It is almost as though Uncle Charlie can forego physical nourishment as long as he can live off his victims.

Maurice Hindle states of Dracula, "For him, sex is power,"[4] and this is as true for Uncle Charlie as it is for Stoker's Count, since Hitchcock frequently highlights Uncle Charlie's sexuality by having him hold phallic objects, including cigars and a champagne bottle. Uncle Charlie is able to gain the cooperation of his victims by making himself irresistible, an allure which is in keeping with Dracula's ability to hypnotize his victims, a mesmerism which is often sexually charged.

Closely linked to Dracula's hypnotic powers is his telepathic link to Mina. This mental telepathy is mirrored by Uncle Charlie's seemingly telepathic bond to Charlie, who decides to telegraph her uncle, asking him to visit at the same time Uncle Charlie decides to travel westward to Charlie and the rest of his family in California. That Uncle Charlie can communicate telepathically points to his ability to transcend spatial limitations, as does his unexplained evasion of the pursuing detectives in the Philadelphia section of the film. Charlie recognizes the mental bridge between herself and her uncle for, on learning that her uncle is on his way, Charlie cries, "He heard me, he heard me." Charlie exclaims ecstatically that "he'll come for me," little realizing that her wish is the equivalent of inviting a vampire into her home of her own free will, for Uncle Charlie does indeed come for her as he has been summoned. It appears that Charlie so desired her uncle to come that her wish has been fulfilled. This likens Charlie to the females in *Dracula* who, it could be argued, subconsciously want the Count to come to them. Dracula does not, in general, invite victims into his castle; rather, his victims must initiate any interaction by calling to him.

So charismatic Uncle Charlie moves west to joins his sister's family, the Newtons, in Santa Rosa, California, just as Dracula travels from his home in Transylvania to London. According to the film's associate art director, Robert Boyle, Hitchcock chose Santa Rosa as the film's location as it "was the kind of place that didn't say where it was. It was American."[5] As *Shadow of a Doubt* was to be Hitchcock's first real American film, in that it was to be the first of his films set in America, as opposed to *Rebecca* and *Suspicion* (1941), Hitchcock wanted to get to the very heart of his adopted homeland, and to Hitchcock, Santa Rosa "spelled America more than any town."[6] It stood for an innocent America into which evil could, and would, enter. This evil is symbolized by the great plume of unnaturally black smoke which is belched out by the train carrying Uncle Charlie to Santa Rosa, literally blocking out the sun and casting a shadow across the station platform, an omen of imminent evil. That Uncle Charlie is a polluting entity is further hinted at through the smoke of his ever-present cigars and the car exhaust fumes with which he tries to gas Charlie.

The Newton house is typical Americana, warm and inviting. It is, according to Robert Boyle, "the kind of house where you didn't lock doors. It beckoned you to come in and be there. So all the influences, good and evil, could enter that house from any place":[7] "which, of course, they do, for the Newton home is the film's locus of terror as Uncle Charlie and Charlie play out a battle of wits and nerve as a police net closes in around them. While Boyle helped realize the big set-piece scenes of other Hitchcock classics, such as the traitor falling from the Statue of Liberty in *Saboteur* (1942) and the chase across Mount Rushmore in *North by Northwest* (1959), for *Shadow of a Doubt* no such stand-out scene was needed; rather, an encroaching sense of evil was required. To begin with, however, Uncle Charlie is a welcome visitor to the Newton home where he is reunited with the females he keeps in thrall to an almost incestuous degree, his adoring sister and Charlie. Interestingly, Mr. Newton, Uncle Charlie's brother-in-law, initially acts like the Transylvanian peasants in Stoker's tale and is superstitious and suspicious of his visitor until he, like so many others, is charmed by his wife's brother.

Throughout Hitchcock's catalogue of work characters resemble each other, as seen in the many instances of mistaken identity in films as diverse in tone as *North by Northwest* and *The Lodger* (1927), in which a visitor to a town is suspected of being a serial killer, though, unlike Uncle Charlie, the lodger is innocent. The doppelganger is an oft-discussed motif of *Vertigo*, but it is an equally important element in *Shadow of a Doubt* in which the doubling of characters takes on a "vividly vampiristic"[8] nature. The two Charlies are doubles of each other, sharing not just a name and a seemingly telepathic bond, but also, as relatives, a bloodline, something Charlie highlights when she exclaims, "We have the same blood."

Blood forms a link between Dracula and Mina too, for during Dracula's infernal baptism of Mina he forces her to drink from him, and Uncle Charlie appears to hint at his literary predecessor, stating, "The same blood flows through our veins, Charlie," thus recalling Dracula's words to Mina: "Flesh of my flesh, blood of my blood; kin of my kin."[9] However, there seems to be more than a familial, blood bond between the two Charlies. This is recognized by the characters themselves, for Charlie states, "We're not just an uncle and niece," which is something her uncle echoes, asserting, "We're no ordinary uncle and niece." Indeed, there does seem to be a romantic element to the relationship which borders perilously on the incestuous. Further, it is strongly hinted from the start that Charlie's closeness to her Uncle is unhealthy and damaging, for both characters are associated with sickness: Uncle Charlie's landlady asks if he is sick; on the train heading to Santa Rosa both the porter and fellow passengers discuss how ill Uncle Charlie seems as he keeps to his cabin as Dracula keeps to the hold on board the ship carrying him to England; and Charlie asks her uncle if he is sick when he disembarks from the train. Also, Charlie describes her whole family as sick. Thus it seems that the intense closeness shared by Charlie and her uncle registers in incest and issues of ill-ness and identity.

In *Dracula*, the Count exhibits a polymorphous quality, assuming various shapes (a bat, a dog and mist) and straddling boundaries: between life and death, and between nationalities as he disguises himself as the Englishman Jonathan Harker. Dracula also blurs the distinctions between various identities found in the family. For instance, during the scene in which he forces Mina to drink his blood as it spurts from his chest, the Count appears as a mother suckling a child, yet simultaneously he also resembles Mina's lover as the scene exhibits a dimension of horrific sexuality. That the roles of lover and giver of life are inextricably linked in the novel is further borne out by the nature of Arthur Holmwood's relationship to Lucy Westenra, for having saved his fiancé's life with a transfusion of his blood, Arthur reveals that he feels he has married the dying Lucy, thus linking life-providing blood with the bodily fluids associated with a wedding night. Such exchanges of bodily fluids represent a "perverse sexuality"[10] that challenges the natural laws of society. Similarly, the unnatural affinity between the Charlies is symbolized in the scene in which Uncle Charlie gives Charlie the ring of one of his victims. The scene calls to mind the initiation scene between Dracula and Mina, as it is apparent to the viewer that the ring symbolizes an extra degree of closeness between uncle and niece. The scene resembles a proposal scene from a romantic movie as Charlie's face lights up on receiving the jewelry, and while she suggests that she and her uncle are "sort of like twins," it is apparent that really they are more "sort of" like lovers, thereby recalling the sexual dimension of the relationship between Dracula and Mina. Charlie desires interaction with her victimizing uncle for she feels he will rescue her from the dull ordinariness of everyday life that she identifies as "dinner, then dishes, then bed," and she treads a thin line between intellectual knowledge and sexual knowledge, coyly teasing him that she knows he harbors a secret, "[s]omething secret and wonderful, and I'll find it out." Charlie is partly correct in this regard for, although he is a serial-killing monster, Uncle Charlie is also a "dark rescuer"[11] who saves Charlie from her stultifying existence, a confining boredom represented by the thin vertical strips of light and shadow that pervade the Newton home, forming imprisoning bars. Into this humdrum Santa Rosa universe, Uncle Charlie brings adventure, charisma and drama.

The arrival of Uncle Charlie sees Charlie head towards sexual maturation. Though Adam Knee states that Charlie is clearly presented as a young adult possessing a sense of responsibility that marks her as emotionally mature,[12] I would argue that her infatuation with her uncle marks her out as emotionally immature, an immaturity which is highlighted through her dress, which becomes increasingly adult as the film progresses, with Charlie graduating from form-concealing baggy coats to figure-hugging suits by the end of the film. This change of costume reveals how Charlie's sexuality blossoms on the arrival of her attractive and charming uncle, for she reacts to his attentions by dressing in a more mature fashion. Sexual allure plays a large part in

Uncle Charlie's success as a serial killer, for the reason he proves irresistible to his female victims is that to them he appears to be something other than he is. Uncle Charlie is a master of dissemblance. Indeed, like Dracula, Uncle Charlie is a symbolic mirror revealing the monstrous potential of seemingly attractive masculinity, and again, like Stoker's Count, Uncle Charlie must be destroyed by the end of the film as he exhibits a "terrible duplicity of appearance"[13] which, when combined with a perverse narcissist egotism and unnatural sexual desires, threatens the cultural values and social distinctions held dear by society. The only times in the film that Uncle Charlie takes his true form both come, significantly, at night—once at the dinner table in which he describes his victims as "fat wheezing animals," and once when he takes Charlie to a bar where he tells his niece, "I brought you nightmares." Uncle Charlie's charm is such, though, that even though the viewer knows of his crimes, we almost forgive him for them. Though he is shrewd and cynical and his pathology runs frighteningly deep, Uncle Charlie presents his reasons for murder, materialistic though they are, with a veneer of idealism that is highly attractive. Uncle Charlie depends on his true murderous nature going unnoticed and so is averse to being photographed because he knows that the camera can unmask him, with the camera as a corollary to the vampire's aversion to mirrors, cameras and celluloid as is entrenched in cinematic vampire-lore. As Michael Walker points out, the manner of Uncle Charlie's unmasking is ambiguous for, despite Uncle Charlie's best efforts to avoid being photographed, Detective Saunders does manage to take his picture and, through sleight of hand, is able to keep hold of the film despite Uncle Charlie's efforts to obtain it. Presumably the picture is sent to detectives in the East for identification, yet nothing more is heard of this photograph.[14] At the end of the film, only Charlie and Detective Graham know of Uncle Charlie's guilt, so does this mean that Uncle Charlie could not be identified from the picture because the photograph turned out to be blank? If so, it seems that the reason Uncle Charlie refuses to be photographed is that he knows that as a vampiric being his image cannot be captured on film, and he refuses to allow his picture to be taken to stop others from learning his secret.

Interestingly, the only female who does not fall for Uncle Charlie's charm is Charlie's younger sister, Anne. As a young girl she is too young to succumb to her uncle's sexual magnetism and rather is repulsed by him, scorning his childish presents and games and refusing to sit next to him at dinner. Another reason for Anne's dislike of her uncle is that she is well acquainted with literary vampires. In an almost throwaway line the bibliophilic Anne is instructed to tell "the story of Dracula" to another character. Hitchcock reportedly changed the shooting script's reference from one to the story of *Dr. Jekyll and Mr. Hyde* to a *Dracula* reference,[15] which more than likely reveals that the director recognized the vampiric elements of his film. It also seems that, having read Stoker's novel, Anne subconsciously sees through her uncle's charming exterior to his true character, unlike Charlie, whom Anne admonishes for not reading as much as she should. Maybe if Charlie had borrowed her sister's copy of *Dracula* she would have been better prepared for her uncle's visit?

Towards the end of the film, Charlie realizes her uncle is a killer. She not only comes to see that he is a serial murderer but also that he wishes to kill her, having cut through her staircase and locked her in a gas-filled garage. This forces Charlie to discover her own murderous potential, as she calmly warns her uncle that she could kill him herself, thus reflecting the vampire's ability to contaminate others, especially innocent females. Indeed, at one point in the film, Charlie does seem to have taken on characteristics of the vampire for, having become suspicious of her uncle, Charlie decides to visit the local library in order to check a newspaper story which she feels pertains to her charismatic relative. Charlie runs to the library, encountering the ire of a local policeman after she jaywalks, a transgression which is quickly followed by another, for Charlie arrives at the library after the end of opening hours and has to beg to be let in, echoing the vampire's traditional asking for admittance. Therefore, Charlie has experienced two negative interactions with those who maintain law and order—a policeman and a librarian—and though the rules Charlie has broken are undoubtedly low-level, they do, nonetheless, signal that Charlie is now willing to act outside of the law and, if necessary, to take on the role of renegade while searching for the truth about her uncle. Charlie's new-found willingness to disrupt society reveals how proximity to Uncle Charlie is corrupting. The librarian allows Charlie to enter the building, whereupon Charlie finds circumstantial evidence that Uncle Charlie is a killer: initials etched on the ring he produced earlier in the film match the initials of one of the Merry Widow Murderer's victims. This is the turning point of the film, for Charlie now knows her uncle's murderous *alter ego*, and what is more, Charlie can prove her suspicions with the ring as evidence. The discovery changes Charlie's perception of the world for she now knows that the man she adores is hazardous to females, with the ring now morphing from a symbol of both romantic and familial affinity to a symbol of her descent into danger. Charlie now acknowledges her uncle's murderous qualities and, momentarily, she exhibits vampire-like qualities of her own, for, following the night-time visit to the library, Charlie sleeps all through the next day and does not wake until sundown. Having transformed to some degree into a dangerous creature, Charlie now has the power to harm her uncle, for the ring, which was a symbol of unity, is now both an object of conflict and a symbol of her empowerment. The ring is proof of her uncle's crimes, and as long as Charlie keeps possession of the ring, she has power over her uncle.

Throughout the film Charlie is described as a "typical girl" and an "average girl from an average family," but now she must act in a way that is not ordinary—by fighting off her "vampire" relative/lover and spying on him for the police in the way that Mina spies remotely upon Dracula as he flees back to Transylvania from London. Proximity to Uncle Charlie has irrevocably changed Charlie, with her innocence gone forever. Once she discovers Uncle Charlie's secret, she can never un-learn what she knows. It is the shifting perception of the female characters—Charlie, and to a lesser extent her mother and younger sister—which produces fear on the part of the viewer. As the central investigative figure of the film, Charlie is required to acquire knowledge and understand the situation around her, and events in the film are understood in relation to her, as they are in relation to any heroine of the female Gothic genre,[16] the genre to which *Shadow of a Doubt* could be said best to belong. Charlie's transition from immature innocent to suspicious investigator echoes her journey from childhood to adulthood, as she learns concurrently about evil, sexuality and responsibility. While her confrontation with Uncle Charlie means she has acquired self-knowledge, it also means that she is now aware of the sinister aspects of society which she had previously either been unaware of or had merely regarded as imaginary tales as told to her by Anne or as her father's childish murder games with his next-door neighbor. Now, though, Charlie realizes that such dark goings-on are real and present in the society in which she lives, for she has glimpsed the "dark heart of patriarchy"[17] which lies at the centre of the female Gothic genre.

The end of the film sees Charlie triumph over her uncle, inhabiting the role of the naive, attractive young woman threatened by the vampire, but one who is also instrumental in the vampire's destruction, similar to Mina's "hypnotic reports"[18] on Dracula's plans and Count Orlok's inability to resist the blood of an innocent past the cock's crow in *Nosferatu*. Having managed to evade the police, who wrongly believe another man to be the Merry Widow Murderer, Uncle Charlie has lined up his next victim, installing the gullible Mrs. Potter on board the train on which he is leaving Santa Rosa. Uncle Charlie differs from Dracula in that he does not wish to spread his domination throughout a new land as Dracula does by moving to London: nevertheless, Uncle Charlie is always on the look-out for new victims, and it is made clear that Mrs. Potter's being on the train with him is no fluke by the coy wave of acknowledgement she gives Uncle Charlie from the other end of the train carriage. However, before Uncle Charlie is able to run off with Mrs. Potter, he has one last chore to complete. Thus he lures Charlie onto the train, waits for it to pull out, and then attempts to throw her from the moving carriage. However, Charlie manages to out-manoeuvre her uncle one final time, and it is Uncle Charlie who dies under the wheels of an oncoming train—presumably decapitated in the traditional manner for the undead. All would seem to end happily ever after for Charlie, her family and the rest of America. Uncle Charlie has been defeated, and Charlie has found a more appropriate love interest in the shape of Mr. Graham, one of her uncle's policeman pursuers. It seems more than likely that Charlie will marry Graham, for it has already been revealed that Mrs. Newton "thinks girls ought to marry and settle down," and who better for a typical American girl to wed than an upholder of the law? However, just as at the end of *Dracula*, ambiguities remain. The film's conclusion seems to suggest that Uncle Charlie's demise is in some way a defeat for Charlie for with her uncle's death comes the end of her own dreams and aspirations for a more exciting life as she will now have to settle for a life of dull domesticity as did her mother, the very life she disparaged at the start of the film. It seems Charlie will lose her identity as her mother did when she went from being the rather grandly named Emma Spencer Oakley to plain old Mrs. Newton, a transformation which Hitchcock depicts as an act of loss, for Mrs. Newton states, "Charles went away and I got married, and . . . Then you know how it is. You sort of lose yourself. You're your husband's wife." That Mrs. Newton never quite finishes her dialogue (because Hitchcock fades to black during her tearful speech of self-reflection) emphasizes her sense of loss and regret at losing her identity and hints that Charlie may face a similar fate since Charlie is expected to follow the pattern established by her mother. It almost seems as though in *Shadow of a Doubt* Hitchcock depicts two different ways in which patriarchy deadens women: the real, physical death which Uncle Charlie brings to his victim-wives and the symbolic death inflicted on women when they marry. The film also suggests that Uncle Charlie's dark legacy will infect generations of Newtons to come. At the end of *Dracula* Jonathan Harker reflects on the death of Quincey Morris in pursuit of the Count and states that he hopes "some of our brave friend's spirit has passed into"[19] the son he has produced with Mina. However, this is forgetting that something else will have passed into his son, namely Dracula's blood. Throughout the novel Renfield repeatedly states, "The blood is the life,"[20] and so it is logical to conclude that contaminated vampire blood flows through Mina's child since Mina is described by Van Helsing as "tainted . . . with that Vampire baptism."[21] Thus, with Charlie cast in the Mina role, it seems that her offspring will inherit some of Uncle Charlie's demonic genes. Indeed, it is suggested that Uncle Charlie's traits are already present in the rest of the younger generation of Newtons, for Charlie's brother enjoys being doted upon as did Uncle Charlie when he was a child, and even Anne's precocious bookishness echoes that of her uncle in his youth. Thus it seems that disquieting patterns of behavior are already manifest. Also, throughout *Shadow of a Doubt* Hitchcock presents a dark view of humanity, suggesting that the potential for evil must be regulated within all of us—and there are hints that there may be something not quite right with the all-American Newton family, of which Uncle Charlie is part, after all. For instance, Mr. Newton is a murder-obsessive, continually plotting imaginary killings, and his wife is emotionally overwrought with an attitude towards her brother that seems almost more romantic than familial, thereby echoing Charlie's incestuous emotional attachment to her uncle. This incestuous adoration is highlighted in the scene in which Uncle Charlie makes eye contact with Mrs. Newton while handling a suggestively shaped champagne bottle. Uncle Charlie points the bottle at his sister, causing her to laugh, which seems to suggest that Mrs. Newton acknowledges the sexual nature of the action. Further, it is not only the Newtons who will continue to be haunted by the legacy of Uncle Charlie, for the final shots of the film show Uncle Charlie's funeral cortege as a clergyman praises his character. It seems that the Santa Rosa townsfolk will continue to talk glowingly about Uncle Charlie, praising his benevolence and fondly remembering the glamour he brought to the town. Thus, in keeping with the vampire tradition, it would seem that death is not the end for Uncle Charlie, for his presence will continue to haunt the living.

Distributed by Universal Pictures, *Shadow of a Doubt* reflects the film studio's history as a distributor of iconic Hollywood interpretations of key Gothic texts such as *Dracula* (1931), *Frankenstein* (1931), *The Phantom of the Opera* (1925 and 1929) and *The Invisible Man* (1933), films that, like *Shadow of a Doubt*, are concerned with themes of double identity and violence. Peter Bogdanovic has stated that *Shadow of a Doubt* has "a more realistic feel than many of Hitchcock's pictures, than maybe any of his pictures,"[22] yet despite the lack of "gloomy artificiality"[23] which is the hallmark of the Gothic film, *Shadow of a Doubt* is, conversely, one of the most indebted to the supernatural of all of Hitchcock's oeuvre. Drawing on the Gothic past of Stoker and Universal, *Shadow of a Doubt* posits vampire references as central to the film's structure and signification, yet the film transports the vampire from the realm of the supernatural to the everyday in order to suggest the evil that can lurk beneath attractive exteriors. Just as *Dracula* portrays the transgression of meanings, identities and natural family boundaries through the movements of vampiric energy and desires,[24] so *Shadow of a Doubt* explores the erosion of both the nuclear family and social boundaries and reveals the corruptibility of the American Dream.

Notes

1. Bettina Rosenbladt, "Doubles and Doubts in Hitchcock: The German Connection" in *Hitchcock: Past and Present*, ed. Richard Allen and Sam Ishii-Gonzales (London: Routledge, 2004), 46.

2. Both Maria Tatar in her *Secrets beyond the Door: The Story of Bluebeard and his Wives* (Princeton, NJ: Princeton University Press, 2004), 140; and James McLaughlin in his essay "All in the Family: Alfred Hitchcock's *Shadow of a Doubt*," in *A Hitchcock Reader*, ed. Marshall Deutelbaum and Leland A. Poague, 2nd ed. (Chichester, UK: Blackwell Publishing, 2009), 146, discuss the symbolic nature of Hitchcock's through-the-window shots.

3. McLaughlin, "All in the Family," 146.

4. Bram Stoker, *Dracula*, ed. Maurice Hindle, rev. ed. (London: Penguin Books, 2003), xxxiii.

5. *Beyond Doubt: The Making of Hitchcock's Favourite Film*, dir. Laurent Bouzereau (Universal Studios Home Video, 2000), DVD Extra.

6. *Beyond Doubt.*

7. *Beyond Doubt.*

8. McLaughin, "All in the Family," 146.

9. Stoker, *Dracula*, 306.

10. Fred Botting, *Gothic* (London: Routledge, 1996), 150.

11. Tatar, *Secrets beyond the Door*, 143.

12. Adam Knee, "Shadow of a Doubt" in *After Hitchcock: Influence, Imitation and Intertextuality*, ed. David Boyd and R. Barton Palmer (Austin: University of Texas Press, 2006), 54.

13. Botting, *Gothic*, 149.

14. Michael Walker, *Hitchcock's Motifs* (Amsterdam: Amsterdam University Press, 2005), 287.

15. Bill Krohn, quoted in Knee, "Shadow of a doubt," 51.

16. Tatar, *Secrets beyond the Door*, 141.

17. Rosenbladt, "Doubles and Doubts in Hitchcock," 56.

18. Stoker, *Dracula*, 358.

19. Stoker, *Dracula*, 402.

20. Stoker, *Dracula*, 152, 249.

21. Stoker, *Dracula*, 388.

22. *Beyond Doubt.*

23. Botting, *Gothic*, 166.

24. Botting, *Gothic*, 150.

2

A Species of One: The Atavistic Vampire from *Dracula* to *The Wisdom of Crocodiles*

Murray Leeder

"THE COUNT IS A CRIMINAL AND OF CRIMINAL TYPE," says Mina Harker in Bram Stoker's *Dracula* (1897). "Nordau and Lombroso would so classify him, and *qua* criminal he is of imperfectly formed mind."[1] She is following Professor Van Helsing's line of reasoning, as he has just characterized Dracula as a born criminal "predestined to crime." Van Helsing also says, "The criminal has no full man-brain. He is clever and cunning and resourceful . . . but he be of child brain in much."[2] These lines seem very puzzling to a modern reader. Dracula certainly is a criminal in that he violates the laws of England, but he is so much more than that. He is a satanic heretic, a centuries-dead warlord, a bloodsucking demon from Hell, so why characterize him as something so everyday as a criminal?

The word "criminal" had different connotations in the late Victorian period, related to attempts to apply Darwinian theory on the social level. The criminal was an atavistic figure of degeneration, less human than human, who might one day rise en masse and undo modern evolution and progress. The Count, whatever else he may be, is a supernatural instantiation of this degenerate super-criminal. Though *Dracula*'s evolutionary subtext is draped in fin de siècle social tensions and in some ways fails to resonate today, it has passed on to subsequent vampire narratives.

In a previous essay, I made this argument in brief with respect to *Fright Night* (1985), where the vampire Jerry Dandridge (Chris Sarandon) is an ancient figure who launches an invasion into the modern world. His house provides a structural model for the relationship of the past and present, with upper floors as a dusty but well-tended private museum and a basement that

is a cluttered mess of the detritus of history. Dandridge shares with Dracula
the need to sleep in a coffin full of his native earth, signifying his inability to
truly belong and escape the savage past of his origins, no matter how much
he pretends at being a modern figure. Dandridge's fiery death sees him transformed into a serpentine figure, something like a dragon or a dinosaur, an in-
triguing detail hinting at his origin as a primordial predator from mankind's
evolutionary past.[3] This chapter will further develop an understanding of the
atavistic vampire through an analysis of a very different, and in many ways
less conventional, vampire film, Po-Chih Leong's *The Wisdom of Crocodiles*
(1998; also released as *Immortality*). Like Stoker's Count Dracula, the vam-
pire/serial killer protagonist of *The Wisdom of Crocodiles*, Stephen Grlscz
(Jude Law), is constructed as an atavist, a throwback in humanity's midst
who blurs the boundaries between humanity and its evolutionary ancestors.
Unlike the Count, however, Grlscz possesses little or no apocalyptic potential,
and is finally seen as a pathetic and sickly anachronism.

Dracula was one of the first vampire tales set in the present day rather than
in a generic Gothic past,[4] and it was also among the first to rationalize the
supernatural with appeals to current science.[5] Various scholars have explored
how *Dracula* is suffused in late Victorian tensions about evolution, degeneration and criminality.[6] Bram Dijkstra calls it a work in which "[t]he cultural
preoccupation around 1900 with the struggle of evolutionary progress against
the forces of bestiality and degeneration was dramatized most coherently
and consistently,"[7] and David J. Skal agrees that "Stoker achieved a zeitgeist
evocation of atavistic debasement that nonetheless proffered a kind of human
immortality, however compromised and hellish."[8]

Via Mina, Stoker references two key thinkers of degeneration to lend cre-
dence to his construction of the Count as a degenerate supercriminal. Cesare
Lombroso (1835–1909), the famed Italian criminologist, reconceived the
criminal (in particular the "born criminal," who like the Count is predestined
to crime) as an "atavistic" throwback to mankind's evolutionary past. Atavism describes the supposed tendency of certain human beings within a large
sample of the population to show characteristics of their evolutionary ancestors. Stephen Jay Gould sums up Lombroso's views on criminality this way:
"Criminals are evolutionary throwbacks in our midst. Germs of an ancestral
past lie dormant in our heredity. In some unfortunate individuals, the past
comes to life again. These people are innately driven to act as a normal ape or
savage would, but such behavior is deemed criminal in our civilized society."[9]
Lombroso implicitly endorsed European bourgeois modernity as the epitome
of human evolution and located in born-degenerate criminals characteristics closer to animals and non-Caucasian peoples, as well as children and
women.[10] He backed up these assertions with detailed measurements taken

from Italian prisoners. In Lombroso's key text, *The Criminal Man*, originally printed in Italian in 1876, one may read that 28 percent of criminals have handle-shaped ears "as in the chimpanzee," and that many criminals display a uniformity of their teeth, "a peculiarity of gorillas and ourang-outangs." Twelve percent of criminals display an unusual number of ribs, either more or fewer, "an atavistic character common to animals and lower or prehistoric human races . . . contrasting with the numerical uniformity characteristic of civilized mankind." Criminal chins are either "small and receding, as in children, or else excessively long, short or flat, as in apes," while criminal ears are often atrophied, assuming a form "common to apes," and their limbs often have the "ape-like character" of a span that exceeds their total height. Some criminals even have a "prolongation of the coccyx, sometimes tufted with hair" . . . a tail! Lombroso also asserts that criminal noses often "rise like an isolated peak from the swollen nostrils, a form found among the Akkas, a tribe of pygmies of Central Africa." The foot is often flat, "as in negroes." Degenerates often display prehensile feet "and an elongated big toe, with which, like the Japanese, they are able to clasp objects."[11]

Lombroso's disciple Max Nordau (1849–1923), the other name Stoker places in Mina's mouth, was the scholar who most famously framed the struggle between evolution and degeneration as an apocalyptic struggle for the future of humanity. Nordau's 1892 opus *Degeneration* is dedicated to Lombroso, and it takes the degenerative hypothesis behind Lombroso's criminology onto a broader social plane. Nordau writes, "Degenerates are not always criminals, prostitutes, anarchists and pronounced lunatics; they are often authors and artists. These, however, manifest the same mental characteristics and for the most part the same somatic features . . . who satisfy their unhealthy impulses [not] with the knife of an assassin or the bomb of the dynamiter [but] instead with pen and pencil."[12] The targets of Nordau's acid pen include Ibsen, Whitman, Tolstoy, Zola, Verlaine, Nietzsche, Wagner, Wilde, Swinburne and Baudelaire, all of whom he assesses as being atavistic criminals wearing the guise of artists and writers. Indeed, the phrase "degenerate art" later adopted by the Nazis is of Nordau's coinage (a supreme irony, considering that Nordau was a Jew and an ardent Zionist). For Nordau and many of his contemporaries, the atavistic criminal was no trivial figure but one brimming with apocalyptic potential who aimed at nothing less than the degeneration of society into primitive anarchy. For Nordau, the fin de siècle represented "the dusk of nations," a decadent end-time pregnant with tensions of all sorts:

> Massed in the sky the clouds are aflame in the weirdly beautiful glow which was observed for the space of years after the eruption of Krakatoa. Over the earth

the shadows creep with deepening gloom wrapping all objects in a mysterious dimness, in which all certainty is destroyed and any guess seems plausible. Forms lose their outlines and are dissolved in a floating mist. The day is over, the night draws on. The old anxiously watch its approach, fearing they will not live to see the end.[13]

This lurid scene represents the world into which Dracula emerges, an active agent of degeneration bent on pulling evolved England down to the level of evolutionarily stagnant Transylvania.

As described by Stoker, the Count's hairy and bestial appearance[14] seems heavily drawn from descriptions of the criminal man. As Jonathan Harker first describes the Count, his features read like a roll-call of Lombroso's suspect features: the "high bridge of the thin nose and peculiarly arched nostrils," a "lofty domed forehead," "hair growing scantily round the temples," "massive eyebrows," and "peculiarly sharp white teeth" that protrude over his lips even when his mouth is closed. Add to this the rank breath; pointed ears; broad, squat fingers and hairy palms,[15] and Dracula emerges as an absolute model criminal. Stoker's use of Lombroso goes far beyond these obvious and superficial borrowings. For Lombroso, the atavistic criminal is the relic of an ancient race. So too is the Count, a sort of living fossil who boasts of his ancestry from the Huns and the superiority of his bloodlines to those of the Hapsburgs and Romanoffs in his only lengthy speech[16]—a proud atavist, he is a criminal who openly admires other criminals. According to Van Helsing, in invading England he is obsessively repeating the actions of his ancestors,[17] much in the same way that Lombroso insists criminals, even ingenious ones, are limited to repetitive patterns of behavior. This is one of our heroes' greatest advantages over the Count, says Van Helsing:

> The criminal always work at one crime—that is the true criminal who seems predestinate to crime, and who will of none other. This criminal has not full man brain. He is clever and cunning and resourceful, but he be not of man stature as to brain. He be of child brain in much. Now this criminal of ours is predestinate to crime also. He, too, have child brain, it is of the child to do what he have done.[18]

We may be comforted to know that we enjoy such advantages over criminals, even vampire ones. But darker implications creep in as well. For if Stoker has his protagonists deploy England's advancement (framed in quasi-evolutionary terms) and such modern technologies as the telegraph, railway, typewriter, phonograph and Winchester repeating rifle against Dracula, he also has Van Helsing affirm that it is England's very progress that makes it a tempting target for the Count: "leaving his own barren land—barren of people—and coming to a new land where life of man teems till they are like the multitude of standing corn."[19] Evolution and progress open the possibility of degeneration and atavism. Jonathan Harker famously states, while trapped inside Castle Dracula and having observed the Count crawl down the side of the castle like a lizard, that "the old centuries had, and have powers of their own which mere 'modernity' cannot kill,"[20] but the truth is even more terrifying: modernity *contains* the ancient, an atavistic specter that might crawl back to the surface at any time, especially when it seems to be the most under control. As R. J. Dingley correctly observes, "The appeal of Bram Stoker's novel, both for its original readers and for us, is that it creates a myth capable simultaneously of exposing and exorcising potential sources of spiritual, political and moral crisis. [It is] at once alarmist and anodyne."[21]

Steven Grlscz in *The Wisdom of Crocodiles* has no grand designs to overthrow civilization and degrade modern progress. He is a very different sort of vampire for a different age, but one whose construction is no less rooted in degenerate conceptions of criminality. One of the cycle of art film–vampire film hybrids in the 1990s that also included Michael Almereyda's *Nadja* (1994), Abel Ferrara's *The Addiction* (1995) and Larry Fessenden's *Habit* (1995),[22] *The Wisdom of Crocodiles* has fallen into obscurity, in spite of containing an early Jude Law leading role. No reference to it, for instance, appears in all 908 pages of the latest edition of J. Gordon Melton's *The Vampire Book* (2011).[23] If it shares something with its art house brethren of the 90s, it also has certain affinities with *The Hunger* (1983), another chic reimagining of the vampire that discarded many of the old conventions in favor of a sun-drenched cinematography and a vampire who is as much a medical specimen as a supernatural monster. Neither film uses the word "vampire" at any point. In fact, if we define a vampire as "a reanimated corpse that sustains its immortality by feeding on blood, and in doing so, drains his victim's life force and transforms the victim into a likeness of itself,"[24] Grlscz fails utterly; he does not seem to be able to create new vampires, and there is no hint that he is a reanimated corpse.

Despite its revisionist qualities, however, *The Wisdom of Crocodiles* retains at least a few important qualities of *Dracula*, including an appeal to contemporary science in order to lend a measure of scientific credibility to its vampire. The film certainly echoes *Dracula* in its London setting and the presence of an Eastern European vampire (Grlscz identifies his vowel-free name as Bulgarian) living unsuspected in the anonymity of the modern metropolis.[25] The film's London is a sleek and cold world of steel, glass and concrete, and the ease with which Grlscz occupies it reflects the "reconfiguration of the vampire from a premodern monster to an urban flâneur, increasingly at home in the city."[26] Grlscz is unencumbered by such conventional vampire weaknesses as sunlight and the cross. He eats food without trouble and appears outwardly human, but he also possesses amazing abilities, some of them uncommon (the ability to write with one hand and simultaneously sketch with the other), and some of which are clearly superhuman (inhuman speed, reflexes, strength and senses). He drinks blood to live, but not just anyone's blood: it needs to be the blood of a woman who loves him, since he actually subsists on a chemical residue produced by the emotion of love. Grlscz works as a medical researcher who focuses on crystals found in human bladders and kidneys that are produced by severe emotional states: rage, resentment, malice, fury, spite, despair. "Emotions are things," he tells Anne Levels (Elina Löwensohn), the film's female protagonist and his intended victim. "Your blood carries every emotion it's possible to feel . . . Love is what I feed on, what I eat." After feeding, he painfully spits up crystals of his own created by the negative emotions contained in the women's blood alongside the love. Simultaneously suggesting a scientist doing medical research and a serial killer taking souvenirs from his victims, he stores these crystals in cases marked with the name of the unfortunate woman who died to prolong his existence. When he goes too long without feeding, Grlscz becomes sickly, resembling someone suffering from anemia (pallid skin), hemophilia (extreme vulnerability to even simple wounds) or perhaps the bodily degeneration associated with the late stages of AIDS.

Like Dracula, Grlscz is driven by the basic, repetitive drives that Lombroso applies to the born criminal. He must endlessly repeat the process of finding a woman, making her fall in love with him and drinking her blood. A natural predator, Grlscz gravitates towards the vulnerable, focusing on one woman after her failed suicide attempt and fixating on Anne after observing her hyperventilating from an asthma attack. Caroline Joan (Kay) Picart and Cecil Greek locate Grlscz as a point of contact between the classic vampire and the serial killer, perhaps the key modern criminal icon.[27] Like Hannibal Lecter, Grlscz conceals his criminal nature beneath surface gentility and charisma and is contrasted against a much more thuggish group of London street criminals who may superficially come closer to Lombroso's criminal type. Grlscz hides his true nature, but he is a well-dressed (in all senses) imposter in humanity's midst. In voiceover, he describes himself as a "species of one . . . a creature . . . a crocodile who needs a job, who needs a bank account, a place to live." The film's title refers to words written by Francis Bacon in 1625 that critique self-centered wisdom as animalistic and inhumane: "Wisdom for a man's self is, in many branches thereof, a depraved thing. It is the wisdom of rats, that will be sure to leave a house somewhat before it fall; it is the wisdom of the fox that thrusts out the badger who digged and made room for him; it is the wisdom of crocodiles, that shed tears when they would devour."[28] Bacon here alludes to the myth that crocodiles cry as they feed, but that these tears do not express emotions (reptiles, it is assumed, possess none). In the film's opening sequence, we see Grlscz feigning sympathy and love as he lures, seduces and ultimately feeds upon his latest victim, a suicidal woman named Maria Vaughn (Kerry Fox), and throughout the rest of the film we are constantly given to wonder whether he possesses human emotions at all or simply mimes them for his own purposes.

In her article "Dracula: The Reptilian Brain at the Fin de Siècle," Valerie Clemens argues that Dracula's characterization is closer to a reptile than more obvious animal candidates like bats and wolves. Like the lizard, she says, "Dracula is actually a very limited being whose activities are entirely dominated by his drives for food, safety and the reproduction of his species."[29] She draws on a theory in neuroscience that was most famously outlined by Paul D. McLean in *The Triune Brain in Evolution: Role in Paleocerebral Functions* (1990), but which is traceable back to the foundation of contemporary neuroscience in the late 19th century, especially the discoveries of Paul Broca. *The Wisdom of Crocodiles* draws on McLean's work explicitly, with Grlscz recounting the basics as he lies in postcoital rest with Anne: "I once knew this doctor, a neurologist. And he told me that we don't have one brain. We have three. One that is human, built over another that is mammalian, built over yet another that's reptilian. So, when a psychiatrist asks you to lie down on the couch, you're being asked to lie down with a horse, and with a crocodile." On another occasion, we hear a snatch of voiceover that presumably comes from Grlscz's neurologist: "Our brains are very old. From a neurologist's point of view, no one is entirely human. At some level, everyone has four legs. At a level below that, everyone has sharp teeth." In McLean's model of the triune brain, the basal ganglia, or the "reptilian formation," are the seat of instinctual and basic impulses, including aggression and territoriality. The paleomammalian formation, or limbic system, has "the capacity to generate free-floating, affective feelings conveying a sense of what is real, true and important."[30] Finally, the neomammalian formation, constituted by the neocortex and thalamic structures, allows rational thinking and advanced judgments, and thereby human relationships and human society.[31] The psychiatric context of Grlscz's explanation to Anne evokes the triune brain model's broad homologies with Freud's triadic model of the psyche: the id as reptilian (base instincts), the ego as paleomammalian (subjectivity) and the superego as neomammalian (higher feelings like morality and shame).

Anne tells Grlscz about having shoplifted a watch as a teenager, an action that she still cannot explain since she had the money in her pocket to buy it. She asks Grlscz, "[W]as that the horse or the crocodile" acting within her as she stole the watch against her better (presumably human) nature? The film emphasizes that it is not merely within monsters like Grlscz that darker impulses are operative. On another occasion, Grlscz states to Healey (Timo-thy Spall), the police inspector he befriends, "What everyone wants is for evil people to be off somewhere insidiously committing evil deeds. Then they can be separate from ordinary men and women and destroyed. But the line that separates good and evil cuts through every human heart. And who is willing to destroy a piece of his own heart?" Salli J. Kline, in a particularly percep-tive observation, writes that in making the Count both a born criminal and a Satanic personification of evil, Stoker "consciously established a connection that was . . . inherent in the degenerate hypothesis all along. The whole pur-pose of the theory was to explain evil in positivistic medical terms."[32] So even though *The Wisdom of Crocodiles* sometimes poses questions of good and evil in moral and religious terms and sometimes in scientific, evolutionary ones (how is it possible to reconcile the crocodile, the horse and the human?), there is no necessary conflict; in fact, the film helps expose the natural affinities between these two sets of discourses.

The film's religious themes play out principally with respect to Healey. The inspector is becoming a Catholic, and his rebirth through baptism is contrasted with Grlscz's inability to escape his nature. His crucifix is stolen by criminals and then recovered and returned to him by Grlscz; in an inversion of the traditional relationship of the vampire to Christianity,[33] the vampire is not repelled by the crucifix and even assists in the detective's spiritual life (albeit, perhaps, for his own reasons). Healey is a noble figure, but he fails both as a policeman and in his moral duties as a man of faith in his inability to recognize a wolf in sheep's clothing (or a crocodile in human garb). He releases Grlscz from suspicion because he finds it impossible to think that anyone would save a woman from committing suicide only to murder her, but Grlscz did just that. Healey is blinded to Grlscz's true nature by his own goodness. If "one of the basic lessons of *Dracula* was to reaffirm the existence of God in an age when the weakening hold of Christianity generated fresh debate about what lay beyond death,"[34] *The Wisdom of Crocodiles* is content to further muddy the waters.

Grlscz's affiliation with science carries implications of its own for Grlscz is a vampire whose existence is not only justified by (pseudo-) science, he is himself a scientist. Grlscz extracts a crystal from a sick young girl in a sequence that echoes scenes in which such cinematic mad scientists as Dr. Gogol (Peter Lorre) in *Mad Love* (1935), Dr. Macfarlane (Henry Daniell) in *The Body Snatcher* (1945) and Dr. Génessier (Pierre Brasseur) in *Eyes With-out a Face* (1960) demonstrate the practical medical benefits to their unethical research by healing sick children. In this case, Grlscz calculates to have Anne witness it as part of his strategy to make her love him: "You were very kind to that little girl," she says as she abandons her defenses. A painting hanging in

Grlscz's apartment depicts a naked woman being tugged at by both a white-robed surgeon and a skeleton, and at one point we even see Grlscz's face reflected on the painting as he lures Anne to her intended death on the phone. It is *Der Arzt* by German painter Ivo Saliger, an allegorical depiction of the physician's struggle against death; both the doctor, grim-faced and standing erect, and the skeleton, kneeling at the woman's feet, appear to be embracing her. If the woman in *Der Arzt* represents life, she is paradoxically faceless, limp and passive. In *Sexual Visions: Images of Gender in Science and Medicine between the Eighteenth and Twentieth Centuries* (1989), Ludmilla Jordanova discusses a body of erotically tinged artworks which depict doctors dissecting beautiful young nude women, often while a symbolic skeleton of death looks on.[35] *Der Arzt* is clearly related to this tradition, and it is similarly representative of the ways Western culture tends to gender science and culture more generally as masculine and active, and nature as feminine and passive. For Roberta McGrath, Saliger's painting presents "an ambivalent image; it is unclear whether woman will . . . pull man down with her into a nether world, or if he will be able to fend her off and avoid death. It is, in any case, certain that woman exists somewhere between masculinity and death and is more closely aligned with death."[36] *The Wisdom of Crocodiles* is free of degenerate female vampires like Lucy Westenra and Dracula's monstrous consorts, and the painting becomes more of a visualization of different aspects of Grlscz's identity: the scientific researcher who evinces genuine compassion for his patients and the monster who must feed or die. The burden falls on Anne to be the subject of this grim tug of war, and echoing McGrath's observations, she does in a sense "pull down" Grlscz into death, which is associated with imagery of falling in the voiceovers that bookend the film.

If Grlscz is a reworking of Stoker's Count, Anne is a millennial incarnation of Mina Harker, less repressed but equally associated with capability, rationality and a sort of potentially corruptible purity. Where Mina was a late-Victorian working woman akin to an emerging New Woman, a schoolmistress noted for her talent as a typist and stenographer and her head for details,[37] Anne is a full-fledged career-woman, a structural engineer who cancels her first date with Grlscz to lay waterproof concrete at a building site. Mina confesses that "some taste of the original apple . . . remains still in [women's] mouths,"[38] and this strategy of locating women's fallen nature in the distant past gets echoed when *The Wisdom of Crocodiles* links Anne's theft of the watch to primitive impulses and the ancient parts of the brain. Mina is rendered polluted, damaged and "unclean" after consuming the Count's blood in a rape-like scene, and when a Eucharistic wafer is placed on her forehead, it burns a mark that does not fade until the Count's death cleanses her tainted blood. Anne's parallel weakness comes from her asthma, which figures both in Grlscz's initial attraction to her and her final decision to help him. Likewise, she continues to wear the stolen watch, she says, "to remind me of my shame." Both women, of course, are intended victims of the vampire yet retain some pity for him as well: "I suppose one ought to pity anything so hunted as the Count," says Mina,[39] and Anne ultimately chooses to care for the dying Grlscz even after learning that he is a monster and killer. As is the case with Mina in some adaptations of *Dracula* (including Orson Welles's 1938 production for *The Mercury Theatre on the Air* and Francis Ford Coppola's *Bram Stoker's Dracula* [1992]), Anne is even allowed to kill him directly.

Grlscz first encounters Anne amid the whirring engines of the Kew Bridge Steam Museum in southwest London, a site dedicated to Britain's industrial heritage. The Age of Steam was certainly when the modern vampire mythology took shape; is this why Grlscz finds such a museum to be a natural hunting ground? As much an anachronism as the antique steam devices of the museum, he is there to fulfill an ancient predatory impulse, first stalking a young female schoolteacher before fixing on Anne instead. Anne, on the other hand, is photographing the interior of the museum for work purposes. Characterized in dialogue as "a modern woman," Anne is nevertheless steeped in traditions of various sorts: she is prone to quoting Confucius, and she even purchases and repairs old sports cars in her spare time (again bridging the old and the new). She keeps a pair of 18th-century silver chopsticks, given to the first grandchild as a sign "that the baby will always be fed, always be safe." Even though Anne acknowledges that her grandfather purchased them from a swindler in Shanghai, she keeps them with her and regards them as lucky charms. In the film's last scenes, Grlscz recovers under Anne's care enough to give in to his blood lust and stalk her, leading to a scene on the roof unavoidably reminiscent of the climax of *Blade Runner* (1982)[40] with Anne dangling off the side of the building while Grlscz holds her by the arm. Anne would rather die in the fall than be Grlscz's victim, and she drives the chopsticks through his hand. Again as in *Blade Runner*, he pulls her to the roof rather than let her fall, and she escapes while he bleeds to death from the wound. The chopsticks, signifying Anne's sentimental nature and her investment in tradition, save her and kill Grlscz. Ernest Fontana notes that in the postscript that concludes *Dracula*, where we are told that Mina gave birth to a son a year to the day after the Count's defeat, she becomes "a vessel of evolution rather than a victim of reversion."[41] No such maternal role is required of Anne, but she too functions in the (profoundly gendered) role of affirming a natural balance of the past and present against the unhealthy relationship inherent to atavism.[42] Her surname, "Levels," implies the healthy balance between the past and present that is not possible for Grlscz, a degenerate aberration who must die to reaffirm stasis.

Clive Leatherdale has written, "No doubt Stoker viewed Dracula as morally offensive in the same way that many Victorian Christians felt about Darwin. The novel can thus be seen as a microcosm of decadent late nineteenth-century England faced with the threat of an evolutionary apocalypse."[43] But these apocalyptic elements of *Dracula* scarcely resonate with modern readers. Despite stray references to the Count as "the father or furtherer of a new order of beings, whose road must lead through Death, not Life" and fears that he "might, amongst [London's] teeming millions, satiate his lust for blood, and create a new and ever widening circle of semi-demons to batten on the helpless,"[44] the Count's actual crimes in England are of remarkably small scale. As Leatherdale also notes, he "is the perfect law-abiding citizen . . . He has labored to learn British values and customs. His house purchases are meticulously above board. It could almost be said that he performs no violence (except in self-defense when under personal attack) or indeed any other offence. His only crime is to 'seduce' women who are not at all determined to resist him."[45] Our heroes ultimately beat Dracula with little collateral damage, with only Lucy Westenra and Quincey P. Morris dying out of the major characters. If the Count is much less successful in dethroning humanity at the top of the food chain than, for example, the vampires in Richard Matheson's *I Am Legend* (1954), F. Paul Wilson's *Midnight Mass* (2004) and films like *Vampire Hunter "D"* (1985) and *Daybreakers* (2009), he still represents something terrifying in ways that go far beyond his actual deeds. He is the walking and (infrequently) talking embodiment of the tide of atavism that writers like Nordau foresaw wiping away all of civilization's accomplishments. Though newer narratives that pit vampires against humans for dominance of the planet surely invoke Darwinian themes (Charles Bromley [Sam Neill] in *Daybreakers* even characterizes his transformation into a vampire as "evolution"), they tend to favour an "us and them" dichotomy that downplays the role of atavism, the survival of the ancient within the modern that is so central to *Dracula*. Perhaps we can ultimately understand Steven Grlscz as being what the atavistic vampire becomes when sapped of that broader fin-de-siècle context: a sickly creature out of his proper time, a pathetic and anachronistic "species of one."

Notes

1. Bram Stoker, *Dracula*, in *Bram Stoker's Dracula Omnibus* (Toronto: Smithbooks, 1992) 279.

2. Stoker, *Dracula*, 278.

3. Murray Leeder, "Forget Peter Vincent: Nostalgia, Self-Reflexivity and the Genre Past in *Fright Night*," *Journal of Popular Film and Television* 36 (2009): 193–94, 199.

4. Valerie Clemens, "Dracula: The Reptilian Brain at the Fin de Siècle," in *Dracula: The Shade and the Shadow*, ed. Elizabeth Miller (Westcliffe-on-Sea, UK: Desert Island Books, 1997), 205.

5. In addition to the evolutionary and criminological contexts discussed here, *Dracula* references such figures of contemporary psychology and neuroscience as John Scott Burdon-Sanderson, David Ferrier, Jean-Martin Charcot and others. In the late-Victorian Gothic wave of Gothic literature, also including famous works by H. Rider Haggard, H. G. Wells, Robert Louis Stevenson, Oscar Wilde, Henry James and more, we often find that "science is Gothicized, and gothicity is rendered scientifically plausible": Kelly Hurley, *The Gothic Body: Sexuality, Materialism, and Degeneration at the Fin de Siècle* (Cambridge: Cambridge University Press, 1996), 20. See also Roger Luckhurst, Introduction to *Late Victorian Gothic Tales*, ed. Roger Luckhurst (Oxford: Oxford University Press, 2005), ix–xxxi.

6. For related treatments of *Dracula* not otherwise cited in this article, see Charles S. Blinderman, "Vampurella: Darwin and Count Dracula," *Massachusetts Review* 21 (1980): 411–28; Kathleen L. Spencer, "Purity and Danger: *Dracula*, the Urban Gothic, and the Late Victorian Degeneracy Crisis," *English Literary History* 59 (1992): 197–225; Judith Halberstam, "Technologies of Monstrosity: Bram Stoker's *Dracula*," *Victorian Studies* 36 (1993): 333–52; David Glover, "'Our Enemy Is Not Merely Spiritual': Degeneration and Modernity in Bram Stoker's *Dracula*," *Victorian Literature and Culture* 22 (1994): 249–65; Athena Vrettos, *Somatic Fictions: Imagining Illness in Victorian Culture* (Stanford, CA: Stanford University Press, 1995), 172–3; Fred Botting. *Gothic* (London: Routledge, 1996), 144–54; Daniel Pick, "'Terrors of the Night': *Dracula* and 'Degeneration' in the Late Nineteenth Century," *Critical Quarterly* 30 (1998), 71–87; Michael J. Dennison, *Vampirism: Literary Tropes of Decadence and Entropy* (New York: Peter Lang, 2001), 82–115; Stephen Kern, *A Cultural History of Causality: Science, Murder Novels, and Systems of Thought* (Princeton, NJ: Princeton University Press, 2004), 223–24; and John Glendening, *The Evolutionary Imagination in Late-Victorian Novels: An Entangled Bank* (Aldershot, UK: Ashgate, 2007), 107–36.

7. Bram Dijkstra, *Idols of Perversity: Fantasies of Feminine Evil in Fin-de-Siècle Culture* (New York: Oxford University Press, 1988), 342.

8. David J. Skal, *Screams of Reason: Mad Science and Modern Culture* (New York: W.W. Norton, 1998), 81.

9. Stephen Jay Gould, *The Mismeasure of Man* (New York: Norton, 1981), 124. For a discussion of the centrality of the Gothic to Lombroso's work, see Nicole Rafter and Per Ystehede, "Here Be Dragons: Lombroso, the Gothic, and Social Control," in *Popular Culture, Crime and Social Control*, ed. Mathieu Deflem (Bingley, UK: Emerald Group Publishing, 2010), 263–84.

10. In later writings on female criminals, Lombroso would characterize female criminals as distinguished mainly by "precocity and a minor degree of differentiation from the male": Cesare Lombroso and Guglielmo Ferrero, *The Female Offender* (New York: D. Appleton and Company, 1898), 113. Questions of female degeneration are of course hugely important in many discussions of *Dracula* and the vampire more broadly, but will largely be elided here for reasons of space.

11. Cesare Lombroso, *The Criminal Man* (Montclair, NJ: Patterson Smith, 1972), 14, 17, 18, 17, 15, 19, 15, 21, 243.

12. Max Nordau, *Degeneration* (New York: D. Appleton, 1895), vii.

13. Nordau, *Degeneration*, 6.

14. Students are frequently surprised to discover how hideous and obviously inhuman the Count of the novel is, being familiar only with the more aristocratic portrayals that stem from John L. Balderson and Hamilton Deane's stage production, originally produced in 1924. Elizabeth Miller disputes the claim that Stoker based the Count's appearance on Lombroso's criminal, since her research into Stoker's notes shows that it was drawn more or less directly from Sabine Baring-Gould's *The Book of Were-Wolves* (1865): see her *Dracula: Sense and Nonsense* (Westcliffe-on-Sea, UK: Desert Island Books, 2000), 26, 45.

15. Stoker, *Dracula*, 14–15.

16. Stoker, *Dracula*, 23–24.

17. Stoker, *Dracula*, 195.

18. Stoker, *Dracula*, 278.

19. Stoker, *Dracula*, 260.

20. Stoker, Dracula, 29.

21. R. J. Dingley, "Count Dracula and the Martians," in *The Victorian Fantasists*, ed. Kath Filmer (New York: St. Martin's Press, 1991), 22.

22. *Nadja; The Addiction* and *Habit* are all discussed in Jamie Sexton, "US 'Indie-Horror': Critical Reception, Genre Construction, and Suspect Hybridity," *Cinema Journal*, 51 (2012): 67–86.

23. J. Gordon Melton, *The Vampire Book: The Encyclopedia of the Undead*, 3rd ed. (Canton, MI: Visible Ink Press, 2011).

24. Margaret L. Carter, *Shadow of a Shade: A Survey of Vampirism in Literature* (New York: Gordon Press, 1975), 3.

25. Interestingly, Anne is played by a Romanian actress with a strong accent, though the character's foreignness is never commented on, while contrarily Grlscz is apparently an immigrant (or at least posing as one) but is played by a British actor. No doubt in an attempt to defray the xenophobia of many vampire narratives, the film characterizes contemporary London (positively) as a city of immigrants—indeed, the director is himself a second-generation immigrant who has split his career between Britain and Hong Kong.

26. Stacey Abbott, *Celluloid Vampires: Life after Death in the Modern World* (Austin: University of Texas Press, 2007), 141.

27. Caroline Joan (Kay) Picart and Cecil Greek, "The Compulsion of Real/Reel Serial Killers and Vampires: Toward a Gothic Criminology," in *Monsters In and Among Us: Toward a Gothic Criminology* (Madison, NJ: Fairleigh Dickson University Press, 2007), 242–46. For more on the links between vampires, serial killers and atavism, see Jörg Waltje, *Blood Obsession: Vampires, Serial Murder and the Popular Imagination* (New York: Peter Lang Publishing, 2005).

28. Francis Bacon, *Francis Bacon's Essays and the Wisdom of the Ancients* (Boston: Little, Brown and Company, 1884), 160–61.

29. Clemens, "Dracula," 207.

30. Paul D. McLean, *The Triune Brain in Evolution: Role in Paleocerebral Functions* (New York: Plenum Press, 1990), 17.

31. Though neuroscience has largely departed from the triune brain model, it remains popular in broader culture. See, for instance, Joseph D. Miller's application of it to *King Kong* (1933) in "Darwin, Freud and King Kong," in *King Kong Is Back*, ed. David Brin (Dallas: BenBella Books, 2005), 93–101; and Howard Bloom's invocation of it in his controversial *The Lucifer Principle: A Scientific Expedition into the Forces of History* (New York: Atlantic Monthly Press, 1995), 25–27.

32. Salli J. Kline, *The Degeneration of Women: Bram Stoker's* Dracula *as Allegorical Criticism of the* Fin de Siècle (Rheinbach-Merzbach: CMZ-Verlag, 1992), 51.

33. However, one might argue that *The Wisdom of Crocodiles* adheres more closely to a counter-tradition emblematized by Anne Rice's novels which likens vampires to martyrs and saints: see Lloyd Worley, "Anne Rice's Protestant Vampires," in *The Blood Is the Life: Vampires in Literature*, ed. Leonard G. Heldreth and Mary Pharr (Bowling Green, OH: Bowling Green University Popular Press, 1999), 79–92, especially when Grlscz dies with stigmata-like wounds.

34. Clive Leatherdale, *Dracula: The Novel and the Legend*, (Wellingborough, UK: Aquarian, 1986), 176.

35. Ludmilla Jordanova, *Sexual Visions: Images of Gender in Science and Medicine between the Eighteenth and Twentieth Centuries* (Madison: University of Wisconsin Press, 1989), esp. 87–110.

36. Roberta McGrath, *Seeing Her Sex: Medical Archives and the Female Body* (New York: Manchester University Press, 2002), 13.

37. For accounts of Mina's complex and paradoxical characterization and her relationship to the New Woman movement, see Jean Lorrah, "Dracula Meets the New Woman," in Heldreth and Pharr, *The Blood Is the Life*, 31–42; and Charles E. Prescott and Grace A. Giorgio, "Vampiric Affinities: Mina Harker and the Paradox of Femininity in Bram Stoker's *Dracula*," *Victorian Literature and Culture* 33 (2005): 487–515.

38. Stoker, *Dracula*, 149.

39. Stoker, *Dracula*, 186. In some adaptations, including *Dracula* (1979) and *Bram Stoker's Dracula* (1992), the mild sympathy Mina has for the Count in the books is turned into outright passion and love.

40. Picart and Greek, 245.

41. Ernest Fontana, "Lombroso's Criminal Man and Stoker's *Dracula*," in *Dracula: The Vampire and the Critics*, ed. Margaret L. Carter (Ann Arbor, MI: UNI Research Press, 1988), 164.

42. One might further note that like the woman in *Der Arzt*, Anne mediates between life and death, equally capable of meting out death to Grlscz and saving the life of a coworker injured in an accident.

43. Leatherdale, *Dracula*, 191.

44. Stoker, *Dracula*, 246, 42.

45. Leatherdale, *Dracula*, 186.

3

Dracula the Anti-Christ: New Resurrection of an Immortal Prejudice

Melissa Olson

FOR A MONSTER THAT TRAVELS the globe feeding on the blood of the innocent, Dracula certainly doesn't seem to be going anywhere. It has been well over a century since Bram Stoker's novel was first published, and during all that time the book has never been out of print. The vampire Count has materialized on television, in films, on cereal boxes, as a bobble-head, and as children's Halloween costumes. He has been a villain, a hero, a misunderstood romantic, a joke. He has his own comic book, ballet, video game, and even a bungee jump event. Despite its age, the tale of the infamous vampire has managed to remain relevant because it has been continually redefined through these new interpretations, both serious and parodic. Because such interpretations are legion, however, it is all too easy to overlook an entry in the *Dracula* catalog that actually contributes something original: the ill-received 2000 horror film, *Dracula 2000*.

As intended, this film embodied a specific cultural moment, a breath that the world held between two millennia. More significantly, however, in their attempt to update Dracula for the new millennium's contemporary, cynical audience, the filmmakers incorporated an imaginatively brazen statement about the infamous vampire: that he is actually Judas Iscariot, betrayer of Christ and the most hated of all Jews. With this bold leap of logic, *Dracula 2000* not only revives the same anti-Semitic prejudices that originally contributed to the myth of vampires, it brings them to a zenith, creating a vacuum for the next generation of vampire movies to fill.

The Chain Reaction: Early Anti-Semitism and Vampirism

In the year 1267, in Pforzheim, there was an old woman who, out of greed, sold an innocent seven-year-old girl to the Jews. The Jews stopped up her mouth, so she could not cry out, cut open her veins, and wrapped her with cloths, to catch up her blood. The poor girl soon died from the torture.[1]

It began with a murder, and a rumor. In 1144, a twelve-year-old apprentice tanner named William was murdered in Norwich, England, on Good Friday. A rumor began to circulate that the boy had been killed by a conspiracy of Jews who intended to mock the Passion of Jesus Christ by killing the boy in the same fashion. The authorities who investigated William's death never found any evidence to support this claim, which did not satisfy the Christian population. They began to riot, attempting their own free-court trial of the accused. The local sheriff managed to intervene and save the lives of the Jewish suspects, but this act only fueled the population's growing suspicion of some sort of collusion between the ruling class and the city's Jews.[2]

This tension did not end with William of Norwich. The rumors grew, as rumors do. Soon it was said that Jews were using the blood of Christian children in their wine and to make their bread. More Jews were accused of more ritual murders, often of children. Most of these cases ended with the torture and execution of the Jewish suspects. Countries began to exile entire Jewish populations over such accusations, and the rumors still continued to grow: it was said that Jews were poisoning Christian wells, that they were responsible for the Plague, and that they willfully and maliciously destroyed the Communion wafer, the Christian symbol of Christ's body.[3] The anti-Semites claimed that Jews were blood-sucking, money-hungry parasites without a homeland, and this reasoning "gradually replaced the Crusades as a pretext for mass exterminations . . . Diligent chroniclers have estimated more than one hundred cases of profanation of the Host, more than one hundred and fifty trials for 'ritual murder,' and the number of cases we do not know about must be infinitely greater."[4]

For some time now, historians and literary scholars have pointed out the alarming connections between these anti-Semitic stereotypes and the myth of the vampire. The vampire hates Christianity, shrinking from and even being wounded by the cross, the Bible, the crucifix. He tries to spread the plague of vampirism, consumes blood, and is often portrayed as a traveler, a foreigner wandering without a home. Of course, it is not as simple as the vampire myth corresponding flawlessly to the anti-Semitic stereotype of Judaism: both myths developed individually before intertwining after young William's death. Judith Halberstam, in her book *Skin Shows: Gothic Horror and the Technology of Monsters*, considers this connection one aspect of the process of "Othering": "The reason Gothic monsters are overdetermined—which is to say, open to numerous interpretations—is precisely because monsters transform the fragments of otherness into one body."[5]

Still, the relationship is undeniable. Jeffrey Weinstock perhaps summarized it best when he argued that the categories of vampirism and anti-Semitism must be considered as having developed together, symbiotically. This argument encapsulates both folklore and specific literary examples, including—and maybe especially—the most famous of all English-language vampire stories, Bram Stoker's *Dracula*.

The Anti-Semitic Dracula

Between 1881 and 1900, the number of foreign Jews in England increased by 600 percent. The response to their presence was both hostile and fearful . . . Perceived as dirty, swarming, and overwhelmingly alien, the Jews were highly visible, and they evoked fear, distrust, and distaste.[6]

It is easy to forget, well over a century after its appearance, that *Dracula* was on the cutting edge of modern literature in its day. As Stacey Abbott writes in *Celluloid Vampires: Life after Death in the Modern World*, Stoker's book was "littered with icons of modern living, such as new technologies, sciences, transportation networks, bureaucracy, and urbanization, all of which would have been instantly recognizable to his late-nineteenth-century readers."[7] Also recognizable was Stoker's implementation of one of the great fears of the time: Jewish immigration. Stoker applied these viewpoints—advancing modernization and a new climate of xenophobia—to the longstanding vampire folklore, creating *Dracula*.

In addition to its modernity, the novel is rife with allusions to anti-Semitic contributions to the vampire myth: while describing her first experience reading the book, Halberstam writes,

Dracula, I thought, with his peculiar physique, his parasitical desires, his aversion to the cross and to all the trappings of Christianity, his blood-sucking attacks, and his avaricious relation to money, resembled stereotypical anti-Semitic nineteenth-century representations of the Jew. Subsequent readings of the novel with attention to the connections in the narrative between blood and gold, race and sex, sexuality and ethnicity confirmed my sense that the anti-Semite's Jew and Stoker's vampire bore more than a family resemblance.[8]

Halberstam goes on to note the many anti-Semitic connections in *Dracula*: "his appearance, his relation to money/gold, his parasitism, his degeneracy, his impermanence or lack of allegiance to a fatherland," and so on. Her argument regarding Dracula's appearance and its connection to degeneracy is particularly interesting: she notes that physically, the Count corresponds to the racial stereotype of Jews at the time of Stoker's book: he has a "hooked nose," "shifty eyes," "massive eyebrows," and "bushy hair." "The face in the nineteenth century which supposedly expressed Jewishness," Halberstam writes, "is also seen to express nineteenth-century criminality and degeneration within the pseudosciences of physiognomy and phrenology. Degeneration and Jewishness, one could therefore conclude . . . were not far apart."[9] Degeneracy was seen as a hereditary quality, and racial profiling had long since attributed it to Jews. In other words: it was not even their fault they were such degenerates. It was just their inherent nature.

Count Dracula produces a similar profile: he is a degenerate not just morally, but because he pollutes the human bloodline with vampirism, reducing humans like Lucy Westerna to the status of monsters. He is also a sexual degenerate, forcing young women to submit to his will and perversions. In assigning blame for these behaviors, Halberstam refers to the section toward the end of *Dracula* when Van Helsing describes the vampire as having a "childbrain"—despite his charm and worldliness, his mind is primitive.[10] Therefore, it's not even his fault. It's just his inherent nature.

The anti-Semitic connection in *Dracula*, specifically, has been explored elsewhere as well, particularly in light of the late 19th century's xenophobia. Jules Zanger, in "A Sympathetic Vibration: Dracula and the Jews," emphasizes this correlation, noting the overwhelming increase in the population of Eastern European Jews in England and the anxieties of such a population shift, suggesting that "*Dracula* derived a significant portion of its power from its ability to dramatise in a socially acceptable form a body of hostile perceptions of the newly arrived Jews."[11]

It is worth noting, in light of the argument that anti-Semitic views of Jewishness and vampirism developed symbiotically, that the connection between these two did not end with the publication of *Dracula*, or even with the 19th century. Accusations of ritual murder continued into the twentieth century, gaining a forceful charge with the Nazi rise to power in the 1930s. Accusations of ritual murder continued across the globe through at least the 1970s. As Jeffrey Weinstock notes, "In the 1960s and '70s, Dennis Prager and Joseph Telushkin report that the blood libel was spread by the leading financial figure of the Arab world, King Faisal of Saudi Arabia, who informed newspaper interviewers that the Jews annually celebrated Passover by murdering a non-Jew and consuming his blood."[12]

The vampire myth expanded and diminished in popularity a number of times in the last century, but it is important to point out that all the while, rumors of ritual murder derived from the anti-Semite's view of Jewishness were still expanding and diminishing, as well. This interdependent relationship between myths led all the way up to the end of the 20th century, when Dracula was once again incarnated onscreen in *Dracula 2000.*

Dracula 2000: Pinnacle of a Prejudice

There is no doubt that *Dracula 2000* is meant to be not just an appearance by the famous character (the vampire has turned up everywhere from *Buffy the Vampire Slayer* to a number of novels, i.e., *The Historian*), but a continuation of Bram Stoker's book. Director/Cowriter Patrick Lussier makes a number of direct references to the novel's plot points, beginning with the opening scene: the ship *Demeter* transporting Dracula to England in the year 1897, just as it did in the book. The mythology of the vampire is similar as well: Dracula can transform into mist, a wolf, and bats, and he has to be invited into a home. He keeps a menagerie of three attractive females who attempt to seduce/kill the film's "Jonathan Harker" character, Simon.

There are also a number of visual cues connecting *Dracula 2000* to both the novel and its previous onscreen manifestations. Dracula's three female vampires dress in white—an echo of the three brides previously seen onscreen. Like Bela Lugosi's character, this Dracula wears a long black cape during the flashbacks to 1897. In the "present" he exchanges the cape for a floor-skimming black coat, though all the characters around him wear hot-weather clothes in reference to the Louisiana weather. A portrait of Abraham Van Helsing hangs in the study of "Matthew" Van Helsing, an homage to a similar portrait hung in Van Helsing's study in *Dracula: A.D. 1972.*

The film doesn't just remake a modernized version of what has come before, however: Lussier takes pains to set this new story apart by blurring the boundaries between sequel and remake. In the first dialogue scene, antiques dealer Matthew Van Helsing actually discusses Stoker's book with his assistant Simon. Matthew is supposedly the grandson of Abraham Van Helsing, who, he explains, "inspired" Stoker's character. Van Helsing good-naturedly rebukes Simon for joking about this history, dismissing it with "How my poor grandfather could have inspired a character out of Bram Stoker's book . . . I'll never know." By creating this distance between the "true" story within the film and the fictional story of the book, Van Helsing cleverly acknowledges the well-known history behind *Dracula 2000* while simultaneously alerting the viewer that this will be something different. Later, when it is revealed that Matthew is actually Abraham kept alive by frequent injections of Dracula's blood, the distance is dropped and the two stories of book and film are blended together.

This idea is further expressed through revival of one of the novel's themes: the juxtaposition of history and technology. Though the book's plot involves an ageless vampire with a courtly Old World manner (he lives in a *castle*), the "new" technology that allows Mina to transcribe the various "sources" is frequently used and mentioned. As Abbott argues,

> Rather than simply establish a structural opposition between a premodern vampire and the modern scientific community, the novel places their conflict, and the vampire itself, at the center of a whirlwind of social and technological change, and emphasizes the ambiguous distinction between the two.[13]

Similarly, *Dracula 2000* contrasts the 19th century with the millennium, particularly via visual contrasts: Van Helsing's antique chessboard is actually a sophisticated machine that hides his leech kit. A state-of-the-art vault, complete with computer program, retinal scanner, and voice recognition, appears to house only cobweb-covered antique artifacts: books, furniture, skulls with alarmingly long canines. When Marcus, the leader of the thieves who rob Dracula's tomb, faces off with the vampire, we see Dracula overpower Marcus, lifting him to drain his blood. As Marcus dies, the fake eyeball used to fool the retinal scanner falls from his pocket, abandoned on the floor.

Though he's dedicated to some degree of authenticity, Lussier has clearly taken pains to "revamp" Stoker's story for a new generation: the film pulses with techno music, gruesome special effects, and flashing cuts to a hedonistic Mardi Gras crowd in New Orleans, where the majority of the story takes place. This setting provides Dracula with an opportunity to enjoy the degradation the world has suffered since the last time he walked it. At one point, Dracula is entranced by a larger-than-life screen playing a music video. As he watches, the screen cycles rapidly through images: tanks going to war, mud-wrestling women, exploding missiles, pierced extremities. "I am a pure assault / You'll never be worse than me, no / So get in the fucking car / We've got a whole world to see," screams the rock star, as images of a burning cross, an atomic bomb, and dancing naked women fill the screen. The Victorian count stares with great pleasure, finally murmuring, "Brilliant." Dracula, the film argues, would be very pleased with the world as we've made it.

It's an interesting exercise in updating a classic tale, and Lussier is certainly enchanted by the idea of what Dracula would think of contemporary society. The problem with *Dracula 2000*, however, is that in addition to all the references to the novel and previous films, it also picks up the anti-Semitic qualities of the vampire/Dracula myth—and even pushes them to extremes. Once again, Dracula is an outsider without a home, a sexually deviant parasite wandering to a new city to spread his disease and death. Degeneracy is a major theme in the film as well, not just because of Dracula's pollution of the human population with his additional vampires and sexual immorality, but also because his blood is spread to non-vampires. Abraham/Matthew Van Helsing has vowed to stay alive until he can find a way to kill Dracula, but to achieve his objective he has done the unforgivable: mixing Dracula's tainted blood with his own. He essentially becomes a "half-breed," and he passes this trait on to his daughter. In his journal, Van Helsing writes, "My unholy addiction has corrupted Mary's blood, and not a day goes by that I don't pray for her immortal soul." Mary was born with "tainted" blood, forcing her to experience violent and sexual visions from Dracula. This is made all the more degenerate because Mary is, in a sense, Dracula's own daughter, giving their relationship an incestuous quality. Dracula's blood isn't just infectious, it's debasing.

Dracula The Anti-Christ

Jesus said unto her, "I am the resurrection, and the life: he that believes in me, though he were dead, yet shall he live."

—John 11:25, King James Bible

"Believe in me. I am the way to eternity."

—Dracula, *Dracula 2000*

The character of Mary represents *Dracula 2000*'s revival of anti-Semitic stereotypes in more ways than one. The major subplot of the film is the battle for Mary's soul, between her Catholic upbringing (Mary is close friends with a Catholic priest, Father David, to whom she goes for counsel) and her involuntary psychic connection to Dracula, who here represents not just a monster, but the flip side of Jesus Christ/Christianity. Once Lussier has established that we're talking about *the* Dracula and reviewed the novel's prejudices, he brings us to the revelation that Dracula is Judas Iscariat, the great betrayer of Jesus and most hated of all Jews.

Lussier does a clever job of connecting the dots between our preconceived notion of Dracula and the fallen disciple, dropping hints throughout the film. As Mary and Simon search for clues to Dracula's origins, they discuss long-held assumptions about the vampire:

Simon: We know he detests all things Christian. Holy water, the cross, the Bible.

Mary: And silver.

Simon: Why silver? It's not uniquely Christian. There has to be something more.

It's a good point—Stoker himself never addressed the reasoning behind Dracula's aversion to Christianity. *Dracula 2000* explains it by claiming that Dracula/Judas hates silver (he flinches at the very sound of metal jangling on the street) because it reminds him of the thirty pieces of silver he received for his betrayal. He hates all things Christian because he betrayed Christ, who, he believes, turned him into a monster as punishment. Conversely, Christian things in the film don't like Dracula either: the pages of a Bible, which Dracula calls "propaganda," fly out of the book toward the vampire, starting little fires wherever they touch. Holy water, of course, burns him. When he throws Mary into a stained glass image of Christ the glass mostly shatters—but the image of Christ's face does not, staring down at him in perceived judgment.

There are also clues to Dracula's true identity in the biblical naming of the main characters. Dracula says, "We are all so much more complicated than our names," and he's right—most of the characters' names have a serious subtext to them. Lucy Westerman is taken right from the novel's Lucy Westerna, but David is an Old Testament figure who battles Goliath and eventually becomes king. Mary, of course, can conjure an image of either Mary Magdalene or Mary, the mother of Christ. Simon and Matthew are the names of two of Jesus's disciples, and while Simon's last name is not directly mentioned in the film, in the credits it is revealed to be Sheppard. His job is to guide and protect Mary through her plight. Mary, Simon, Matthew, and to a lesser degree David, are the "good guys" of the film, and except for Matthew, who must die because he betrayed his race by injecting vampire blood, they are the only characters who get to live. They are positioned as on the side of Jesus, which logically points toward Dracula, their enemy, as Jesus's own enemy.

As it transpires, Dracula isn't just another incarnation of anti-Semitic prejudices, and he isn't even just Judas Iscariat. Dracula/Judas is also portrayed as literally the anti-Christ, the flip side of Jesus. We get our first hint in the opening scene between Van Helsing and Simon. When he brings Van Helsing a new crossbow, designed to shoot silver arrows, Simon attempts to translate the inscription:

Simon: All fear he who walks beneath the crown of eternal night.

Van Helsing: No, no, it's not "crown." It's halo. "Beneath the halo of eternal night."

This juxtaposition of the words "eternal," "halo" and "crown" (as in "of thorns") subconsciously reminds the viewer of Jesus's suffering on the cross—yet the weapon is intended to kill Dracula, therefore referring to him.

Most significantly, however, Dracula is positioned as the anti-Christ in his dialogue at the end of the film. The vampire speaks directly to the stained-glass portrait of Jesus, "I drink the blood of your children, but I give them more than just eternal life. I give them what they crave most: all the pleasure

You would deny them . . . forever. You made the world in your image. Now, I make it in mine." He equates vampirism with Christian salvation; or, given the context of the relationship between anti-Semitic stereotypes and vampirism, he equates Jewishness with the inverse of Christianity.

Mary, with her corrupted blood, is torn between these two extremes. Though early in the film she doubts the strength of her own Catholic faith, in the end, this faith saves the day. During their final battle, Dracula has already bitten Mary, turning her into a vampire. She continues to fight, however, by stabbing him in the stomach.

> Dracula: Didn't your father tell you, Mary? I can't die. He won't have me.
>
> Mary: Did you ever ask?
>
> Dracula: For what? For forgiveness? Do you really think I'd go back to Him?
>
> Mary: He still loves you.
>
> Dracula: Does He? Just as He still loves you? Then go back to Him . . . and see if He'll still have you!

With that, Dracula moves to throw Mary off the roof. However, she wraps a cord around his neck and takes both of them off the roof together. It is literally a leap of faith: she's trusting that God, in his infinite forgiveness, will allow Dracula/Judas to die this time. (As she is still a vampire, Mary herself crashes to the ground in relative safety.) Dracula stares down at her, seemingly astonished at her actions, then whispers, "I . . . release . . . you." Mary becomes human again. Then he burns in the morning sun, frozen with his arms spread in the classic crucifixion pose.

The implication is that Mary's faith has so impressed Dracula that he permits her to give up her connection to vampirism, and that Dracula has at last been allowed to die. The latter is left ambiguous, however, by Mary's voiceover at the end of the film. She states that she will guard Dracula's ashes just in case, and she adds that she now knows who she is: her father's daughter. This statement could refer to Van Helsing the vampire hunter or to God the Father—but not to Dracula, who has released Mary from her connection to him. Mary is no longer a half-breed, and she can return to her life—and presumably, her Catholicism. In the decision between vampirism/Judaism and Christianity, Mary has made the "right" choice.

Epilogue: Dracula after *Dracula 2000*

In his introduction to *Monster Theory*, Jeffrey Cohen argues that we are what we presently fear: the monster "is born only at this metaphoric crossroads, as an embodiment of a certain cultural moment—of a time, a feeling, and a place."[14] He suggests that this connection works both ways: we are what we presently fear, just as what we presently fear is what we are. Dracula has always been a perfect example of this argument, as a textbook case of fears (Otherness, Jews, invaders, blood-sucking) manifested in one of our most recognized monsters. As part of both Cohen's monstrosity and Halberstam's Othering, he has flexed and adapted to a century's minute changes in fear. By the millennium, when much of the global population held its breath to see if the world was going to end, Dracula's identity turned sharply toward religion: not just the anti-Semitic stereotypes that had followed him since his creation, but also questions of faith and evil.

This changing identity is evident in the vampire movies that have appeared since *Dracula 2000*. There has been a major topical shift. "In particular, the *Blade* films, *Underworld* (2003), *Van Helsing* (2004), and *Underworld: Evolution* (2006) have contributed to a reconception of generic conventions and iconography that undermines the laws of religion and folklore in favor of the laws of science and technology."[15] Abbot doesn't delve too deeply into the topics of fear and monstrosity, but she does note that studies in genetics have had a high media profile in the last decade, and such films "demonstrate this cultural preoccupation with both the science and the ethics of genetics and DNA."

Dracula has appeared onscreen twice more since 2000, in *Van Helsing* and *Blade Trinity* (2006). The former is set in the 19th century, but it has been reconfigured as an adventure film in which Van Helsing has a "Q"-like sidekick who supplies gadgets and potions that kill monsters. The latter repurposes the Dracula character to tell a modern story about using genetic experimentation to destroy the plague of vampires once and for all. *Dracula 2000* brought the anti-Semitic–vampirism connection to a boil, after which it apparently began to evaporate. With the end of the twentieth century, our fears have shifted— and therefore our monsters have shifted. And given the nature of the vampire myth's original development, not a moment too soon.

Notes

1. Jacob and Wilhelm Grimm, *Deutsche Sagen* [German Sagas] (1816/18), no. 354.
2. Leon Poliakov, *The History of Anti-Semitism: From the Time of Christ to the Court Jews*, Richard Howard, trans. (New York: Vanguard Press, 1965), 58.
3. Jeffrey Weinstock, "Circumcising Dracula: The Vampire as Anti-Semitic Trope," *Journal of the Fantastic in the Arts* 12 (2001): 95.
4. Poliakov, 62–63.

5. Judith Halberstam, *Skin Shows: Gothic Horror and the Technology of Monsters* (Durham, NC: Duke University Press, 1995), 92.

6. Jules Zanger, "A Sympathetic Vibration: Dracula and the Jews," *English Literature in Translation 1880–1920* 34 (1991): 35.

7. Stacey Abbott, *Celluloid Vampires: Life after Death in the Modern World* (Austin: University of Texas Press, 2007), 16.

8. Halberstam, *Skin Shows*, 92.

9. Halberstam, *Skin Shows*, 93.

10. Halberstam, *Skin Shows*, 93.

11. Zanger, "A Sympathetic Vibration," 36.

12. Weinstock, "Circumcising Dracula," 94.

13. Abbott, *Celluloid Vampires*, 16.

14. Jeffrey Cohen, *Monster Theory: Reading Culture* (Minneapolis: University of Minnesota Press, 1996), 4.

15. Abbott, *Celluloid Vampires*, 198.

Filmography

Dracula 2000, Dir. Patrick Lussier, Perfs. Gerard Butler, Justine Waddell, 2000. DVD (Echo Bridge Home Entertainment, 2011).

Dracula: A.D. 1972, Perfs. Christopher Lee, Peter Cushing, 1972. DVD (Warner Brothers Pictures, 2005).

4

Eat Me! The Morality of Hunger in Vampiric Cuisine

Simon Bacon

T HE RELATIONSHIP OF FOOD to the subject that eats it is an inherently symbiotic connection constituted in the tension between what we define as being food and how we are then defined by that food. It is a consummation between that which is consumed and that which consumes it. As noted by theorist Roger Scruton, "Food is the place where the needs of the body and the needs of the soul should converge, to offer nourishment and meaning in equal measure."[1] This consummation then is not just a physical one: it also has a spiritual dimension. With a suitably biblical flourish Angel F. Méndez Montoya states, "[I]n the beginning was the Word. It was only when human beings appeared that the Word became food on a table."[2] The notion of the Word made flesh made food is further examined by Montoya when he quotes Alexander Schmemann:

> Schmemann claims that from the beginning of creation humanity is presented as "a hungry being," within a world that is offered by God as a divine banquet. As created by God, the whole cosmos bears the inscription of its maker, but in a way that expresses a cosmic feast: "all that exists lives by 'eating.' The whole creation depends on food."[3]

Our place within and in relation to the universe is then in a fundamental way related to food, whether as bodily or spiritual sustenance. The importance to our notions of selfhood and agency contained within this intimate relationship, between what we are and what we eat, is made all the more prescient when the tables are turned and we become that which is eaten. This chapter, whilst predicated upon notions around the issue of hunger, is more focused upon how the very nature of what it is to be human is tied up with the ideas of need and satiation; with what it is to be the one that "hungers" and what it is to be the object of that innate and insatiable drive. Specifically, I will concentrate on two particular constituent elements of hunger: that which is desired and the one who desires it. To examine the implications contained within this, I will look at a creature whose very nature is defined by the "need to feed," and whose evolutionary imperative is to satisfy this constant craving with the blood of humans. It has, in various shapes and forms, been with us since the dawn of civilization itself: the vampire.[4]

Our Vampire, Our "Other" Selves[5]

The figure of the revenant immediately touches upon notions of impurity and abjection, as Sarah Sceats notes: "[V]ampires are antisocial; they are associated with taboo, transgression, and degradation; they are feared, reviled, or sought for the highly erotic under-current and contagious nature of their appetites."[6] Elaine Showalter takes this even further, disrupting the traditional binaries of the monstrous and abject and aligning it with the blurring of "sexual, psychological, and scientific boundaries."[7] This manifests itself in spatial and spiritual terms and in the loss of differentiated notions of selfhood: as she explains, Dracula lives in Transylvania, "on the borders of three states," which we might read as states of living, dead, and undead, or of masculinity, femininity, and bisexuality.[8] Though possibly one of the most transgressive aspects of them, not mentioned above, is that which is related to one of the most taboo of subjects, that of cannibalism. Cannibalism points not only to the ambivalence of eating any kind of flesh. As William Ian Miller notes,

> Food-prohibition systems are so restrictive with regard to eating animals that one could argue that these systems are but superficial manifestations of deeper, more generalized conceptual structures which define our relation to the rest of the animal order. Is it that we are nervous about being an animal and also eating animals?[9]

This is what David Williams further identifies when he observes, "[E]ven more abnormal and horrifying than the reversal of the hierarchy of eaters and eaten is the breakdown of the categories involved in cannibalism, the eating of the equal."[10] The consumption of living flesh, then, confounds the neat and contained parameters of what is food and related concepts of human identity, consequently blurring the boundaries between both. Here the liminality of the vampire is at its most abject for it is simultaneously not only human and nonhuman, alive and dead, but it corrupts the pure with the impure. In partaking of living flesh it reverses the natural order of consumption, meaning that the dead eat the living, but also, on some level it, Ouroboros-like, eats itself.[11] As such it then reconfigures and transmutates the often-used statement "You are what you eat" into a somewhat more ominous and darkly sinister presentiment: "You are what you are eaten by." Such culinary reciprocity reveals an interdependence and interconnectivity between the terms "subject" and "object" and takes the relationship beyond the focus on the subjective "I," being the one who is doing the eating, to a mode of mutual recognition or a substantive symbiosis that demands a much more serious consideration of the ethical consequences enacted within the act of being the "dish of the day."[12]

There is then a notion here not just of seeing the other as food but as an extension of the self in that both are necessarily categories of the same order. Emmanuel Levinas sees such acts of mutual recognition as a "genuine meeting of the 'between' that characterizes the 'I/Thou' relationship."[13] Here the "I/Thou" relationship is one that presupposes a commonality between the subject and the object, and specifically one of a shared humanity or comparative consciousness that would require a certain level of mutual reflexivity and awareness. However, the philosopher Martin Buber extends this to an "I/It" duality, taking this connection beyond the scope of just biological similitude to one that can include that of animate/inanimate. Seeing the I/It relationship as a fundamental part of human experience in, and to, the world, Robert Bernasconi explains, "There follows from this beginning the splitting of the 'primal encounters,' giving rise both to the thing and to the I,"[14] which Andrew Kelly further expands to a basic level of survival, and even identity formation: "In order to nourish myself, to survive, I must live in the world of it. The world of the statesman or the economist would collapse if it were considered solely in terms of Thou."[15] As such, with its feet in both camps as it were, it is not an impossible stretch to continue the relationship to include the liaison between alive/dead or even alive/undead. Levinas, though, sees this meeting taking place only between human subjects, as epitomized in the "face to face" encounter, when the face is not something to be perceived but something one "speaks to."[16] This speech is on the level of unconscious knowledge, more of an a priori interdependence of social beings where the "I" is "responsible to and for the other who faces me."[17] From this positioning, and with the inclusion of Buber's thought, our most basic relations to all living and nonliving subjects are, then, inherently ethical ones, and this has serious ramifications for Levinas.[18]

Anselm K. Min interprets Levinas's idea thus: "[O]nly in ethics do we encounter a reality which we cannot contain, thematize, represent, or in any case reduce to our own subjectivity and which is, therefore, truly transcendent."[19]

It is, then, the nature, or the quality, of this recognition between the "I" and the "Thou" that allows for the human subject to exceed itself. Specifically, Levinas sees this as an encounter with a subject/object that is of a different order to the Self. He observes, "It is not through psychoanalysis, leading back to myths, that I can dominate the totality of which I am a part—but by encountering a being who is not in the system, a transcendent being."[20] This encounter must be with a Thou or It that is outside or exceeds what would be seen as normal or normative categorization. Subsequently, the possibility of human transcendence, that which can take the self beyond itself, can only be found in what Levinas sees as the most extreme form of this encounter where recognition is not a passive but a strategically active agent, and this comes in the shape of what he saw as the "hungry" Other. This is the Other that not just needs or even just desires our attention but aggressively demands it.

Consequently, as further noted by Min, it is the Other "that shakes up our ordinary onto-theological consciousness in its complacency, closure, and arrogance."[21] It is the hungry Other who, in its needs and existence, and its existence that is defined by those needs, reveals this excess that we cannot contain, and, therefore, suggests the possibility of the infinite within us. Min continues to explain this notion thus: "[T]he Infinite is revealed . . . only in the 'surplus' in the exigency of responsibility for the Other."[22] It is in our responsibility for, and to the other, whose demands can never be fulfilled or whose hunger can never be satiated, that the possibility of the infinite opens up within us. This produces an excessively reciprocating binary or symbiotic relationship, where the extreme demands of the earthly body create the potential for a spiritual one. Indeed, Levinas describes bodily compassion as "insatiable," which itself, in its attempts to "saturate" the hungry, becomes hunger in itself which "increases to infinity."[23] As such, in an inverse equivalence, the greater the need placed upon us, the greater the possibility of bodily transcendence. It then becomes vital, for any form of transcendence—or equivalent spiritual excess—to be possible, for there to be an equal but opposite physical, or even existential, lack. This antithetical bodily need is then constituted in the figure of the insatiably hungry. This, I would suggest, is found specifically within the figure of the vampire and would also indicate one possible reason why the vampire has always been such a ubiquitous part of European and world culture.

Face to Face with a Vampire

As indicated before, this supposition would, of course, present problems for Levinas, as vampires, in his formulation, are not considered true human subjects, and, consequently, a vital component of the I/Thou relationship is the fact that the "face is alive."[24] Nevertheless, and not just in the light of the thoughts arising from my earlier consideration of Buber's reading of this, I would argue that revenants necessarily cross the borders between the human and nonhuman, alive and not-alive, and exceed life, death and undeath, as Showalter noted earlier, simultaneously. Their excessive and liminal nature necessarily disrupts the borders of the Self, or what Levinas sees as the "immanence" of the ego. Such immanence is self-contained and directed solely inward and, therefore, towards the world rather than beyond the corporeal. To escape the finitude of the immanent necessitates an encounter to take the "I" beyond that boundary. As Michele Saracino comments, "Levinas knows the holistic reality of being a saint, which is based on a undeniable call from beyond—a call that turns one's sense of self inside out for others."[25] As such, in their beyond-ness, vampires even more keenly intimate the possibility of states of human becoming, or transcendence, beyond normalized categorizations. In this configuration the vampire can be seen as both an extreme form of otherness but also, essentially, as a part of the human self. It is a part of the self that is externalized and, consequently, seen as something foreign and strange, or as the alienated self. As such it makes manifest what can be seen as the expelled or abjected parts of ourselves. Freud posits that such creatures are repressed parts of the self, breaking through from the subconscious;[26] whereas other psychoanalysts, such as Melanie Klein, see them as projected parts of the self, "those parts that cannot be allowed to remain psychically internalised to contaminate the 'good' parts of the subject."[27] Both interpretations reveal the inherent disruptions and disturbances of the borders between the inside and outside. Kleinian object-relations in particular posit that all notions of self and identity are formulated in relation to objects in the world around us, intimating, if not explicitly, the interdependence of the I/It about which Buber speaks. The consequence of this porosity of borders is that what was once fully contained within the interior breaks through, or is expelled into, the exterior, signifying the necessary release of the dangerous or unclean self. This can then be seen to configure to Julia Kristeva's notion of the abject.

Kristeva can be seen to have developed the earlier ideas of culture and taboo put forward by Mary Douglas in her book *Purity and Danger: An Analysis of the Concepts of Pollution and Danger*. Douglas identifies the causes of societal anxiety and pollution, stating,

> Four kinds of social pollution seem worth distinguishing. The first is danger pressing on external boundaries; the second, danger from transgressing the internal lines of the system; the third, danger in the margins of the lines. The fourth is danger from internal contradiction, when some of the basic postulates

are denied by other basic postulates, so that at certain points the system seems to be at war with itself.[28]

Kristeva, utilizing ideas of the individual put forward by both Freud and Klein in conjunction with Douglas, produced a psychology of society and the notion of the "Othering" of the self in her essay *Powers of Horror*.[29] Here she describes the abject which "seems to emanate from an exorbitant outside or inside . . . which, familiar as it might have been in an opaque and forgotten life, now harries me as radically separate, loathsome. Not me."[30] The expulsion of the abject is vital to maintaining the "good" self; but because of its intimate connection to us, it will not leave us alone but constantly "harries" us. Whilst it is an essential part of any sense of self, or the "desire for meaning," it also initiates a tension between the self and that which is expelled, creating the ground state from which Levinas's escalation of excess might lead to a becoming. As Kristeva further notes about the act of abjection: "I expel *myself*, I spit *myself* out, I abject *myself* within the same motion through which 'I' claim to establish *myself*."[31] Thus we can read conversely that the more the abject tries to de-establish us through its desire or hunger, the more we become ourselves, positing the possibility of an excess of self or what can also be seen as a transcendence of self. Somewhat curiously, and indeed presciently for this discussion, Kristeva further describes abjection as "a resurrection that has gone through death. It is an alchemy that transforms death drive into a start of life, of new significance."[32] The death drive, or that which would consume everything, points the way to rebirth. Through death lies resurrection, but only through the act of absolute consummation with the abject or expelled other.

Freud himself intimates such a correlation between death and life when he says in *Beyond the Pleasure Principle*, "[I]f, therefore, we are not to abandon the hypothesis of death drives, we must suppose them to be associated from the very first with life drives."[33] The vampire simultaneously embodies both the hungry other that demands our complete attention and also the abjected self that wants to completely consume us. Both relationships are inherently ethical, requiring a recognition of the responsibility of the "I" to the "Other," which is predicated upon the desire to be seen and recognised as both a subject and other, but also the "I" as seen through the eye of the "Other." Here the self goes beyond the limits of the "I" through being seen by the "Other," enacting a form of recognition that through the eyes and body of the hungry constitutes a possession or a devouring which performs a mode of consummation between the other and ourselves. Such an excess of continual need and fulfillment makes us more than ourselves and, as such, creates the potential means of a new signification that can transcend our original bodily state. Such an eschatology of the self, then, begins to infer the forms of excess that Levinas describes in *Totality and Infinity*, where it "institutes a relation with being beyond the totality or beyond history, and not with being beyond the past and the present . . . [being] a relationship with a surplus always exterior to the totality, as though the objective totality did not fill out the true measure of being."[34]

You Are Hungry: Therefore I Am

The intimate connections that exist between the "I" and the "Thou," as indicated by Klein, Kristeva and Levinas, can also implicitly infer a step beyond what could otherwise be seen as just a mere confrontation between subject and object into what Jelisaveta Blagojevic defines as the "unbearable orb of intimacy."[35] This exceeds the self-recognition by the self of itself in the "Other," or itself being "Othered," and configures this recognition as a space, or proximity, which transforms such acknowledgement into an act of consummation, which sees the abject in a position of unfulfilled yearning. This is not just the yearning for admittance into the "orb," but an imperative necessity to be reintegrated; an overwhelming desire and need to be incorporated back into the self. This compelling need, or hunger, of the expelled object or the self-alienated abject is not just one for sustenance but one for reincorporation or reintegration. Kristeva, in her work on Melanie Klein, identifies her ideas on the relationship of the Self to exterior objects, including those projected from the self, and subsequently observes that they allow us "to theorize a 'reparative reason' and a 'reparative individualism.'"[36] This has larger ramifications for Klein and Kristeva where such an act of purposeful reintegration "reconciles and organizes a society that is founded more on concern and respect for other people than on repressions and instrumentalism."[37] Concern and respect here can be equated with recognition where ones sees the other in an empathic equivalence.

However, this compelling need and yearning for reparation can also be viewed as an un-fillable void. As such, this can be seen to find equivalence in what Jacques Lacan perceived as the wish for the fantasized total unity with the mother and where human subjects are centered upon the need for reparation and reincorporation but are in fact focused upon the fundamental gap or void within this which will always be missing.[38] Fabio Parasecoli, in his book *Bite Me: Food in Popular Culture*, also acknowledges this and identifies the resultant emptiness as being: "as if a bottomless hunger was placed at the core of what we are: whatever we acquire, ingest, and consume could never fulfil it . . . [manifested in] the insatiable voraciousness of vampires, their unspeakable desire, and their existence beyond social or cultural boundaries."[39] This reemphasizes the fundamental nature of the vampire on a symbolic, psychic and even physical level where it expresses the most basic need to negotiate the difference between our "real" selves and our socially constructed personas. The "true" self, through its socially unacceptable, or transgressive, behavior, is denied or disavowed, and so, through processes of ejection and projection, it almost inevitably becomes the other that "bites" back. Once differentiated, against its will, it will not leave us alone, and constantly calls upon us to see it and recognize it. The vampire's demand upon us then is not so much one of indiscriminate consumption, or addiction, but one of innate need that expresses its wish to be seen and reintegrated.[40] At the same time this also reveals and accentuates our need to be able to "see." Consequently, this then becomes configured within the "I" and the "Other" and the equal and opposite, echoing "abysses" that each produces in the other. Here the infinite void "created" by insatiable need becomes recognized and thus forms, through an ethical reciprocity, the infinite excess within the giver. Therefore, whilst being defined by its "need to feed," the vampire's hunger, contrary to popular belief, is not a question of living to eat but, in its imperative drive for reparation and recognition, one of eating to live.

Subsequently, the reconfiguration of the unconstrained voraciousness of the "undead" leads to a reappraisal of its eating habits from one of flesh-eating carnage to a sanctified one of communion and interdependent necessity. If blood is then seen as the essence of life itself, as explained in *Leviticus*, "For the life of the flesh is in the blood; and I have given it to you upon the altar to make atonement for your souls; for it is the blood that maketh atonement by reason of the life,"[41] the immanent act of taking this essence *into* the body produces an equal but opposite transcendence where the life essence is expelled *out of* the body. The traditional interpretation of the vampire as a blood-thirsty killer then becomes vital to the idea of human becoming, for its constant craving for our life force, or essence, allows, through the reciprocity of excess, for the possibility of existence beyond the confines of the flesh. Veronica Hollinger identifies this importance of the figure of the vampire to human transcendence when she comments, "[T]he vampire . . . also signals a return, a re-birth into another mode of existence."[42] This interpretation of vampiric hunger would seem to offer a possible explanation of the continuing cultural fascination with vampires where it is not one predicated on fashion but a more fundamental and inherent psychic and spiritual need. Yet this symbiotic dependence, predicated on such a fine balance of desire and satiation, contains within it the worrying proposition regarding any shifts within the relationship, and it is one that is particularly prescient at the beginning of the 21st century when the bloodsuckers of old have been reinvented.

All That Glitters Is Not Gold

The question the contemporary cinematic vampire poses is what happens if the predator of old no longer wants to indulge itself and curbs its inhabitable hunger for human blood . . . and turns vegetarian? This worrying precedent can be traced from the 1980s and Anne Rice's novel *Interview with the Vampire*. Here the character of Louis de Pointe du Lac, played by Brad Pitt in the 1994 Neil Jordan film, configures the first, mainstream, self-loathing vampire, and shows himself to be as weak, conflicted and self-destructive as the humans he is supposed to hunt and feed upon. Subsequently, he dines only on rats and on other small animals. Possibly even more perturbing is his Master, or Sire, Lestat de Lioncourt, the self-styled libertine of vampirism, who proclaims, "I was resolute that I would never drink innocent blood."[43] Such an anachronistic, ethical "bloodlust" can only be a harbinger of worse to come. Subsequent popular representations, such as Blade in *Blade* (Norrington, 1998), *Blade II* (del Toro, 2002), and *Blade Trinity* (Goyer, 2004); and Selene in *Underworld* (Wiseman, 2003) and *Underworld Evolution* (Wiseman, 2006), reverse the expected sympathy for the devil into a love for mankind, showing how contemporary revenants are getting, if not exactly human, then definitely more and more humane and, as a result, less and less abject. No more so than in the Cullen family, as featured in *The Twilight Saga* by Stephenie Meyers.[44]

The *Twilight* story has taken the world, or rather the teen world, by storm with an incredible number of book, film, and merchandising sales. However, the most disturbing part of the phenomenon—beyond a hundred-year-old man, Edward Cullen, born in 1901, dating a teenage girl, Bella Swann—is the fact that the main vampire family are all vegetarian. Obviously, both these terms need qualifying for the Cullens are not what traditionally would be considered either a family or vegetarian. The "family," headed by Dr. Carlisle Cullen and his wife Esme, are related in blood rather than by blood. Three of the five "children," Edward, Rosalie and Emmet, were "sired" or turned by Carlisle, but only when they were on the verge of death, an act driven by salvation rather than salivation. The remaining two Cullen "siblings," Alice and Jasper, chose to join the family of their own accord because of a shared ethical outlook upon human life and the world in general. This, somewhat anachronistically in the words of Meyer herself, sees "all of them bonded by their desire to live more compassionately than normal vampires did."[45] As such, they actually constitute the only "normal" or non-dysfunctional family in Forks, Oregon, where the action takes place, comprising both a loving father, a mother, and five well-adjusted children. Part of this "adjustment" is seen in the fact that they are all vegetarian. Of course, as vampires, they are unable to digest vegetables, so what vegetarianism in fact means is that they do not drink human blood but only that of "free-range" animals. Within the structure of the books and films this produces a very specific result both in their inherent nature as a family and as vampires. As explained by one of the characters in the final installment of the saga *Breaking Dawn*, "[I]t seems to me that intrinsic to this intense family binding—that which makes them possible at all—is the peaceful character of this life of sacrifice."[46] The fundamental cause of this "peaceful character" is directly attributed to their "[a]bstaining from human blood . . . [which consequently] makes us more civilized."[47] This donning of the cloak of civilization positions them in a very peculiar place because if vampires are no longer consuming human flesh, is it still legitimate to denote them as vampires at all?

The question becomes more interesting when one realizes that this is not a natural expression of their innate character but an act of extreme, self-imposed abstinence, for the Cullens *really do* want to drink human blood. We see this in the second film, *The Twilight Saga: New Moon* (Weitz, 2009), when they hold a birthday party for Bella and she accidentally cuts her finger whilst opening a present. As a drop of her blood falls to the floor, Jasper has to be physically restrained from pouncing on her, and the entire family stands and stares longingly at her bleeding finger, forcing Carlisle to shout, "Get Jasper out of here" and then explain apologetically to Bella, "Jasper hasn't been away from human blood as long as the rest of us." The excessive nature of this self-denial is further expressed by Edward in the first *Twilight* novel when he says, "I wrestled all night, while watching you sleep [Bella], with the chasm between what I knew was right, moral, ethical, and what I wanted."[48] Edward's true desire is not restraint but unrestrained consumption; he literally wants to eat Bella alive. His self-imposed asceticism, along with the diet of the entire family, denies all the essential definitions of what a vampire is. A vampire is primarily defined by its physical manifestation as our bad selves, as noted above, and by its insatiable desire for human blood. In *Twilight*, however, the vampire becomes the antithesis of this, being the model for the All-American family, embodying the "good" objects that need to be incorporated and the repression of the unrepressed. This is further shown when, at one point, Edward pleads with Bella, "I don't want to be a monster."[49] One could then ask what happens if our monsters no longer want to be monsters; or if the abject is no longer what we are not but what we want to be? Where are we if the Other no longer demands anything from the Self, but it is the self that desires what the Other is? The psychological processes of this are explained by Suzy McKee Charnas: we reassure ourselves that the monster isn't so bad when you get to know him—he's misunderstood and in fact is often less horrible than we are; or we demonize or deify the monster into an invincible figure with whom we then identify so that we can feel as powerful as he is.[50] This, however, does not extend or take the Self beyond its earthly borders but rather takes all that exceeds, or transcends, the I and contains it within the subject. Such immanence negates a realm outside of everyday experience and denies the life of the spirit that Levinas sees as possible only "in relation to the Other, where being is surpassed."[51]

The Beginning in the End

This chapter has shown that Levinas's notion of the possibility of human transcendence is configured through the "I/Thou" relationship, and specifically in the excessive demands of the Other. The figure of the vampire can be seen as the perfect embodiment of this insatiable Other due, in part, to its liminality but also in its excessive character that configures both human and nonhuman objects, which also manifests the self expelled from the self. This further indicates the necessary categorical equality between the I/Thou, human/vampire relationship which is particularly shown through the act of eating, which Ernest Jones observes in regard to the revenant thus: "[T]he practice of drinking his [human] blood or eating his flesh . . . again shows the reciprocal talion nature of the relationship between the dead and living."[52] Consequently, the crossing, or permeability, of borders, which it inherently embodies, allows not only for an equal and opposite echoing of the infinite within the subject and the object, but also provides an example of possible human becomings beyond any normative categories. The new breed of vampires in the 21st century, primarily seen in the *Twilight Saga*, both novels and films, indicates a worrying turn away from this fundamental and necessary relationship. Further, the contemporary cinematic trend for people-friendly or moral vampires increasingly transforms them so that our monsters are made not only like humans but even more than human so that they are no longer "abhorrational" but aspirational figures. In this dramatic shift the vampire is now not what we define ourselves against, but what we want to become. It then ceases to be a call for mutual recognition, which is both reparative and potentialized, but an entropic and internalizing act of self-negation. As a result, the Cullen family from *The Twilight Saga* do not signal an acceptance of the Other but a disavowal of the self which sees human becoming configured through denial rather than acceptance and, as such, no longer a becoming at all. This sees the Other made in the image of the self, and so it can never be a form of transcendence, just an abysmal, narcissistic immanence. For humanity to go beyond itself, it must have monsters that embody all that it cannot contain, or accept, of itself. We can then become all that we can be, as recognised by Levinas, and not just all that we want to be. What Levinasian transcendence needs is the insatiable hunger of Dracula, not the political correctness of Dr. Carlisle—or, to paraphrase a well-known song from the 1960s, "What the world needs now" is not "love sweet love" but "blood sweet blood."[53]

Notes

1. Roger Scruton, "Eating the World: The Philosophy of Food," *OpenDemocracy* (2003), www.opendemocracy.net/ecologyfoodwithoutfrontiers/article_1224.jsp.

2. Angel F. Méndez Montoya, *Theology of Food: Eating and the Eucharist* (Chichester, UK: John Wiley & Sons, 2009), v.

3. Montoya, *Theology of Food*, 19.

4. For the history of human-vampire relations, see Montague Summers, *The Vampire* (London: Senate, 1928); Paul Barber, *Vampires, Burial, and Death: Folklore and Reality* (Binghamton, NY: Yale University Press, 1988); Alan Dundes, *The Vampire as Bloodthirsty Revenant, in The Vampire: A Casebook* (Madison: University of Wisconsin Press, 1998); and Bruce A. McClellend, *Slayers and Their Vampires: A Cultural History of Killing the Dead* (Ann Arbor: University of Michigan Press, 2006).

5. Taken from Nina Auerbach's often-quoted book *Our Vampires, Ourselves* (Chicago: University of Chicago Press, 1995) where she attributes the characteristics of vampires to the concerns and anxieties of the times and cultures that produce them.

6. Sarah Sceat, "Oral Sex: Vampiric Transgression and the Writing of Angela Carter," *Tulsa Studies in Women's Literature* 20 (2001): 114.

7. Elaine Showalter, *Sexual Anarchy: Gender and Culture at the Fin de Siècle* (London: Virago Press, 1992), 179.

8. Showalter, *Sexual Anarchy*, 179.

9. William Ian Miller, *The Anatomy of Disgust* (Cambridge, MA: Harvard University Press, 1997), 46.

10. David Williams, *Deformed Discourse: The Function of the Monster in Medieval Thought and Literature* (Exeter, UK: University of Exeter Press, 1996), 145.

11. The Ouroboros is a symbol of a serpent or dragon eating its own tail, and it represents the cycle of live, birth, death and regeneration.

12. See also Jacques Derrida, *Of Hospitality*, trans. Rachel Bowlby (Stanford, CA: Stanford University Press, 2000). Jelisaveta Blagojevic, "I Think, Therefore I Think the Other: Derrida's Poetics of Hospitality," *Journal for Politics, Gender, and Culture* 3 (2004): 223–35, offers an interesting interpretation of the mentioned book.

13. Michael Morgan, "Levinas and Buber: Dialogue and Difference," *Notre Dame Philosophical Reviews* (August 2010), http://ndpr.nd.edu/review.cfm?id=4822.

14. Robert Bernasconi, "'Failure of Communication' as a Surplus: Dialogue and Lack of Dialogue between Buber and Levinas," in *Levinas and Buber: Dialogue and Difference*, ed. Peter Atterton et al. (Pittsburgh, PA: Duquesne University Press, 2004), 67.

15. Andrew Kelley, "Reciprocity and the Height of God: A Defense of Buber against Levinas," in Atterton et al., *Levinas and Buber*, 228.

16. Emmanuel Levinas. "Is Ontology Fundamental?" in *Emmanuel Levinas: Basic Philosophical Writings*, ed. A. T. Peperzak et al. (Bloomington: Indiana University Press, 1999), 1–10. See also Atterton et al., *Levinas and Buber*.

17. Morgan, "Levinas and Buber," 1.

18. Here, as inferred by Buber, the act of recognition of another, whether it is a fellow human or inanimate object, constructs it as a subject or fellow "being."

19. Anselm K. Min, "Naming the Unnamable God: Levinas, Derrida and Marion," in *Self and Other: Essays in Continental Philosophy of Religion*, ed. Eugene Thomas Long (Dordrecht: Springer, 2007), 101.

20. Emmanuel Levinas, *Entre Nous: On Thinking-of-the-Other*, trans. Michael B. Smith and Barbara Harshav (New York: Columbia University Press, 1998), 34.

21. Min, "Naming the Unnamable God," 101.

22. Min, "Naming the Unnamable God," 101.

23. Levinas, "Is Ontology Fundamental?" 51–57.

24. Levinas, "Is Ontology Fundamental," 51–57.

25. Michele Saracino. *On Being Human: A Conversation with Lonergan and Levinas* (Milwaukee, WI: Marquette University Press, 2003), 98.

26. Sigmund Freud, "Repression," *The Standard Edition of the Complete Psychological* Works, vol. 14, trans. James Strachey (London: Hogarth Press, 1915), 143–58.

27. Juliet Mitchell, The Selected *Melanie Klein* (New York: Free Press, 1986), 19–21.

28. Mary Douglas, *Purity and Danger: An Analysis of the Concepts of Pollution and Taboo* (New York: Routledge, 1966), 123–24.

29. The fear of social and individual pollution and its necessary expulsion/exclusion is also explored in Mary Douglas's work on Leviticus and the Middle Ages in particular: see Douglas, *Purity and Danger*.

30. Julia Kristeva, *Powers of Horror: An Essay in Abjection*, trans. Leon S. Roudiez (New York: Columbia University Press, 1982), 1.

31. Kristeva, *Powers of Horror*, 3 (emphasis in original).

32. Kristeva, *Powers of Horror*, 15.

33. Sigmund Freud, "Beyond the Pleasure Principle, Group Psychology, and Other Works," in Freud, *The Standard Edition*, 57.

34. Emmanuel Levinas, *Totality and Infinity: An Essay on Exteriority*, trans. Alphonso Lingis (Pittsburgh, PA: Duquesne University Press, 1969), 22–23.

35. Blagojevic, "I Think," 223–35.

36. Julia Kristeva, *Melanie Klein*, trans. Ross Guberman (New York: Columbia University Press, 2001), 234.

37. Kristeva, *Melanie Klein*, 234.

38. See Bruce Fink "Notes from 'The Lacanian Subject': Between Language and Joiussance," in Avoiding the Void (2010), http://avoidingthevoid.wordpress.com/2010/01/04/notes-from-the-lacanian-subject-between-language-and-jouissance-by-bruce-fink/.

39. Fabio Parasecoli, *Bite Me: Food in Popular Culture* (Oxford: Berg, 2008), 51.

40. See Rob Lathem, *Consuming Youth: Vampires, Cyborgs, and the Culture of Consumption* (Chicago: University of Chicago Press, 2002), regarding vampires and consumption; and the films *Habit*, dir. Larry Fessenden (Genius Entertainment, 1997) and *The Thirst*, dir. Jeremy Kasten (Starz, 2007), with regard to vampires and addiction.

41. Leviticus, 17:11.

42. Veronica Hollinger, "Fantasies of Absence: The Postmodern Vampire," in *Blood Read: The Vampire as Metaphor in Contemporary Culture*, ed. Joan Gordon and Veronica Hollinger (Philadelphia: University of Pennsylvania Press, 1997), 212.

43. Anne Rice, *The Vampire Lestat* (London: Sphere, 2009), 18.

44. The saga consists of four books—*Twilight*; *New Moon*; *Eclipse*; and *Breaking Dawn*—published 2005–2008 by Lane, Brown & Company. Each is to be made into a film, with the last part divided into two episodes: *Twilight*, Catherine Hardwicke, dir. (Summit, 2008); *The Twilight Saga: New Moon*, Chris Weitz, dir. (Summit, 2009); *The Twilight Saga: Eclipse*, David Slade, dir. (Summit, 2010); *The Twilight Saga: Breaking Dawn: Part I*, Bill Condon, dir. (Summit, 2011); and *The Twilight Saga: Breaking Dawn: Part II*, Bill Condon, dir. (Summit, 2012).

45. Stephenie Meyer, *Breaking Dawn* (Boston: Little Brown & Co., 2010), 29.

46. Meyer, *Breaking Dawn*, 666.

47. Meyer, *Breaking Dawn*, 559.

48. Stephenie Meyer, *Twilight* (Boston: Little Brown & Co., 2006), 303.

49. Ruth Ferla, "A Trend with Teeth," *New York Times*, July 2, 2009, www.nytimes.com/2009/07/02/fashion/02VAMPIRES.html?pagewanted=all 3).

50. Suzi Mckee Charnas, "Meditations in Red: On Writing the *Vampire Tapestry*," in Gordon and Hollinger, *Blood Read*, 59.

51. Levinas, *Totality and Infinity*, 302.

52. Ernest Jones, *On the Nightmare* (New York: Liveright Publishing, 1951), 116.

53. "What the World Needs Now Is Love" is a 1965 popular song with lyrics by Hal David and music composed by Burt Bacharach. First recorded and made popular by Jackie DeShannon, it was released on April 15, 1965.

Filmography

Blade, dir. Stephen Norrington (New Line Cinema, 1998).
Blade II, dir. Guillermo Del Toro (New Line Cinema, 2002).
Blade Trinity, dir. David S. Goyer (New Line Cinema, 2004).
Twilight, dir. Catherine Hardwicke (Summit Entertainment, 2008).
The Twilight Saga: New Moon, dir. Chris Weitz (Summit Entertainment, 2009).
The Twilight Saga: Eclipse, dir. David Slade (Summit Entertainment, 2010).
Underworld, dir. Len Wiseman (Screen Gems Sony, 2003).
Underworld Evolution, dir. Len Wiseman (Screen Gems Sony, 2006).

II
RACE, GENDER AND THE VAMPIRE

5

The Madonna and Child: Reevaluating Social Conventions through Anne Rice's Forgotten Females

Donna Mitchell

THIS CHAPTER WILL ANALYZE and reevaluate the social conventions placed upon the female in patriarchal society, specifically through the characters of Gabrielle and Claudia in Anne Rice's *Vampire Chronicles*. Rice became a respected figure within the Gothic literary genre most notably for this series, the first of which was published in the 1970s. The success of these novels, which propelled her male protagonists to a cult-figure status that still exists today, unfortunately saw her female characters overshadowed by their male counterparts. By applying feminist ideas, as well as psychoanalytic and post-structuralist theories to the texts, this chapter will examine them from an alternative perspective that uncovers two of Rice's forgotten females as examples of the rigid social constrictions placed on women. Gabrielle signifies an unconventional portrait of motherhood, while Claudia represents the eternal child who is forever vengeful towards her patriarchal constraints. Both characters' time within the novels is quite transient, yet their memory ensures that their presence remains long afterward. They are the most complex and significant females in *The Vampire Chronicles*, and their characteristics shape the standard classification of the Ricean female from which their predecessors are formed.

Still mortal when introduced to the reader, Gabrielle is first mentioned through Lestat's proclamation of his love for her. She is portrayed as a silent figure who is cold and distant towards her husband and children. Sigmund Freud claims that the nature of the mother's relationship with her children is a direct outcome of her marital relationship.[1] As Gabrielle's bond with her husband is quite hostile, so too is her bond with the rest of the family, with the exception of Lestat. Their bond suggests that her true identity is separate from the traditional domestic realm within which she cannot establish her existence. In *The Second Sex*, Simone de Beauvoir raises the idea that the mother's bond with her child is an investigation of herself, as the child becomes "a double, an alter ego, into whom the mother is tempted to project herself entirely."[2]

Gabrielle confesses she feels Lestat is the male version of herself, as she claims that by her living vicariously through him, he is "the man in [her]."[3] This is the first hint of an oedipal complexity within their relationship. It represents a different signification of their original union during pregnancy many years beforehand, as well as a premonition of the future ties that will form between them. Similarly, Lestat sees Gabrielle as the mirror image of himself in both personality and physicality. His dependence on her for the development of his identity can be defined through Jacques Lacan's idea of the mirror stage, as is discussed in *Écrits*. The mirror stage starts when an infant is about six months old when he begins to recognize his own image as such in a mirror. Although the child may be unable to walk or stand yet, he will "overcome his prop in order to . . . view the image [and] fix it in his mind."[4] Lacan states that this mirror phase is crucial as it forms the ego, prior to its social determination. Furthermore, Lacan favors the archaic link to the mother's gaze as the mirror in the continuous development of the child's self-perception that is "mediated by the other's desire."[5] This inaugurates for the child the moment of experiencing that he is the object of her desire and love. The child cannot later recognize himself as a desirable object until he knows he is the exclusive object of her desire at this stage.[6] In accord with Lacan's theory, Gabrielle becomes Lestat's mirror in the text, as her undivided love is a major contributor to the development of his character and ego. Her joint roles as mother and lover combine the two images of female desire, thus making this reflection even more powerful.

The nature of their relationship threatens social order, as it alludes to the desire for an incestuous union between mother and son. In *Totem and Taboo*, Freud discusses the issue of incest, claiming that "even the most distant grades of relationship [have always been] recognized as an absolute obstacle to sexual union."[7] In *The Interpretation of Dreams*, this concept is psychoanalytically examined in relation to Freud's theory of the Oedipus complex, in which he claims that the young boy harbors a repressed desire to possess his mother sexually and kill his father. Freud defines it as being a sexual preference from an early age, whereby "a boy's first childish desires are for his mother," which causes the father to become a "disturbing rival" to the son. This desire is usually the result of the Mother's natural instinct to spoil her son, and "as the child is well aware of this partiality, he turns against that one . . . who is opposed to showing it."[8] Gabrielle's interest in Lestat grows as she recognizes his dissimilarity to his father and brothers. Her dependency on him portrays de Beauvoir's idea of the mother-son relationship, whereby the mother relies on her son to be "her liberator [who will] defend her against the domination of her husband."[9] As well as supporting Lestat in any arguments with his father, Gabrielle also defies her husband incessantly, which illustrates her lack of conformity towards the traditional expectations of marriage within a patriarchal society. This mutiny allows her a taste of freedom from the social restraints placed on the female.

Entrusting Lestat as her confidant, she commits her strongest rejection of the maternal role when she breaks women's silence and confesses the true horror of labor to Lestat, claiming that it was only during the "vulgar act of giving birth, that I understood the meaning of utter loneliness."[10] Aware of her social obligation as a married woman to have children despite the risks associated with childbirth, her confession depicts John Donne's paradoxical reference to the womb as being a "house of death" for many women who do not survive the experience, as noted by Ann Dally in *Inventing Motherhood: The Consequences of an Ideal.*[11] By confessing her feelings regarding childbirth, Gabrielle reveals the true loneliness of the experience and, in doing so, breaks the feminine tradition of secrecy. De Beauvoir exposes the pain and fear of the act with her idea that the mother sees "this [newborn] projection of herself as a foreshadowing of her death."[12] This notion is echoed in Gabrielle's description that she "felt trapped in the pain, knowing the only release was the birth or [her] own death."[13]

Following her rejection of the social expectations on the expectant mother, Gabrielle confesses that her greatest desire is to reject the many sexual inhibitions placed upon women. She voices her wish to get drunk and be naked and to embrace her primitive instincts. Her longing to escape life and return to nature is evident in her confession that she wants to bathe naked in a stream and afterward take multiple lovers to her bed. This is a very significant moment for her character and is core to her gaining independence from male supremacy, as she claims that "in this moment . . . I belong to no-one."[14] These words clearly indicate that she feels trapped within the constraints that society has put on her life as an upper-class woman. She becomes the aporetic embodiment of de Beauvoir's feminine and emancipated woman as she wishes to enchain man "by means of the desire she arouses in him, in submissively making herself a thing," while simultaneously wanting to be "active, a taker, and [to refuse] the passivity man means to impose on her."[15]

The process whereby Lestat gives immortality to Gabrielle symbolizes a deconstructed image of childbirth as it demands an irreversible unification of their beings in both body and blood, which consequently brings their relationship to an intimate climax. This blurring of identity is the ultimate incestuous act, and it sees Lestat define Gabrielle as both his "flesh and blood and mother and lover."[16] The act of feeding his blood to her is a deconstruction of the act of breastfeeding a newborn infant. A reversal in their familial roles is seen here as Gabrielle is temporarily dependent on him for her survival and sustenance. De Mausse defines this process as a parent-child reversal. The child becomes a substitute for the adult figure, leading to a reversal in familial roles.[17] While de Beauvoir argues that "it is in maternity that woman finds her physiological destiny,"[18] it is not until Gabrielle's immortal rebirth that she reaches her physical potential, as her new identity allows her finally to gain the social freedom that she has always desired.

By removing her from society, Lestat has given Gabrielle the liberty to defy her former molds of wife and mother, and so she can now experiment with her outward appearance. In doing so she epitomizes Judith Butler's argument in *Gender Trouble*, which uses various theorists to explore the idea that gender and sexuality are performative constructs, as Gabrielle embraces her new identity by taking on an androgynous persona. Her newfound supernatural strength gives her the ability to explore the world as she has always wanted. She immediately revels in this independence and casts no nostalgic thought on her previously maternal role. Both her lack of mourning for her family life and disregard for her other children illustrate how she differs from the traditional version of the mother. Lestat acknowledges Gabrielle's emancipation from her old identity when he describes her outward appearance as now having "no chains . . . free to soar."[19] During this transition, Gabrielle temporarily feels the acceptance that she has always longed for, as Lestat describes her in raw and honest terms as being "simply who she was. She was Gabrielle."[20] It is only at this stage that he calls her by her name instead of "Mother," as the dynamic of their relationship continues to progress towards an almost romantic one. He also looks upon her narcissistically as a mirror image of his immortal self. This mutual identification supports the earlier notion of Gabrielle being Lestat's mirror during his infantile mirror stage, and it also confirms the Lacanian concept that its influence continues right through to the child's adulthood.

Gabrielle's struggle for identity continues throughout her immortal life as she welcomes the opportunity to define herself without social restraint. The Gothic technique of doubling, first made popular by Edgar Allen Poe, is seen here in her complete consumption of her victims. Repeating the reverse breast-feeding act, Gabrielle now gains sustenance from her first victim as she drains his blood completely. She exemplifies Butler's claim that "a woman's fantasy [is] to take the place of men"[21] as she strips him down and puts on his clothes. In doing so she steals not only his life but also his masculinity: "as

[when] she put on his garments, she became the man."[22] She continues this reinvention of herself by cutting her long, blonde hair into a short, masculine style, thus mirroring Lestat to an even greater extent than before. The power struggle between the two characters seems to begin when Gabrielle chooses to wear men's clothing instead of her usual restrictive and elaborate gowns. Lestat's dissatisfaction with her actions epitomizes de Beauvoir's argument that the woman's body seems to a man to be his property, covered with ornamental attire so as to transform her into an idol. De Beauvoir claims that the function of this ornamentation is to make her share more intimately in nature, while at the same time removing her from the natural world. In other words, nature is present within the woman, but has been remolded nearer to man's desire.[23] Lestat reluctantly confesses that their power struggle is also partly due to the fact that Gabrielle made a better vampire than he, as "she was colder than I. She was better at all of it."[24] In addition to this, Lestat is aware from the beginning that he is the more dependent of the two as "unlike her, [he] cannot stand to be alone."[25] In an effort to appease him, Gabrielle wears her hair long and loose again, and dresses in proper, feminine clothing, pretending to be "a great and beautiful lady for a little while."[26] This demonstrates de Beauvoir's masquerade theory that women use their femininity in a deliberate way in order to renounce any desire for possession of the phallus that can be obtained only through castration. De Beauvoir claims that "this fear of retribution is the consequence of woman's fantasy to take the place of men, more precisely, the father."[27]

As Lestat is now Gabrielle's creator and father, Gabrielle's masquerade functions mainly as an illusion to disguise her challenge of his position. Lestat has already acknowledged that she is the superior predator, so Gabrielle's masquerade is necessary to maintain the status quo of their fragile union. His desired vision of Gabrielle is identical to de Beauvoir's vision of "the good wife," which de Beauvoir claims is man's most precious treasure for which he is responsible and in which he takes more pride than he does any other possession, as she is the measure through which his power is illustrated to society.[28] Therefore Lestat's wish to adorn Gabrielle in bourgeois clothing and jewels is due to his belief that she is a mirror image of his social representation. Unfortunately for him, Gabrielle resists this role and focuses on only representing her true self. Her lack of cooperation illustrates her dissimilarity to the typical woman who de Beauvoir claims would usually allow herself passively to be shaped by the husband she represents,[29] meaning that Gabrielle's peaceful times with Lestat are transient. Furthermore, Gabrielle's relentless silence has transitioned into her immortal life, so she cannot express her principles properly to Lestat. As, according to Freudian theory, language is the development of the superego, Gabrielle's constant struggle with verbal

communication suggests an internal resistance to its development. Consequently, her later decision to discard social regulation in favor of the tran-
quility of nature can be seen as the ultimate rejection of her superego. This
supports Freud's judgment that women develop a weaker conscience or
superego than their male counterparts.[30] As the nature of Gabrielle's silence
is self-inflicted, it symbolizes an absolute inner harmony with her id, as she
wishes to fulfill her savage but instinctual need for blood without the intru-
sion of social conscience or patriarchal judgment.

Gabrielle's obsession with the natural world occurs because she considers it an alternative to patriarchal society. When she decides to spend her
daytime rest within the earth itself, Lestat witnesses the ease with which the
union takes place. He notes how the earth envelops her effortlessly "as if [it]
belonged to her" and afterward, that "the leaves settled as if nothing had
disturbed the spot."[31] Her fear for the preservation of nature is expressed
through her desire for vampires to use their supernatural power to carry out
vigilante justice on the world's population, as she sees humankind as being
predominantly male and fears it will inevitably destroy the natural world.

She anticipates the vampire Akasha at this point as she argues that eventually a leader will ascend and encourage those suppressed by social law to rise
up against it. Akasha will represent a return of the repressed, as she becomes
a substitute mother and lover for Lestat many years after he has parted ways
with Gabrielle.

While Lestat takes comfort in the order of the patriarchal social system,
Gabrielle longs for the freedom and chaos of a more primitive world. Aware
that these different beliefs are major factors in their lifestyle choices, Lestat
and Gabrielle finally recognize the need to go their separate ways as "she
could not give me what I wanted of her. There was nothing I could do to
make her what she would not be . . . *what she really wanted was to be free.*"[32]
It is only at this stage that Lestat finally accepts Gabrielle's need for freedom
from him too, as he is the only tie that binds her to a society that she hates
so passionately. The complexity of her evolution within the text shows how
Gabrielle represents a new performative paradigm of the previously under-
developed maternal role in Gothic texts. Her inability to fit into the mold of
the mother is even greater after this progression which, as Laurence Rickels
points out in *The Vampire Lectures*, could be the reason why their family unit
cannot continue on. Rickels argues that "the body is the mother. By declaring the mother off-limits, the body has been declared off-limits."[33] In other
words, the state of Gabrielle and Lestat's relationship was always doomed, as
Gabrielle's maternal role ensured that she was off-limits to him even before
he welcomed her to vampirism.[34] This means that the progression of the relationship itself is now also problematic, as it is no longer familial or incestuous

in nature. As it cannot develop any further, it simply ceases to exist, and they go their separate ways. Gabrielle briefly returns many years later to support Lestat's struggle against Akasha, but she quickly returns to her preferred life within the natural world afterward.

Lestat's subsequent creation, Claudia, is, in the words of Anne Rice, "a metaphor for the raging mind trapped within a powerless body."[35] She enters the text initially as one of Louis's victims, but it is Lestat who cements her place within it when he sees her as both a ruse to keep Louis bound to him as well as an opportunity to create a doppelgänger of himself. As Rice's vampires have no sexual identity and can no longer engage in sexual relations once they have transitioned to immortality, gender boundaries become blurred and her male characters tend to become more feminized. This theory is proven by Lestat's actions which consequently see him become a maternal figure within the text. The act of turning Claudia imitates the mother who hopes "to compensate for her inferiority by making a superior creature out of one whom she regards as her double."[36] He sees in Claudia the opportunity to mold both a deadlier version of himself as well as a version of Gabrielle over whom he can exert complete control. Simultaneously, Claudia's rebellion against Lestat's authority and subsequent plot to bring about his demise reflect de Beauvoir's claim that the potential mother—in this case Lestat—sees procreation as "a foreshadowing of her death."[37]

Claudia's relationships with Lestat and Louis are almost incestuous in nature and are best explained using Carl Jung's theory of the Electra complex as discussed in *The Theory of Psychoanalysis*, which defines the young girl's "typical affection for the father . . . with a correspondingly jealous attitude towards the mother."[38] It is the feminine version of the Oedipus complex and was inspired by Sophocles' tragedy *Electra*. Jung claims that though it is a typical complex that develops in early childhood, it is also quite transient in nature, as the sexual development of the child means that "what surrounds us daily . . . loses its compelling charm and thus forces the libido to search for new objects [to] prevent . . . inbreeding."[39] This theory is also supported by Rickels, who claims incestuous relations are a typical characteristic of the Gothic family that is "held together unconsciously by the incest taboo"[40] as it "is not kept unconscious, is not repressed . . . It is the Law . . . *Every body is* made infinitely available to everybody else.[41]

Claudia's existence within the family unit is initially peaceful due to her unquestionable acceptance of their authority as her mind is still that of a child. Her love for Lestat ensures her desire to please him, so she silently follows his instruction and soon matches his skill at hunting. But their relationship becomes endangered when Claudia's mind matures and she subsequently gains a better understanding of her situation. Although she is still ignorant of the exact details of her transition to immortality, she assumes the responsibility lies with Lestat. This brings about a powerful hatred on her behalf and sees their relationship irreconcilably damaged as he considers her to be a threat to his authority. He tries to intimidate her back into submission, but only succeeds in ensuring her wrath. Their conflict reaches a climax during an argument in which Lestat quotes Ferdinand from Webster's *Duchess of Malfi*: "Cover her face; Mine eyes dazzle; She died young."[42] In doing so he condemns himself, as Claudia interprets the words as an unrepentant confession. The disharmony within their family at this stage mirrors that of the play's world, as Claudia decides to exact her revenge on Lestat and begins her deadly plot, declaring, "[T]he secret is that I want to kill him . . . I want him dead and I will have him dead. I shall enjoy it."[43] The ensuing betrayal sees their family torn apart and destroyed. Claudia's rebellion against and betrayal of Lestat is a very definite example of the Electra complex, which de Beauvoir expands upon by discussing the development of an inferiority complex within the young girl, as well as a growing resentment of the father's position within the family. The young girl's reaction to this situation can be defined as the "masculine protest," which calls for her to either masculinize herself, as seen in Gabrielle's case, or make use of her feminine weapons to wage war on the male,[44] as illustrated by Claudia. As Lestat is both the matriarch of their family as well as the patriarchal leader of their coven, he must face her wrath on both accounts. This leads Claudia to use her innocent facade and sexuality to persuade Louis into aiding her betrayal of Lestat.

Simultaneously, her relationship with Louis is quite sensual in nature as they often exchange intimate kisses and caresses, with Louis claiming on more than one occasion that they are "father and daughter. Lover and lover."[45] Over time they start to see each other as married spouses, as Louis tells her that "we are wed."[46] However, Claudia's resentment towards him grows as steadily as her despair at being trapped within a child's body, and eventually, when her hatred of him blossoms, she confesses, "I love you still, that's the torment of it. Lestat I never loved. But you . . . do you know how much I hate you!?"[47] When Claudia's diary entries are found many years later, Louis learns that her love towards him was, in part, a Machiavellian scheme to gain his loyalty and help her take revenge on Lestat. The passages reveal her innermost feelings towards her "evil parents"[48] and her immortal state for which she actually "holds Louis far more accountable than Lestat"[49] but realizes that "Louis will do as I wish, even unto the very destruction of Lestat, which I plan in every detail . . . so there my loyalty lies, under the guise of love even in my own heart."[50] Her vengeful intent is twofold as she knows that this betrayal will also devastate Louis, as it will weigh heavily on his conscience and lead to his eventual downfall: "so that his soul, if not his body, is the same size at last as my own."[51] Although she is murdered before she can witness this downfall, her memory remains a constant presence within the texts. While Lestat is haunted by the memory of Gabrielle and occasionally Claudia, it is Louis who bears the burden of Claudia's loss as eventually he "lives in torment" and "thinks of nothing else."[52]

Claudia's constant silence is one of her most captivating characteristics, one that became a standard feature of many Ricean females to succeed her in *The Vampire Chronicles*, as illustrated by Gabrielle's silent desolation, Pandora's silent indifference, and Akasha's inanimate, centuries-long sleep, as well as the tragically mute Mekare. Louis notes the progression of her silence over the years. As a newborn vampire, her mind is that of a child struggling to adjust to her new circumstances, so he initially interprets it as a bemused silence. He later fears for her sanity, stating that "she was mysteriously quiet."[53] He struggles to understand her disposition as "mute and beautiful, she played with dolls . . . mute and beautiful, she killed."[54] Her psychological evolution is illustrated by her sudden interest in reading Aristotle and playing Mozart on the piano. Now fully aware of the innocent disguise that her silent and youthful femininity gives her, she mirrors Gabrielle by using it to lure concerned adults to her side as victims. Lestat is initially indifferent to her silence, but he becomes wary of it once he recognizes her growing resentment towards him. He realizes that hers is no longer a submissive silence, but rather an ominous threat, which he tries to counteract with his menacing promise to "break [her] into a thousand pieces."[55]

The numerous comparisons between Claudia and dolls throughout the text raise the notion of de Beauvoir's interpretation of Freud's penis envy. De Beauvoir states that "to compensate . . . and serve [the young girl] as alter ego, she is given a foreign object: a doll [that] will serve the girl as substitute for . . . the penis."[56] The confusion with this act is that "the doll represents the whole body" while simultaneously being "a passive object," which will inevitably lead the young girl to "identify her whole person and to regard this as an inert given object."[57] De Beauvoir argues that this passivity is the essential characteristic of the "feminine" woman and is "a trait that develops in her from her earliest years,"[58] thus perpetuating the docile nature that patriarchy enforces upon women. She notes that through the doll, the young girl gains her idyllic representation of physical femininity and so wishes to be pretty and admired just like her doll. In order to do so "she must make herself an object" and renounce her autonomy, so as to become "a live doll [that] is refused liberty."[59]

Claudia's struggle within male supremacy is best analyzed through the various doll analogies in the text. Louis repeatedly celebrates her doll-like appearance, despite his knowledge of her psychological development. In doing so, he condemns her to the social consequences of her exterior semblance:

"Doll, doll, I called her. That's what she was. A magic doll."[60] Claudia is given countless dolls throughout her immortal life. While she primarily loves them as a child, she soon sees them as a symbol of her own social misrepresentation: "Yes, I resemble her baby dolls . . . Is that what you still think I am?"[61] Her constant resistance to the male figures of her world illustrates how the bindings of patriarchy are an inescapable reality for the female. Her character also portrays how female resistance to the social norm is not strong enough to conquer these perpetual limitations.

As the conversion to immortality is a form of rebirth and gender blurring for vampires, the transition sees them return to an infantile state, with Claudia being used as an alternative doll substitute for Lestat's and Louis's lost sexuality. Similarly, Claudia's obsession with dolls at first, and later with the doll-maker, Madeleine, portrays her penis envy within a society that demands compliance based on her child-like exterior. She sees Madeleine as a maternal figure, but also as a lady-doll over which she has power, thus challenging the dynamics of patriarchy. Her obsession begins when she visits Madeleine's shop and asks the doll-maker to create a lady doll for her. She notes how all of the baby dolls have "the same face, lips"[62] as an effigy of her deceased daughter to whom Claudia is physically similar. Claudia regards Madeleine as a kindred spirit who was also denied a mother-daughter bond. Madeleine's inability to mourn her daughter as well as her infatuation with Claudia explains her immediate willingness to become a vampire. Their relationship is based on tragedy, and one which Rickels suggests is a portrayal of the disconnection between mother and child within the text.[63]

Claudia also mirrors the creature in Mary Shelley's *Frankenstein* on many occasions, not only through her fortuitous fate as the experimental creation of a senseless eccentric, but also through her tragic demise. The initial reason for her creation was to make Lestat's other progeny happy, as Claudia soon realizes that "he made me . . . to be [Louis's] companion."[64] She becomes as fixated on maternal love and absent mothers as *Frankenstein*'s creature who "was forever deprived of the delights that such beautiful creatures could bestow."[65] She spends her immortal life mourning the loss of her mortality as well as the love of her biological mother. In a final similarity and morbid reversal of the birth of *Frankenstein*'s monster as well as the Everywoman in Shelley Jackson's *Patchwork Girl*, her death sees her body dismembered as she begs Armand to relieve her of her childish anatomy. He recounts how, on her request, he decapitated her so as to reattach her head to the body of an adult vampire and give her the form that she had always desired, but instead he created "a writhing jerking catastrophe" that was "a botched reassemblage of the angelic child she had [once] been,"[66] so he left her out in the sunlight to be destroyed.

While their identities may be quite difficult to define in simple terms, together Gabrielle and Claudia represent an antithesis of the conventional female figure in both textual and social terms. Marianne Hester notes how patriarchy is reliant on consent or force as well as ideological pressures for its survival.[67] Gabrielle represents the mother's constant struggle against these ideological pressures in both the private and public sectors. The true horror of her situation is revealed when she removes herself entirely from society to embrace the natural realm, only to be replaced through the doubling technique by Claudia and Akasha. Claudia's definition within the female spectrum is even more ambiguous, as the disconnection between her physicality and mentality illustrates the female's struggle for identity within a world which constantly tries to define her in simplistic terms that adhere to social classifications. In both cases, life with Lestat ends when the women no longer wish to define themselves according to his patriarchal preferences. Their subsequent displacement from the social world within the text illustrates the potential consequences of female rebellion against male supremacy.

Notes

1. Simone de Beauvoir, *The Second Sex* (London: Vintage, 1997), 532.

2. De Beauvoir, *The Second Sex*, 205–28.

3. Anne Rice, *The Vampire Lestat* (London: Time Warner Books, 1985), 72–73.

4. Jacques Lacan, *Écrits* (New York: W.W. Norton & Company, 1966), 76.

5. Lacan, *Écrits*, 77.

6. Jean-Michael Rabaté, *Jacques Lacan: Psychoanalysis and the Subject of Literature* (Basingstoke, UK: Palgrave, 2003), 30–194.

7. Sigmund Freud, *Totem and Taboo* (New York: Moffat, Yard & Co., 1918), 9.

8. Sigmund Freud, *The Interpretation of Dreams* (New York: Basic Books, 2010), 274–75.

9. De Beauvoir, *The Second Sex*, 596.

10. Rice, *The Vampire Lestat*, 46.

11. Ann Dally, *Inventing Motherhood: The Consequences of an Ideal* (London: Burnett, 1982), 31.

12. Dally, *Inventing Motherhood*, 515.

13. Rice, *The Vampire Lestat*, 46.

14. Rice, *The Vampire Lestat*, 48.

15. De Beauvoir, *The Second Sex*, 727.

16. Rice, *The Vampire Lestat*, 174.

17. Dally, *Inventing Motherhood*, 61.

18. De Beauvoir, *The Second Sex*, 501.

19. Rice, *The Vampire Lestat*, 181.

20. Rice, *The Vampire Lestat*, 174.

21. Judith Butler, *Gender Trouble: Feminism and the Subversity of Identity* (London: Routledge, 1990), 65.

22. Rice, *The Vampire Lestat*, 189.

23. De Beauvoir, *The Second Sex*, 190–1.

24. Rice, *The Vampire Lestat*, 189.

25. Rice, *The Vampire Lestat*, 310.

26. Rice, *The Vampire Lestat*, 364.

27. Butler, *Gender Trouble*, 51.

28. De Beauvoir, *The Second Sex*, 207.

29. De Beauvoir, *The Second Sex*, 208.

30. Sharon Heller, *Freud: A to Z* (Hoboken, NJ: John Wiley & Sons, 2005), 124.

31. Rice, *The Vampire Lestat*, 348.

32. Rice, *The Vampire Lestat*, 381.

33. Laurence A. Rickels, *The Vampire Lectures* (Minneapolis: University of Minnesota Press, 1999), 342.

34. Rickels, *The Vampire Lectures*, 344.

35. Katherine Ramsland, "The Lived World of Anne Rice's Novels," in *The Gothic World of Anne Rice*, ed. Gary Hoppenstand and Ray B. Browne (Bowling Green, OH: Bowling Green State University Press, 1996), 21.

36. De Beauvoir, *The Second Sex*, 533.

37. De Beauvoir, *The Second Sex*, 515.

38. Carl Jung, *The Theory of Psychoanalysis* (New York: Journal of Nervous and Mental Disease Publishing Company, 1915), 69.

39. Jung, *The Theory of Psychoanalysis*, 70.

40. Rickels, *The Vampire Lectures*, 342.

41. Rickels, *The Vampire Lectures*, 342.

42. John Webster, *The Duchess of Malfi* (Manchester, UK: University of Manchester Press, 1977), 49.

43. Anne Rice, *Interview with the Vampire* (London: Time Warner Books, 1976), 137.

44. De Beauvoir, *The Second Sex*, 74.

45. Rice, *Interview with the Vampire*, 112.

46. Rice, *Interview with the Vampire*, 269.

47. Rice, *Interview with the Vampire*, 284.

48. Anne Rice, *Merrick* (London: Chatto & Windus Press, 2000), 249.

49. Rice, *Merrick*, 350.

50. Rice, *Merrick*, 349.

51. Rice, *Merrick*, 350.

52. Rice, *Merrick*, 340.

53. Rice, *Interview with the Vampire*, 108.

54. Rice, *Interview with the Vampire*, 108.

55. Rice, *Interview with the Vampire*, 121.

56. De Beauvoir, *The Second Sex*, 306.

57. De Beauvoir, *The Second Sex*, 306.

58. De Beauvoir, *The Second Sex*, 307.

59. De Beauvoir, *The Second Sex*, 308.

60. Rice, *Interview with the Vampire*, 113.

61. Rice, *Interview with the Vampire*, 224.

62. Rice, *Interview with the Vampire*, 224.

63. Rickels, *The Vampire Lectures*, 320.

64. Rice, *Interview with the Vampire*, 130.

65. Mary Shelley, *Frankenstein* (London: Penguin Books, 1818), 138.

66. Anne Rice, *The Vampire Armand* (London: Chatto & Windus Press, 1998), 271.

67. Marianne Hester, *Lewd Women and Wicked Witches: A Study of the Dynamics of Male Domination* (London: Routledge, 1992), 44.

6

Female Empowerment:
Buffy and Her Heiresses in Control

Karin Hirmer

Mythology: Contextualizing the Vampire

VAMPIRES AND "THEIR APPEAL [ARE] dramatically generational."[1] The *Buffy* generation was socialized in the 1990s, when "power and control" was one of the major issues in all cultural products. *Buffy* was about female empowerment, and its seven seasons were a coming-of-age story. It is no surprise that the reaction of many *Buffy* fans to the latest installments of on-screen vampire drama is often highly critical. The infamous YouTube video "Buffy vs. Edward" displays the conflict between two generations.[2] Yet it is interesting that the wrath of the fans mainly hits Edward, the male protagonist of *Twilight*, whereas there would be much more reason to focus it on Bella, the anti-Buffy. Whatever has happened to the female protagonists of vampire drama?

Since the 1990s there have been two major changes relevant to this chapter: the quality of TV shows, and the new vampire as the neighbor. With the appearance of *Buffy the Vampire Slayer* and *The Sopranos*, TV shows started to change drastically. Scripted TV shows became more complex, more daring and certainly better founded. *Buffy* was one of the first shows with a devoted geek fandom that appreciated the show's devotion to detail and coherence. Today's vampire shows, *True Blood*, *Moonlight*, *Being Human* and *The Vampire Diaries*, acknowledge *Buffy*'s iconic status and respond to devoted fans who prefer logic and coherence.

The creators of the Buffyverse make clear in the very first episode of *Buffy*, "Welcome to the Hellmouth," that there is a great emphasis on mythology.

Giles, who later becomes a main character in his own right, mainly serves the purpose of exposition throughout season 1, thus ensuring that context is always provided. He explains to Xander and Willow,

> The books tell that the last demon to leave this earth fed of a human; mixed their blood. He was a human form, but affected by the demon's soul. He bit another, and another, and so they walk the earth, feeding—killing some, mixing their blood with others to make more of them. Waiting for the animals to die out, hoping for the old ones to return (*Buffy*, S01 E01).

None of the newer shows have a knowledgeable character like Giles, who researches things ahead of time; and as a result, explanations, if any, are usually presented in hindsight. *Buffy* is sometimes illogical in means of production—for example, when it comes to the library cage, which actually should not hold anything. However, the show is fully aware of the tradition it follows, as evidenced by the episode "Buffy versus Dracula" (S05 E01). The show's creators also have paid close attention to continuity, like making "The First," a villain who first appeared in "Amends" (S03 E01) when it tried to make Angel commit suicide, the "Big Bad" of the last season.

"The essence of genre is the fundamental recipe of repetition and difference."[3] The rightfully cancelled *Moonlight* tried to combine vampire fiction with a film-noir tradition, but it largely failed to be innovative enough to draw a large audience. The show reflected vampire mythology but reduced it to a point where it almost did not matter anymore. An interview at the beginning of the show was supposed to characterize Mick as wanting to belong, wanting to live out in the open.

> Interviewer: Do you sleep in a coffin?

> Mick: No, that's an old wives tale. I sleep in a freezer. And while we're on the subject: garlic is tasty on pizza; toss holy water on me, I get wet; crucifixes, okay, if you like that kind of thing; oh, and I definitely can't turn into a bat. ("No Such Thing as Vampires," S01 E01)

This interview reveals the show's dilemma: Mick states that the coffins are old wives tales but does not explain why he sleeps in a freezer or what vampires did before there were freezers. The show's creators relied too much on repetition to set up a genre show, and they failed in making it different.

The more successful shows build on repetition, genre and mythology, but they deviate largely in order to come up with a new approach. *True Blood*, a very raunchy show on HBO, follows the darkness of the genre and is also quite coherent in its storytelling, but it is the visualization of the Sookie Stackhouse novels that has helped to create a unique atmosphere, somewhere between the Gothic tradition and the sensual notion of the South. Mythology is presented only when necessary; the main focus is on the vampires having come out into the public, since the invention of artificial "True Blood" allows them to survive without human blood. This is the only show in which vampires fully live out in the open, although season 8 of *Buffy* (the comics) follows that path in giving Harmony a reality TV show, and more and more people seem to know about vampires in *The Vampire Diaries*.

Storytelling in *The Vampire Diaries* has a tendency to be complicated rather than complex. Particularly in its first season, *The Vampire Diaries* is more a teenage drama than anything else. It has many similarities to *Dawson's Creek*, which was also created by Kevin Williamson: love triangles, high-school dilemmas, and dead-serious characters. The mythology comes in second place, although the creators drew on fog and ravens in the "Pilot" (S01 E01) as a reminder of the show's Gothic tradition. However, "Let's put a ring on it" is the solution to most problems: most vampires have a ring to protect them in broad daylight; and jewelry with Vervane in it makes humans vampire-repellant. With each episode, *The Vampire Diaries* finds its own approach to vampire mythology. Season 2, for instance, revolves around the idea of a Shamanic curse, which explains why vampires cannot walk in the sunlight and werewolves can only turn at the full moon. ("Masquerade," S02 E07)

The latest installment of vampire shows is *Being Human*, a U.S. remake of a U.K. series that centers on a werewolf, a vampire and a ghost (the only female protagonist) who share a flat. This show puts far more emphasis on difference than on repetition, and it has been quite successful in creating a coherent mythology in its first two U.S. seasons—with vampires being able to walk in the sunlight but not liking it due to their hypersensitivity, for example.

Moreover, *Being Human* is the best example of the second big change in vampire shows since the 1990s: the shift of the vampire from dangerous "Other" to a neighborly and sympathetic person. *Being Human* takes this literally by making a werewolf, a ghost and a vampire into flat mates, setting them up in the ultimate non-Gothic environment. The show addresses the crucial dilemma of these new nonhumans in its title: What does it mean and require to be human?

All four recent shows have moved on to this concept of the vampire as the neighbor,[4] even if the vampire doesn't live out in the open. The vampire, no longer "the other," becomes the object or the subject of these shows, leaving the humans marginalized and certainly less interesting.

One other side effect of vampires at the center of attention is that their characters become essential to the shows' narratives, and new species need to be added to contrast and fight with them. Even Buffy is not just a vampire slayer, but also a demon slayer: the third episode features a witch as the "demon of the week" to establish this ("Witch," S01 E03). And after season 2, with Angel as the Big Bad, the show sees a demon-cyber-hybrid, a goddess, a witch, and evil itself as the villains Buffy has to defeat. The various species in *True Blood, The Vampire Diaries* and *Being Human* serve yet another purpose. They support the idea that each character has its own agenda. Sure, there is still the Big Bad of the season, which can either be deviant vampires, like Russel in *True Blood*, Klaus in *The Vampire Diaries*, or Bishop in *Being Human*; or other mythological figures, such as Maryann the maenad. However, the main narrative draws on the fact that all the different characters represent different motifs and constantly shifting alliances.

The main consequence of vampires as a group of characters who are not dusted as soon as their arch is over is that vampires now have to find a place in society. In *Being Human* and *Moonlight*, this is still dealt with on a personal level, as no one knows of the vampires' existence. The clearest attempt to establish themselves as an ethnic minority is undertaken by the vampires in *True Blood*. In *The Vampire Diaries*, vampires mainly have to justify and fight the Founders' Council, who clearly have a more traditional and "prejudicial" perspective on vampires: they kill, and thus they should be killed.

Mental Control

Adding to this conflict is the issue of mental control: "control *of* the mind, to control *by* the mind, even the control of *others'* minds."[5] There is a difference in power relations if the individual human has his own will. "The Thrall" matters—if vampires can enthrall or compel humans, there are consequences for the concept of free will and agency. The control of others' minds was a central theme for the creators of the *Buffy* series; but on *Buffy*, only Dracula has the thrall. At the end of season 4, Big Bad Adam briefly has mental control over Riley, but the latter overcomes it. Jennifer Stuller states that

> in the Buffyverse, the individual human or demon in question is provided with the agency to decide what kind of life to live and what kind of person they want to be . . . Along with female power, redemption is one of the overriding themes of the Whedonverse.[6]

I would argue, though, that the focus in *Buffy* is on the choices humans make, or in a broader sense: the people with a soul. In the four most recent shows it is the vampires who struggle with the choice to be good or evil, and depending on their will, humans without powers are subject to the thrall (all but Sookie, as she is a fairy, and *Moonlight* in general). Since supernaturals cannot compel each other, with the exception of the Originals in *The Vampire Diaries*, power obviously is on the nonhuman side, and so is the need to control it. In the pilot, Stefan writes about his struggle in his journal: "I lost control today. Everything I've kept buried inside came rushing to the surface" ("Pilot," S01 E01). And the female protagonists of these shows, or human characters in general, have to deal with external forces of evil, rather than overcoming their own ambiguity.

Power vs. Control: The Narrative of Control, Power and Emotions

Buffy has to face forces of evil regularly. The show's "demon-of-the-week" episodes are mainly about learning how to kill the monster. Whenever a new villain appears, the first thing the Scoobies do is hit the books. Thus "knowledge is power," and it is used for so-called predictive control.

Figuring out how to use power is very often the plot, but the underlying narrative is how to control this power. One major issue here is dealing with emotions, as Carolyn Korsmeyer states in "Passion and Action": "The treatment of emotions in *Buffy* covertly links the fanciful fictional world with ongoing philosophical issues concerning the relative power (or lack thereof) of reason and emotion to determine choice and action."[7]

Emotions empower the Scoobies: often when Buffy is losing a fight, her opponent annoys her, and she wins. The same happens to Sookie, when she is threatened or someone she loves is in danger; and Caroline beats Damon because she "is angrier" (*The Vampire Diaries*, "Disturbing Behavior," S03 E04).

But it is not only anger that motivates action and agency and thus helps to channel an already existing power; it is love when Buffy stabs Faith for Angel, and grief which makes Willow go further in doing magic than ever before. And here it becomes clear that "power" is a misnomer. Rarely does the individual's power increase—it has been there all the time. But emotions make the characters direct it toward a specific goal—and they gain control.

Differentiation: Power, Control, Responsibility Trust

The whole Scooby Gang undergoes a process of initiation in developing an identity, learning their powers and gaining control over them: Willow has to control her power not to become Evil Willow, Oz has to control the wolf within and Xander grows up to be the one stable center of common sense.

As Xander states in the last season of *Buffy*, "Power is what you have, control is what you do with it." Controlling your power and finding out who you are is at the center of existence. Clearly, control and power are two coexisting and interdependent concepts that exist on the same level but refer to different angles of perception. In contrast to many definitions that see "(1) control [as] a subclass of power, (2) power [as] a subclass of control, (3) control and power [as] synonyms, or (4) . . . no logical connection between the two,"[8] this definition claims a fifth possibility: control and power are two coexisting and interdependent concepts which are on the same level but refer to different aspects of perception.

Power is not a particularly overt act. It can exist without being used. For example, attempted control is as valid an act as the decision not to do anything. Consequently, control might shift with every action; whereas power, as it must be perceived, is longer lasting. Also, a basic assumption of control is that it is a central need of human existence (in contrast to power). Individuals need to exert control to exist; no act can be motivated without a belief in control: in order to give up control willingly, a person must trust another. With control comes responsibility. Only if this responsibility is taken seriously can trust be maintained or earned. Moreover, those in power will be held responsible: whoever is perceived to be in power is also perceived to be capable of effective control. The hierarchy I would like to develop here is this: Power is established by the perception of an external source—the control of this power—and comes with responsibility for those who are controlled, including oneself. Successful control earns trust.

Particularly in season 7 of *Buffy*, the female characters Willow, Buffy and Faith deal with these aspects of control. Willow's dilemma is that she has great Wiccan powers, but she cannot control herself when using them. She says, "What if I give up all this control stuff and I go all veiny and homicidal again" ("Beneath You," S07 E02). She is afraid that her powers are connected to the dark place, and she does not want to go there anymore. Thus the question here is not how to have power, but how to use it. Buffy faces a similar struggle: she feels the weight of responsibility, but she cannot be sure if her way is the right one. And even if she were sure, the others have lost trust in her judgment—they do not want her to be in control because she insists on fighting—on agency. The Slayerettes and the Scoobies turn to Faith as their new leader, but she soon encounters the same problems Buffy had as leader. In the end Buffy is right; pep talked by Spike, she takes control and regains agency, and this leads all to a happy ending.

Buffy's, Willow's and Spike's powers never change. They might doubt them, they might not know what to do with them, but it is controlling them that matters in the end. The only power that is indeed created is the new Slayers, and that this is something out of control that can be seen in season 8.

Identity and the Competence Systems

Eventually, the right choice is knowing who you are and not compromising your values. A big factor in determining why Buffy always wins is the "Team in I." As I stated, all of the Scoobies undergo their own initiation at some point or another.

> Though old-standard Jungian archetypes are recognizable in the Buffyverse . . . the heroine, the sidekick, the lover, the sage, the trickster, and the great mother, all become champions whose unique capacities are of equal heroic importance. They are much more than a team—they are a heroic entity.[9]

Buffy wins because she rejects the "she stands alone" doctrine of the Slayers. The heroic entity of which she is a part functions perfectly because its members fulfill all aspects of power and control.

Theoretically, overt behavior can be categorized into three competence levels: physical, emotional and intellectual competences.[10] These competence systems are a basis for power and identity. An individual will develop that competence that he or she perceives as the most promising. Skinner says in *Perceived Control,*

> Perceived control reflects the fundamental human need for competence. From this perspective, all humans come with an inborn desire to interact effectively with the environment and so to experience themselves as competent in producing desired and preventing undesired events.[11]

Buffy concentrates on her physical competences; Willow clearly stands for intellectual competence and Xander develops a high emotional competence. Buffy uses contributory control: the team wins the fight, not she alone. (The best example is the season 4 finale "Primeval," S04 E21.) The heroic entity combines perfectly because, as a team, they fulfill all aspects of power and control, although not in the traditional gender roles.

Buffy concentrates on her physical competence, although she is smart (in season 3 she has very good SAT results); her deficiencies are in the emotional realm—she struggles with complex emotions, finds herself detached and misunderstood. Willow clearly stands for intellectual competence (Wiccapower is a mental power); her emotions manipulate her Witchcraft, and she has to learn to deal with it. Xander, who has neither physical powers (compared to Buffy and her vampires) nor intellectual competences (he never even considered going to college), is the one to fill this void by developing a high emotional competence; he saves the world with his love. With his emotionality, he is the only one to reach Willow in her veinyness.

True Blood and *The Vampire Diaries* take a step back from empowerment and emancipation. Both Sookie and Elena have their strengths in the emotional competences sector: Sookie because she can read minds and understands people, Elena because everyone loves her. Unfortunately neither manages to strategically use her power to network with others. Although Elena is at the center of all friendship, and the people belonging to her circle of friends—Caroline, Bonnie, Damon and so forth—occasionally gang up, each one of them has his or her own agenda. Similar forces keep Sookie's potential Scoobies apart. This makes them into quite old-fashioned damsels in distress, with a classic feminine competence system.

Gendering Control Archetypes, Stock Characters and Their Powers

Physical competence is traditionally associated with masculinity, emotional competence with femininity and intellectual competence with both; whereas witchcraft, for instance, would be feminine, abstract ideas would be masculine. The new TV shows do not challenge this gendering the way Buffy did, and certainly they reflect less on it.

Xander is rather effeminate in the first few seasons—clearly the guy that gets bullied in school. Anya is the first one to see him as a man; perhaps that is why he falls in love with her. But at the beginning of season 5, Xander rejects this role in his "I'm sick of being the one getting the syphilis" speech ("The Replacement," S05 E03) and claims control over what happens to him. Additionally, carpentry, a physical competence, is used in the same season to support his masculinity.

Buffy, with her enormous physical competence, being generally associated with the male role, has problems finding a male counterpart equal to her, and it is no wonder that her relationships fail. Riley leaves her at the end of season 5 because he thinks she does not love him. The truth is, she does not need him.

The Vampires

More than anything, Buffy's case is a comment on overachieving women who in a world of postfeminist backlash encounter insecure men. The crisis of masculinity has been significant in popular culture since the 1990s, and the search for male role models continues. The contrastive program, which I see as partly responsible for the recent craving for vampires, is that the vampire—especially our main male characters—fulfills an ideal of masculinity: strong, but also sensitive, the man who really sees you.

Spike [to Buffy]: I love what you are. What you do. How you try. I've seen your kindness and your strength. I've seen the best and the worst of you. And I understand with perfect clarity exactly what you are. You are a hell of a woman. ("Chosen," S07 E22)

Similarly, *Moonlight* has made an attempt at the irresistible male partner: the one who remembers your wardrobe.

Beth: The night that we first met, or met again, whatever. What was I wearing.

Mick: Blue jeans, white stripe shirt, cream jacket.

Beth: What about my shoes?

Mick: You were barefoot.

Beth: How can you remember that?

Mick: Because I love you. ("Sonata," S01 E16)

As ridiculous as this is, the idea of the female protagonist as being special continues. In *The Vampire Diaries*, Damon tells Elena, "I love you Elena, and because I love you I can't be selfish with you" ("Rose," S02 E08). And of course, neither Bill nor Eric ever fail to emphasize how unique *True Blood*'s Sookie is.

These male vampires, Angel and Spike (*Buffy*), Bill and Eric (*True Blood*), Stefan and Damon (*The Vampire Diaries*), Mick (*Moonlight*) and Aidan (*Being Human*) fall into two categories of what have become stock characters. First and foremost there is the brooding, sympathetic vampire, as can be seen in table 6.1, accompanied by quite a lot of stock scenes.

The other, less moral vampire has also developed into a stock character. Usually, such vampires, like Spike, Damon and Eric, are in love with the female protagonists. Spike does not develop into a good person because of or for Buffy. But he gets his soul back for her, and it doesn't do him much good. Damon (telling name, too) is bad, but only because he has always been rejected. He loves Elena, does everything for her and is the good one when Stefan acts out in season 3. Eric, of course, also loves Sookie. All of them have a few things in common: they have less of a moral attitude, are more pragmatic and like to be vampires. And once they stop acting out, because they get a soul (Spike), or have amnesia (Eric) or have an unstable personality (Damon), they are rewarded with love. *Moonlight* also has one of these (Jason), but there's no love triangle, which might also be due to the fact that it was cancelled so early. The rest of the male vampires are mainly evil (in *Buffy* anyway, as vampires have no soul).

If there is any emancipation to be found in the newer shows, it is on the female vampire side. Where there used to be two general types—crazy

Table 6.1.

	Angel	Mick *ML*	Bill *TB*	Stefan *VD*	Aidan *BH*
Sired by woman	✔	✔	✔	✔	no
Soul (or part)	✔	✔	✔	✔ (currently lost)	✔
Crazy Ex	✔	✔	✔	✔	✔
No Biting Humans (except villains)	✔	✔	✔	✔ (currently bad)	✔ (recently)
Drinks HER blood	✔	✔	✔ (pleasure)	✔	✔ (Celine)
Haunted	✔	✔	✔ (genuine?)	✔	✔
Control or Shame	✔	✔	✔	✔	✔
Breaks up with her	✔	✔	no, but sets Eric free	✔	✔
SHE kisses his vampire face	✔		✔	✔	✔
Worse than all others when "on blood"	✔			✔	✔
Role Reversal	✔		✔	✔	✔

(Drusilla; Bill's ex, Loretta; Mick's ex, Coraline) or morally vague and oversexualized (Harmony, Katherine)—female vampires now develop into rounder and more varied characters. The only good one (in the end) in *Buffy* is Darla, who sacrifices herself for her baby, Connor, on *Angel*. Maternity saves humanity, obviously a parallel to *Twilight*. In *The Vampire Diaries*, Katherine and Elena are juxtaposed. A perfect scene is the beginning of "Masquerade" (S02 E07), in which Elena has sex with Stefan, and there is a crosscut to Katherine having sex with the werewolf Mason. Visually and semantically, true love is crosscut to sex as an instrument of power. This makes Katherine into an archetypal femme fatale, and she admits to this: "I was looking out for myself Elena, I will always be looking out for myself. If you were smart you'd do the same." ("Katerina," S02 E09). Yet Katherine later looks at a picture of her family, slain by Klaus, and this provides her with a new depth. Even rounder characters are those of Caroline (*The Vam-*

pire Diaries) and Jessica (*True Blood*), both of whom struggle with teenage cravings, trying to be a good person and being a babe.

The Female Protagonist

"While a heroine is the protagonist, generally speaking somebody swoops in to save her. A hero is a more complex figure and has to deal with all the rites of passage."[12] Table 6.2, displays analytical aspects of control in the form of a comparison between Buffy, Sookie (*True Blood*), Beth (*Moonlight*) and Elena (*The Vampire Diaries*). Sally (*Being Human*) has been left out since she is a ghost and can hardly be held accountable for her lack of agency.

Buffy is the only one with active power and the only true female hero. *True Blood*'s Sookie has a passive power—mindreading—and since the end of season 4, active fairy power, but this is still for defense as she cannot control it yet. As stated above, Elena's only power is to be loveable and moral, and

Table 6.2.

Female Hero	Heroine
active power	none, or passive power
primary control	secondary control
competence and control systems	vicarious control
moral dilemma	moral certainty
agent	attempt to be agent, needs rescuing
strategic due to responsibility	acts on moral/emotional impulse
internal locus of control	external locus of control
high self-efficacy	extreme: self-learned helplessness
Buffy	Elena *VD*
	Beth *ML*
Sookie *TB*	

therefore she tries to use vicarious control.[13] As this is not working so well, she tries to become more like Buffy ("Smells like Teen Spirit," S03 E06) and gains some fighting skills. Beth Turner basically is a "Lois Lane" character: a curious journalist who gets herself in trouble and then needs to be rescued.

Primary control (I try to change the world) can only be done with a certain power at hand; secondary control (I try to adapt myself to the world) is more logical for a heroine. If the heroine attempts to act as an agent, often on a moral impulse, she either needs a powerful other to help her (vicarious control), protection or—and this is the general case—she needs to be rescued. Sookie is a listener, with the ability to read people's minds. She is perfectly fit to exert secondary control (to adjust herself and her actions to the world), a form of control traditionally associated with women. When she tries to show agency in "Spellbound" (S04 E08), she immediately gets shot and needs to be rescued by the werewolf Alcide.

Only those without power can afford to have a black-and-white morality (like Xander); the one in charge needs to see the bigger picture, to be strategic. Therefore Elena and Beth can be annoyingly moral, and very often they have to adjust their perspective afterward. Yet both types have a certain set of values, which makes them genuinely good. To be fair, Buffy too is saved some decisions as Giles does the ugly work, like killing Ben. Or in season 8, Faith has to kill a dangerous Slayer as Buffy does not kill humans.

Consequently, the female hero should have an internal locus of control (she can control the world), whereas the heroine should have an external one (others control the world). As this is very often not the case, Elena and company sometime appear to be rather stupid in their behavior. A lot of actions can be summarized under "another attempt to get herself killed."

Then again, high self-efficacy is part of a successful identity. When Buffy falls into self-imposed helplessness in the fight against Glory (S5), it is simply frustrating to watch. And the return to agency makes the ending happy, even if she dies for a while.

Following this differentiation between heroine and female hero, apart from Buffy, Sookie is the only human woman who develops into something like a female hero: making her own decisions and possessed of an active power, she does not have to be rescued all the time.

Morals, Ethics, and Social Control

All in all, *True Blood*, *The Vampire Diaries* and *Being Human* have each been successful in their own way in exploring new vampire screen time. *True Blood* has been criticized for its sensationalism, but watching it closer we see it has more layers than chick porn and Tarantinoesque violence (or an accumulation of both, like Bill's "I hate you so much I turn your head 'round 180 degrees" sex with his ex). Its characters are rather complex, as is its mythology. The most interesting part is indeed its moral ambiguity. Vampires may be evil, but that does not mean that humans are good. To ensure the vampires' "decent behavior," the show has come up with a mass of social codes. Social control is extremely high among the vampires—these demons live in an organized and highly regulated society. Human life in contrast seems anarchistic: a disruptive, individualistic society, where people feel lost and disconnected. Violence is everywhere, and the ethnic minority of vampires tries to establish itself as peaceful. Sookie might know better, but being surrounded by death on a daily basis makes it easier to overlook your boyfriend killing someone. Vampire, werewolf or serial killer—it does not make such a great difference, as life is worth less anyway.

The Vampire Diaries and its female central character, Elena, starts out with a rather traditional view of good and evil, with only a few characters in the in-between. As stated above, Elena's power is being moral, but this power is incoherent in a nonreflective way: what is true one week does not necessarily have to be true the next week. In "Kill or Be Killed" (S02 E05) she fights for Caroline, and obviously it is no problem that the latter has just killed two innocent deputies. Or Elena tells Damon that she will never forgive him in "Bad Moon Rising" (S02 E03), then takes it back a few episodes later. The biggest problem with Elena's morality, though, is that it does not make any sense to keep her alive, when this means that Klaus can create more hybrids and will, therefore, kill many more innocent humans. Elena could sacrifice herself, and many lives would automatically be saved. Moreover, there is no reasonable explanation why vampires have a right to live at all. All of them kill at one point or another. In the Buffyverse, where capital punishment by being staked to dust is the norm, morals and ethics have a certain ambiguity, regardless of which *Buffy* follows a coherent inner logic of character development.

"Where do we go from here?"

"This isn't about demons at all, is it? It's about women. It's about power and it's about women and you just hate those two words in the same sentence, don't you?" ("Long Way Home," S08 E04)

It is questionable whether Buffy is really as feminist as she is claimed to be, given that "feminism" is such a vague ideology. At the end of season 7, though, she definitely tries to establish a non-patriarchal system by sharing her power; and in contrast to other TV shows discussed here, *Buffy*'s female hero is an überfeminist. It is quite shocking how *Moonlight* and *Vampire Diaries* portray their female protagonists as moral centers then fail to base their morals on any abstract ideas.

This new assessment of power (or no power) positions the central romances of the shows discussed as reactionary reruns of relationships common to the 1950s: the woman is the moral pillar of society, weak and in need of protection. The man, as the powerful partner, has to take responsibility for her. The only problem is that the men are not trustworthy, and the women are essentially doomed. Perhaps, with the exception of Buffy.

Notes

1. Nina Auerbach, *Our Vampires, Ourselves* (Chicago: University of Chicago Press, 1995), 5.

2. YouTube, "Buffy vs Edward: Twilight Remixed—[Original Version]," Rebelliouspixles (2009), www.youtube.com/watch?v=RZwM3GvaTRM.

3. Claire Mortimer, *Romantic Comedy* (New York: Routledge, Kindle edition, 2010), 2.

4. Ken Gelder, "Our Vampires, Our Neighbours," unpublished paper presented at the International Conference on Vampires: Myths of the Past and the Future, University of London, Institute of Germanic and Romanic Studies, November 2–4, 2011.

5. Daniel M. Wegner and James W. Pennebaker, eds., "Changing Our Minds: An Introduction to Mental Control," *Handbook of Mental Control* (Upper Saddle River, NJ: Prentice-Hall, 1993), 1.

6. Jennifer K. Stuller, *Ink-Stained Amazons and Cinematic Warriors: Superwomen in Modern Mythology* (London: I.B. Tauris, 2010), 88–89.

7. Carolyn Korsmeyer, "Passion and Action: In and Out of Control," in *Buffy the Vampire Slayer and Philosophy*, ed. James B. South (Chicago: Open Court, 2003), 160.

8. Jack P. Gibbs, *A Theory about Control* (Boulder, CO: Westview Press, 1994), 58.

9. Stuller, *Ink-Stained Amazons*, 97–98.

10. Intellectual competence system: persuasion, information, disinformation, lying, talking, thinking, deception. Emotional competence system: love, threat, loss, stereotypes, shame, withdrawal of love, embarrassment. Physical competence system: sex, violence, movement.

11. Ellen A. Skinner, *Perceived Control, Motivation & Coping* (Thousand Oaks, CA: Sage Publications, 1995), 8.

12. Stuller, *Ink-Stained* Amazons, 78.

13. That is, she attempts to associate with powerful others in order to gain control through them. Instrumental submissive behavior is likely.

TV Shows

Being Human, 2011–Present. Toby Whithouse, Syfy/ Space.
Buffy the Vampire Slayer, 1997–2003. Joss Whedon, WB/UPN.
Moonlight, 2007–2008. Ron Koslov, Trevor Munson, CBS.
The Vampire Diaries, 2009–Present. Kevin Williamson, CW.
True Blood, 2008–Present. Alan Ball, HBO.

7

Lightening "The White Man's Burden": Evolution of the Vampire from the Victorian Racialism of *Dracula* to the New World Order of *I Am Legend*

Cheyenne Mathews

A S VAMPIRE MYTHS SPREAD from Eastern European folklore to the literature of Victorian England, the vampire's visage changed from dark and ruddy to pale and refined to suit its audience as John William Polidori's "The Vampyre" introduced an aristocratic vampire and James Malcolm Rymer's *Varney the Vampire* portrayed a "perfectly white—perfectly bloodless" villain.[1] The vampire, however, maintained the threatening, subversive class status of the Other that arose from its development in Slavic superstitions as Bram Stoker's *Dracula* depicted as its antagonist a Transylvanian count aiming to corrupt and conquer London. In his novel, Stoker reinforces the imperialist idea of taming the savage Other, a notion prevalent in Victorian England and epitomized by Rudyard Kipling as the "White Man's Burden." Stoker presents allegedly scientific arguments to support this idea and further mythologizes the vampire as inferior by creating a hierarchy in which upper-class white men outwit the "child-brain" of Count Dracula, who remains marginalized despite a wealth and physical appearance equal to that of his hunters. Richard Matheson's modern American novel *I Am Legend*, however, deviates from this trope by portraying the vampire not as a symbol of Otherness but as a symbol of humanity's decreasing social capital as the white, male protagonist, Robert Neville, strives to maintain order amidst a decaying civilization. Matheson, like Stoker, employs the rationalism of science but uses such arguments to deconstruct the mythology of the vampire while reconstructing the supernatural figure as a signifier of man's limitations. Both texts invoke vampirism as a discourse of disease that in each era reflects scientific and economic constructs of nationalist and capitalist hierarchies that Vladimir Ilyich Lenin viewed as "the parasitism and decay of capitalism which are the characteristic features of its highest historical stages of development, i.e., imperialism."[2] The vampire's shifting status from pagan mythology to the fiction of Stoker and Matheson exemplifies the class antagonism engendered by Marxist sociohistorical development, in which "every class struggle is a political struggle."[3] As the various manifestations of the vampire reflect the class struggles of its era, the vampire can be read as a congruous figure to Marx's chronicle of the rise of capitalism and its projected downfall through communist revolt.

The fluid perception of the vampire as the Other during shifting religious, social, and political paradigms illustrates German theorist Karl Marx's idea that "[t]he history of all hitherto existing society is the history of class struggles" as oppressor and oppressed "stood in constant opposition to one another, carried on an uninterrupted, now hidden, now open fight, a fight that each time ended, either in a revolutionary reconstitution of society at large, or in the common ruin of the contending classes."[4] In such fights, bourgeois capitalism conquered an aristocratic feudal system, but this social reconstitution only reconfigured slavery as paid wage-labor, creating a subjugated working class exploited by the ruling bourgeois minority. Vampire myths reflect this opposition, and as each generation drafts a new legend the vampire undergoes a physical, mythological, and ideological evolution from a figure of displaced fear to a biological, and thus social, imperative of survival while compelling readers to question whether threats to political and economic stability come from an unknown devil or from an inner egoism.

Before the Middle Ages, revenant stories already existed in the folklore of most cultures, including Africa, China, and ancient Rome and Greece. According to occultist and folklorist Montague Summers, however, in the Greco-Roman tradition "almost without exception, it is the happy dead, the blessed ones, Elysian heroes who return and are in this manner nourished with blood to lend them life and strength."[5] The popular construction of the vampire as a profane and evil entity did not develop until the medieval clash between the old religion of the Slavic peasants and the newly converted Christianity of the ruling class. As the aristocracy turned to Christianity, the Slavic peasantry defiantly upheld their pagan superstitions, which included Whitney's interpretation that "[d]ead wizards, werewolves, heretics, and other outcasts become vampires, as do also the illegitimate offspring of parents themselves illegitimate, and anyone killed by a vampire."[6] In the early legends of the vampire, those who were pariahs in life returned after death to perpetuate their misfortunes and mischief, often revisiting and plaguing the family members and other citizens who had excluded them.

The notion of such outcast revenants developed into a doctrine to explain disease, death, and decay in a society in which medicine only existed in basic forms. The vampire, who once held an inconsequential role in arcane pagan beliefs, emerged as explication for the discrepancy between old and new, superstition and science, and fiction and fact. The peasantry ascribed the curious effects of bodily decomposition to a vampiric transformation during which the departed's complexion changed from pale and sickly to healthy and ruddy; blood drained from the nose and mouth, and hair and fingernails continued to grow after burial. After their transfiguration these vampires returned to their villages, harboring a "deep resentment of the living" and spreading plagues and pestilence in retribution for their ostracism while they were alive and that ostracism's resultant exclusion from love, life, and society.[7] This myth of the vampire as a carrier of communicable disease spread from Eastern Europe to England, where Summers documents medieval fears that "when a Vampire revisits some unfortunate town or district his ravages are, owing to the appalling fetor of the corpse, in every case apparently followed by an outbreak of the plague,"[8] creating a superstitious scapegoat for unexpected maladies and misfortune and introducing the vampire's stigma of an impure outsider into English culture.

Although "after the twelfth century the vampire tradition seems to have entirely died out in England, and with the rarest exceptions not to have reappeared until the nineteenth century when there was so marked a revival of interest in occultism,"[9] its resurgence coincided with England's emergence as a nationalistic, capitalist power, a position achieved through a fetishization and subjugation of foreign peoples. As social and political stratification shifted in the late 18th and early 19th century, so did vampiric depictions of class and culture, which the literature of Victorian England recast from a bloated, decaying body into the suave gentleman popularized by Bram Stoker's Count Dracula. Although Stoker's creation is the icon of blueblood bloodfiends, the Count's origins stem from Stoker's predecessor, physician John William Polidori, who conceived of an aristocratic vampire in his 1819 story "The Vampyre," replacing the fat, rosy corpse of Slavic folklore with a pale, slender, and attractive nobleman. In contrast to the base creatures who brought death and disease, Polidori endowed his vampire with a "winning tongue," "apparent hatred of vice," and a "deadly hue of his face, which never gained a warmer tint."[10] By giving his character the paleness of the privileged, Polidori signified the taming of the savage Other who ravages peasant villages into a sophisticated noble who disguises his degeneracy with genteel manners.

In his 1897 novel *Dracula*, Bram Stoker also reinvented the vampire as a wealthy, land-owning gentleman, but this shift to aristocratic status only reinforced the vampire's marginalization by portraying a new era of class struggle in which the phantom of the medieval feudal system became the apparition of a decaying aristocracy hunted by a burgeoning bourgeoisie. Because this new status quo developed through centuries of cruelty and corruption, according to Marx, "it now exists as a consistent system, whose principle is the dehumanised world."[11] This dehumanized world is the desire of Count Dracula, who proclaims, "My revenge is just begun! I spread it over centuries . . . and others shall yet be mine—my creatures, to do my bidding and to be my jackals."[12] With his obvious infection of others and his ability to dissolve into an airborne mist of elemental dust, Dracula follows the trope of disease from earlier legends, but his vengeful epidemic is spread in a more insidious manner that has been interpreted as a metaphor for the predatory existence of the aristocracy. For Dracula, the lower classes serve only two purposes: sustenance and service. When not feeding on or transforming his victims, he either scares the Transylvanian townspeople into submission or bribes them into subjugation. After he arrives in England, he hypnotizes Renfield, a patient in a mental asylum, to act as a faithful servant to "lord and master" Dracula.[13] Reflecting the parasitism of the upper classes, Dracula ascertains the social weaknesses of others and asserts his dominance over those obviously inferior to him in status—women, the poor, and the mentally deficient.

This aristocratic agency finds its ruin at the hands of solicitor Jonathan Harker, Doctor John Seward, and man of science Abraham Van Helsing, who signify Marx's concepts of "[l]aw, morality, [and] religion," which are to the aristocrat "so many bourgeois prejudices, behind which lurk in ambush just as many bourgeois interests."[14] Through this class antagonism, Stoker erects a clear delineation between the hunted and the hunters, which Charles S. Blinderman reads as "a contest between two evolutionary options: the ameliorative, progressive, Christian congregation, or the Social Darwinian superman in the form of the ultimate parasitic degenerate, Count Dracula."[15] In the name of progress and morality, the men become a law unto themselves and use their bourgeois prejudices as the rationale to destroy Dracula although their self-interest really lies in usurping the power of the aristocracy.

The guise of moral vigilantism also veils a Victorian racialism aimed at subverting the spread of Dracula's contaminated foreign blood. In the Victorian era, fear of social disease superseded the fear of physical disease held by the Slavic peasants, and a popular trope in Victorian literature is the threat of "English invasion by force," in which foreign savages threaten to taint British bloodlines.[16] As imperialist efforts tried to suppress such threats, supporters championed the expansion of the British Empire, which they believed existed "not for the benefit—economic, strategic, or otherwise—of Britain, but in order that 'primitive' peoples, incapable of self-government could, with British guidance, eventually become Christian and civilized."[17]

By constructing Dracula not only as an aristocrat but also as a foreign one, Stoker doubly emphasizes the vampire as an inferior social entity and reinforces Summers's observation that "vampirism only appears in countries which are in a spiritually backward condition, as in some areas of Eastern Europe."[18] The novel's Transylvanian setting fetishizes the spiritual primitivism of an Eastern Europe in which "every known superstition in the world is gathered at the horseshoe of the Carpathians, as if it were the centre of some sort of imaginative whirlpool."[19] In this spiritually backward world, the townspeople are incapable of overthrowing Dracula's dominance because they lack scientific and social advancement. The burden lies upon the hunters to eradicate Dracula's menace by using their Christian principles and English erudition to outwit and overpower him.

Rudyard Kipling's poem "The White Man's Burden" satirized this conflict between primitive and progressive nations, but imperialists adopted the titular phrase to justify colonization as the natural duty of the British to civilize what Kipling called "new-caught sullen peoples / Half-devil and half-child."[20] Van Helsing and his crew use this oppressive imperialist rhetoric to dehumanize Dracula because "politically, imperialism is, in general, a striving towards violence and reaction."[21] The imperialist discourse objectifies Dracula both physically and psychologically by describing him as a demon and a child. References to the Count depict him as a "creature,"[22] a "monster,"[23] "the Thing that is not human—not even beast,"[24] and "that Devil"[25] with a "child-brain,"[26] while physical descriptions of the "tall man, thin and pale"[27] emphasize his "extraordinary pallor,"[28] a "ghastly pale,"[29] "the awful pallor,"[30] and "the livid white face."[31] The hunters view Dracula's paleness as a signifier of his impurity and monstrosity, but it is also a reflection of his enemies, a hypocrisy that he points out, saying, "You think to baffle me, you—with your pale faces all in a row, like sheep in a butcher's."[32] Constructing Dracula as something separate and foreign from themselves allows the hunters to relegate the Count to an inferior status and rationalize the measures taken against him.

Van Helsing further subordinates the Count by using scientific arguments drawn from Italian criminologist Cesare Lombroso to refer to Dracula's primitive physiognomy and "child-brain" as determinants of his actions. In Lombroso's theories, "individuals engaged in criminal acts not by choice but because they were 'atavistic' and had never evolved past the uncivilised nature of our primitive forebears."[33] Physically, Dracula possesses the "very marked physiognomy" of Lombroso's archetypal criminal with his "lofty domed forehead" and "fixed and rather cruel-looking moustache," while his animalistic nature appears in his "peculiarly sharp white teeth" and "massive" eyebrows, two traits traditionally attributed to werewolves.[34] Mentally, Dracula "was spoken of as the cleverest and most cunning" in life, but "[t]hat mighty brain and that iron resolution went with him to the grave."[35] Although Dracula's intelligence survived his physical death, his memory was incomplete, so he now has the limited brainpower of a criminal and can focus on only one crime at a time, such as infecting Mina Harker with vampiric blood or plotting his retreat from England to Transylvania. Although he cites scientific evidence, Van Helsing echoes the Slavic belief that criminals and outcasts become vampires after death while also simplifying the politics of their conflict, saying, "This criminal has not full man-brain. He is clever and cunning and resourceful; but he be not of man-stature as to brain. He be of child-brain in much, now this criminal of ours is predestinate to crime also; he too have child brain, and it is of the child to do what he have done."[36] Van Helsing downplays the economic and national antagonism between his compatriots and Dracula by depicting the hunters as mere disciplinarians scolding a wayward child.

Regardless of such rhetoric, the hunters know that slaying Dracula is a serious political and economic matter because of the "domination, and violence that is associated with it, such are the relationships that are the most typical of the 'latest phase of capitalist development.'"[37] With more exposure to English life, Dracula increases his knowledge and power, thus becoming more virulent to a bourgeois revolution. Despite his limited memory and childish actions, Dracula is, according to Van Helsing's broken English, "finding patience just how is his strength, and what are his powers. He study new tongues. He learn new social life; new environment of old ways, the politic, the law, the finance, the science, the habit of a new land and a new people who have come to be since he was."[38] Dracula may learn these new ways, but he lacks the social advantages bestowed upon the hunters by their British birthright, which even Renfield, the lunatic, acknowledges, saying, "You, gentlemen, who by nationality, by heredity, or by the possession of natural gifts, are fitted to hold your respective places in the moving world."[39] Equating national identity with natural attributes, Renfield elevates the hunters above their prey, who finally succumbs to their stake during his daylight repose. Upon Dracula's death, Mina Harker observes on his face "a look of peace, such as I never could have imagined might have rested there," which Leslie S. Klinger reads as an effect "to make the hunters appear relentless, hardened, remorseless—strengthening the impression that good British (and American) men triumphed over the evil vampire."[40] Through the annihilation of the aristocracy, imperialism prevails and capitalism advances as Stoker immortalizes Romania as a fetishized terrain of savage vampirism and constructs a British and American bourgeoisie as the primary socioeconomic power.

The scientific arguments in both philosophy and the physical sciences posited in *Dracula* show the experimental errors of science, however, as they only appear to bolster Victorian attitudes of social superiority and renounce the childlike superstition of less-developed societies. Critic S. T. Joshi says, "Like many later Victorians, Stoker saw in the radical advancements of science during his time a means to defeat superstition once and for all. Van Helsing and his band use every scientific means at their disposal to combat the overwhelming power of the vampires."[41] Stoker's text actually contradicts this claim, failing to fully break the discursive cycle of superstition and science. In the author's preface to an Icelandic edition, Stoker admonishes the valuing of science as an absolute, writing, "But in our times it ought to be clear to all serious-thinking men that 'there are more things in heaven and earth / than are dreamt of in your philosophy,'"[42] misquoting Hamlet in warning that some things escape explanation, despite serious thought and its inherent skepticism of anything that cannot be proven as absolute. While briefing the hunters before their mission, Van Helsing voices the same dissension over the guarantees of science, saying, "All we have to go upon are traditions and superstitions . . . because, after all, these things—tradition and superstition are everything . . . A year ago which of us would have received such a possibility, in the midst of our scientific, sceptical, matter-of-fact nineteenth century?"[43] Stoker does advocate the advancements of science, but he also acknowledges science as inseparable from superstition. The two belief systems feed upon each other, reviving old beliefs and siring new theories to be proven or disproven.

Rather than completely eradicating superstition, Stoker supplants it with a new socio-nationalist ideology. By equating foreign or aristocratic standing with criminality and devilry, he perpetuates a nationalist discourse that is as vampiric and invidious as Dracula himself. The reform imposed upon Dracula by the British "is a deception, a 'pious wish,' since the bourgeois representatives of the oppressed nations go no 'further' forward, the bourgeois representatives of the oppressing nation go 'further' *backward*, to servility, towards imperialism, concealed by the cloak of 'science.'"[44] In the name of science and progress, the British hunters aim to annihilate Dracula's foreign threat, but they only replicate the existing oppressive classist discourses through their bourgeois ascendancy to power. This rise to power is the result of a capitalist system that, through the contending classes, "has grown into a world system of colonial oppression . . . And this 'booty' is shared between two or three powerful world marauders armed to the teeth (America, Great Britain, Japan) who involve the whole world in *their* war over the sharing of *their* booty."[45] By containing the spread of Dracula's vampirism, the hunters reinforce the imperialist colonial oppression that eventually results in even greater conflict.

Richard Matheson's 1954 novel *I Am Legend* again depicts the vampire as a reconfigured social entity, this time in the wake of such a capitalist war, and presents another stage of Marxist historical class struggle as a bourgeois character, Robert Neville, combats a rising class of vampire proletariat. The novel is set in 1976, three years after the human population is decimated by an airborne disease spread through dust storms produced by bombings during a recent war. This man-made atrocity and its consequent fallout are endemic to the universal suffrage that, for Marx, "seems to have survived for a further moment so as to sign its testament with its own hand before the eyes of the whole world, and to declare in the name of the people themselves: *All that exists deserves to perish.*"[46] Written in an era that was both recovering from World War II and facing the escalating conflicts of the civil rights movement, Matheson's novel is an indictment against national and racial antagonism, blaming man for his own destruction and criticizing the military-industrial complex as a disease of domination spawned by an imperial pursuit that has insidiously consumed global relations. Finally, in the aftermath of these conflicts, everything has perished, save for Robert Neville.

Neville, the last man on Earth, passes his days hunting and killing those who have been turned into vampires by the virus and spends his nights researching and scientifically debunking vampire mythology. Neville tries to avoid superstitious inquiries, telling himself, "I should collect all the questions before I try to answer them. Things should be done the right way, the scientific way."[47] Through repeated experiments, Neville discovers the vampirism is a bacillus, "a cylindrical bacterium. It creates an isotonic solution in the blood, circulates the blood slower than normal, activates all bodily functions, lives on fresh blood, and provides energy."[48] The virus has both physiological and psychosomatic symptoms that reduce superstition to mere science. Garlic acts as an allergen, and mirrors and religious paraphernalia remind the victim of his or her impure affliction.

In his quest for a scientific explanation and cure for vampirism, however, Neville sacrifices his humanity for his supremacist politics, for the political civilization of a nationalist country, according to Rabindranath Tagore, "is scientific, not human. It is powerful because it concentrates all its forces upon one purpose."[49] Neville's one purpose is a survival fueled by resentment, revenge, and loathing of the vampires. He assumes power by classifying the vampires as objects for experimentation rather than as afflicted people, enforcing a nationalism that "is always watchful to keep the aliens at bay or to exterminate them. It is carnivorous and cannibalistic in its tendencies, it feeds upon the resources of other peoples and tries to swallow their whole futures."[50] Through his thirst for revenge, Neville is as cannibalistic as Dracula, for the destruction of vampires becomes the purpose for his existence. Although Dracula and Neville belong to different classes of aristocracy and bourgeoisie, respectively, they still share the aim of a dehumanized world perpetuated through a consistent class system.

Mitigating the mythology allows Matheson to focus on the social component of vampirism, a communistic construct in which "it becomes evident that the bourgeoisie is unfit any longer to be the ruling class of society . . . it has to feed [its slave], instead of being fed by him."[51] The vampire is no longer a parasitic aristocrat feeding off the masses; it is now a rising slave class trying to survive under the militant ravages of Robert Neville. While Stoker depicts vampirism as the pursuit of individual ambitions, Matheson portrays it as a collective response to a capitalist system that, at its apex of imperialism, has finally reached "the eve of social revolution."[52] Neville initially denies the possibility of revolution, criticizing the vampires because there is "no union among them."[53] Neville believes they are too disorganized and unmotivated to wage a serious attack against him, reflecting the Marxist idea that "[t]he bourgeoisie is naturally bound to fear the stupidity of the masses as long as they remain conservative, and the discernment of the masses as soon as they become revolutionary."[54] The vampires do become revolutionary, however, as Neville learns when he encounters another survivor, Ruth, and discovers she is part of a cadre of infected humans who have determined to establish a new society immune to fear of persecution by Neville.

These vampires are not the harbingers of plague like their Slavic predecessors or the enforcers of an aristocratic hegemony like Dracula. Instead, they are victims of Neville's violence and vestiges of the inevitable political war of imperialism, which Lenin describes:

> The tens of millions of dead and maimed left by the war . . . open the eyes of the millions and tens of millions of people who are downtrodden, oppressed, deceived and duped by the bourgeoisie with unprecedented rapidity. Thus, out of the universal ruin caused by the war a world-wide revolutionary crisis is arising which, in spite of the protracted and difficult stages it may have to pass, cannot end in any other way than in a proletarian revolution and in its victory.[55]

Matheson shows this victory in his vampires' adaptive acceptance of their situation. The afflicted have risen from a ruinous, war-inflicted disease to establish a new world order that, with the capture and confinement of Neville, refuses to be oppressed and duped any longer by a self-serving bourgeoisie.

The cycle of social revolution depicted in *I Am Legend* mimics the cycle of scientific evolution, for primitive and progressive societies are as inseparable as superstition and science. When Neville hypocritically criticizes the guerilla tactics of his captors, Ruth explains, "New societies are always primitive . . . You should know that. In a way we're like a revolutionary group—repossessing society by violence. It's inevitable,"[56] echoing Lenin's ultimate question about imperialism: "When the relation of forces is changed, how else, *under capitalism*, can the solution of contradictions be found, except by resorting to *violence?*"[57] For the infected ones, as for Neville, survival is the only imperative. Despite the primitivism of their new establishment, violent revolt is the only possible means of control in the erection of a new socialist state.

In this revolt, Matheson shows the parallel between vampirism and communism that emerged with the rise of the bourgeoisie and the implementation of capitalism through political, economic, and scientific rhetoric that denied agency to certain social groups. In his research, Neville references *Dracula*'s Van Helsing, who says, "The strength of the vampire is that no one will believe in him."[58] To Neville, vampires are a "tenuous legend passed from century to century . . . *That* was imagination, *that* was superstition, there was no such thing as *that*. And, before science had caught up with the legend, the legend had swallowed science and everything."[59] Matheson's allusion to *Dracula* reinforces Stoker's prescient observation that "continuing research in psychology and natural sciences may, in years to come, give logical explanations of such strange happenings which, at present, neither scientists nor the secret police can understand."[60] The strength of the proletariat has been similarly discounted, as "[o]fficial science tried, by a conspiracy of silence, to kill the works of Marx, which by a theoretical and historical analysis of capitalism showed free competition gives rise to the concentration of production, which, in turn, at a certain stage of development leads to monopoly."[61] As the only surviving man, Neville holds a monopoly on existence. Through official science he tries to kill the myth of the vampire, but his attempts at self-preservation, Matheson's allegorical concentration of production, fail to suppress the uprising of the contending class.

Society, like bacteria, can and must mutate in order to survive, and for Marx, such evolution "can only create its poetry from the future, not from the past. It cannot begin its own work until it has sloughed off all its superstitious regard for the past . . . In order to arrive at its own content the revolution of the nineteenth century must let the dead bury their dead."[62] Although Neville successfully disproves the superstitions surrounding vampirism, in doing so he creates a new terror of a monster that plagues one's nightmares. Through his ruthless hunting and slaying of the infected, Neville becomes the Boogeyman for the afflicted others, who cannot flourish if he continues to haunt them. As he awaits execution in the new society, Neville realizes "[t]o them he was some terrible scourge even worse than the disease they had come to live with. He was an invisible specter who had left for evidence of his existence the bloodless bodies of their loved ones,"[63] exemplifying Tagore's warning that those who "sedulously cultivate moral blindness as the cult of patriotism will end their existence in a sudden and violent death."[64] To achieve their communist revolution and reconstitute a new society, the afflicted must bury Neville and the fear associated with him.

In Matheson's new world order, the vampire is no longer the Other, a degenerate outsider threatening to taint the purity of the moral majority. Instead, the hegemonic, upper-class, white male portrayed in Neville is "the abnormal one now. Normalcy was the majority concept, the standard of many and not the standard of just one man."[65] The recognition of the proletariat as the majority party in the means of control and production is the basis for Marx's manifesto. The proletariat must unite in favor of an equal distribution of power rather than accepting capitalism, and the imperialism imparted through it, as the normal economic and political structure. The "White Man's Burden" no longer lies in conquering and converting others to his will but in relinquishing the control promoted through elitism and systemic corruption.

From the Slavic origins to this modern incarnation, normalcy has been the defining factor of the vampire in a cycle of superstition, science, and social hierarchies. During such inevitable ideological shifts, Marx says, "All fixed, fast-frozen relations, with their train of ancient and venerable prejudices and opinions are swept away, all new-formed ones become antiquated before they can ossify. All that is solid melts into air, all that is holy is profaned, and man is at last compelled to face with sober sense, his real conditions of life, and his relations with his kind."[66] In *I Am Legend*, the discursive cycle of superstition and science comes full circle, engendering a "new terror born in death, a new superstition entering the unassailable fortress of forever."[67] This struggle reinforces the sociohistorical, economic, and political significance of the Marxist call for the eradication of class antagonisms, "for the *forms* of the struggle may and do constantly change in accordance with varying, relatively particular, and temporary causes, but the *essence* of the struggle, its class *content, cannot* change while classes exist."[68] Taking up the torch lit by Stoker, Matheson illuminates the essence of this struggle, warning that social corruption can come not only from unknown, foreign threats but also from within as a search for empirical explanations spawns new superstitions to replace one oppressive ideology with another. If the vampire, like the subjugated proletariat, succeeds in overthrowing capitalist, nationalist discourse, then man can no longer objectify his fears through the unknown Other, and he will have to face his own capacity for evil and conditions for oppression.

Notes

1. James Malcolm Rymer, *Varney the Vampyre; or, The Feast of Blood* (New York: Dover, 1972), quoted in Leslie S. Klinger, "The Context of Dracula," in Bram Stoker, *The New Annotated Dracula*, ed. Leslie S. Klinger (New York: Norton, 2008), xxix.

2. Vladimir Ilyich Lenin, *Imperialism: The Highest Stage of Capitalism* (New York: Penguin, 2010), 9.

3. Karl Marx and Friedrich Engels, *The Communist Manifesto* (New York: Penguin, 2004), 15.

4. Marx and Engels, *The Communist Manifesto*, 3–4.

5. Montague Summers, *The Vampire in Lore and Legend* (New York: Dover, 2001 [1928]), 17.

6. William Dwight Whitney, "The Century Dictionary (1889–1891)," in Summers, *The Vampire in Lore and Legend*, 1.

7. Summers, *The Vampire in Lore and Legend*, 7.

8. Summers, *The Vampire in Lore and Legend*, 88.

9. Summers, *The Vampire in Lore and Legend*, 99.

10. John William Polidori, "The Vampyre," (April 1819), in Charlotte Montague, *Vampires: From "Dracula" to "Twilight"—The Complete Guide to Vampire Mythology* (New York: Chartwell, 2010), 43.

11. Karl Marx, *The Portable Karl Marx*, ed. Eugene Kamenka (New York: Viking Penguin, 1983), 93.

12. Stoker, *The New Annotated Dracula*, 418.

13. Stoker, *The New Annotated Dracula*, 351.

14. Marx and Engels, *The Communist Manifesto*, 18.

15. Charles S. Blinderman, "Vampurella: Darwin and Count Dracula," *Massachusetts Review* 21 (1980): 411, 428.

16. Montague, *Vampires*, 153.

17. Klinger, "The Context of Dracula," xx.

18. Summers, *The Vampire in Lore and Legend*, 119.

19. Stoker, *The New Annotated Dracula*, 16.

20. Rudyard Kipling, "The White Man's Burden," *Internet Modern History Sourcebook* (New York: Fordham University, 1997), www.fordham.edu/halsall/mod/kipling.asp.

21. Lenin, *Imperialism*, 113.

22. Stoker, *The New Annotated Dracula*, 76.

23. Stoker, *The New Annotated Dracula*, 98.

24. Stoker, *The New Annotated Dracula*, 326.

25. Stoker, *The New Annotated Dracula*, 465.

26. Stoker, *The New Annotated Dracula*, 456.

27. Stoker, *The New Annotated Dracula*, 429.

28. Stoker, *The New Annotated Dracula*, 47.

29. Stoker, *The New Annotated Dracula*, 151.

30. Stoker, *The New Annotated Dracula*, 355.

31. Stoker, *The New Annotated Dracula*, 362.

32. Stoker, *The New Annotated Dracula*, 418.
33. Stoker, *The New Annotated Dracula*, 455–56.
34. Stoker, *The New Annotated Dracula*, 44–46.
35. Stoker, *The New Annotated Dracula*, 342.
36. Stoker, *The New Annotated Dracula*, 456.
37. Lenin, *Imperialism*, 28.
38. Stoker, *The New Annotated Dracula*, 433.
39. Stoker, *The New Annotated Dracula*, 345.
40. Stoker, *The New Annotated Dracula*, 498–99.
41. S. T. Joshi, "Introduction," in Bram Stoker, *Bram Stoker: Five Novels: Completed and Unabridged* (New York: Barnes & Noble, 2006), ix.
42. Stoker, *The New Annotated Dracula*, 6.
43. Stoker, *The New Annotated Dracula*, 338.
44. Lenin, *Imperialism*, 139.
45. Lenin, *Imperialism*, 5.
46. Marx and Engels, *The Communist Manifesto*, 92.
47. Richard Matheson, *I Am Legend* (New York: Orb, 1995), 27.
48. Matheson, *I Am Legend*, 143.
49. Rabindranath Tagore, *Nationalism* (New York: Penguin, 2010), 9.
50. Rabindranath Tagore, *Nationalism*, 8–9.
51. Marx and Engels, *The Communist Manifesto*, 19.
52. Lenin, *Imperialism*, 1.
53. Matheson, *I Am Legend*, 23.
54. Marx and Engels, *The Communist Manifesto*, 109.
55. Lenin, *Imperialism*, 6.
56. Matheson, *I Am Legend*, 166.
57. Lenin, *Imperialism*, 121.
58. Matheson, *I Am Legend*, 28.
59. Matheson, *I Am Legend*, 29.
60. Stoker, *The New Annotated Dracula*, 5.
61. Lenin, *Imperialism*, 18.
62. Marx and Engels, *The Communist Manifesto*, 89.
63. Matheson, *I Am Legend*, 169.
64. Rabindranath Tagore, *Nationalism*, 22.
65. Matheson, *I Am Legend*, 169.
66. Marx and Engels, *The Communist Manifesto*, 7.
67. Matheson, *I Am Legend*, 170.
68. Lenin, *Imperialism*, 91.

8

You're Nothing to Me But Another . . . [White] Vampire": A Study of the Representation of the Black Vampire in American Mainstream Cinema

Zélie Asava

THIS CHAPTER EXPLORES THE representations of race and gender in two examples of black vampires: the male character Blade, *Blade* (Norrington, 1998), *Blade II* (del Toro, 2002), and *Blade: Trinity* (Goyer, 2004); and the female character Akasha, *Queen of the Damned* (Rymer, 2002). I have deconstructed these representations to find alternative ways of seeing these vampires through an analysis of the films in terms of critical race/ethnicity studies, feminism and queer theory. There is still a great absence of black vampires or even black people in horror films as a whole—a problem mentioned in jest in *Scream 2* (Craven, 1997). This chapter examines why the black vampire is an important presence in Hollywood cinema and an important challenge to dominant racial discourses.

The *Blade* films are distinct from other black vampire films in that they are centered around and empathize with the actions of a vampire hunter, Blade (Wesley Snipes), who is half-human and half-vampire. His black mother was bitten by a white vampire, Deacon Frost (played by Stephen Dorff), while pregnant with Blade, a bite which killed her and infected the fetus with the vampire virus. Blade fights a war against vampires to avenge his mother's death, find the vampire who killed her (and made him a "half-breed") and protect humankind. The first film's twist comes when Blade discovers that Frost is that vampire he seeks and that Frost's sexual partner is the vampire who once was Blade's beloved mother.

Blade's story (produced by Snipes's company Amen Ra Films) was designed to be a trilogy of films in an epic style, a modern multicultural Shakespearean tragedy. It has the elements of a tragedy, including the figure of the hero, Blade, with one fatal flaw that will bring him down: human emotions. Such a view of the film shows it to be an attempt to place a black man in a socially prestigious role, a serious role. But the *Blade* series is also low-brow action films that trade on our most base desires and fears. Arguably, in terms of plot, the same could be said of many of Shakespeare's plays.

Blade is a bag of contradictions, with a constantly shifting, ambiguous identity. This is a much more honest portrayal than simply giving him a "mask of perfection."[1] He doesn't flatter the fantasies of an audience looking for a flawless black hero, and thus his characterization remains true to the horror/fantasy/action genre. Blade is a distinct character in that not only is his life a daily struggle but he must also fight an internal battle to come to terms with his origins, and so he inhabits a place in-between definitions. He is a sharp dresser, short with his words, and he works alone, with the exception of Whistler (a white man who found him as a boy and trained him to hunt vampires; played by Kris Kristofferson). Yet he is also a salvatory figure, a sacrificial subject on a mission to eliminate evil from society.

His characterization as a Shaft-like figure is perhaps due to the context of the comic book *Blade* (begun in the 1970s) from which the film is derived. The film version was the first to treat vampirism as a scientific virus akin to AIDS. Its scientism takes the vampire genre out of mythology and into realist territory. *Blade II* continues Blade's story as he fights to contain and exterminate a new biologically mutated breed of vampires (the "reapers") who are multiplying fast and threatening the extinction of both the original vampires and humanity. He works with "the bloodpack," a small vampire army originally formed to hunt him, as their leader in a joint war on the reapers. In *Blade: Trinity*, Blade teams up with the "Nightstalkers," a group of vampire hunters who aim to destroy all vampires and who face the ultimate battle with Dracula. These films are revolutionary because they place Blade, a black man, in the role of hero and as savior of the world; it is he alone who can prevent the annihilation of humanity, although he does have one constant ally: his (white) friend and fellow vampire-hunter, Whistler.

Queen of the Damned is allegedly the story of Akasha (Aaliyah), the mother and queen of all vampires. In actuality, the film tracks the journey of the white vampire Lestat to find meaning in being an undead. Lestat (Stuart Townsend) starts a rock band, enjoys huge success and falls for Jesse Reeves (Marguerite Moreau), a white girl who works for Talamascar (a secret Masonic organization that records supernatural activity). In the middle of all this he enjoys a brief affair with Akasha that leads him to his "true" destiny: love with Jesse. Ordered by Akasha to kill Jesse he instead "turns" her (i.e., makes her a vampire) and in her finds an eternal soul mate, the one thing he needed to give his life meaning. This film invests Akasha with such evil as to make her into some sort of satanic creature. This is of course true to her character as a vampire, and yet it also seems symptomatic of a wider problem in mainstream American cinema: a refusal to celebrate black women as lead actresses in films, and a refusal to engage fully with interracial love. Akasha's overtly sexual love affair with Lestat is considered acceptable screen material, yet a lasting romance between the two is not. Blade (like most black male characters in Hollywood) is denied the right to have a similarly sexual interracial relationship even though he is clearly attracted to Nyssa (Leonor Valera, a white female vampire), in *Blade II*.

In each of these films one is left with many contradictions. For example, the use of a black actress (rather than a white one, which has long been the tradition in Hollywood) to play an Egyptian queen in *Queen of the Damned* is commendable and a reminder of the long-denied existence of an ancient African royalty. But her representation is also a damning portrayal of Africans as cannibalistic, evil and anarchic, which, of course, is a cinematic tradition going back to *Birth of a Nation* (Griffith, 1915), *King Kong* (Schoedsack, Cooper, 1933) and Tourneur's 1943 film *I Walked with a Zombie*, in which whiteness is portrayed as the good by means of placing it in opposition to "them," the foreign, the Other (e.g., the Oriental/African/Caribbean/black).

The Political Significance of Black Vampires

The vampire myth has been extensively written about as a metaphor for perverse sexuality, for social fears—fear of the Other, fear of evil, fear of the unknown, fear of the spread of disease (particularly AIDS)—and as a metaphor for colonialism. The two books which influenced the modern notion of what it is to be a vampire, Bram Stokers's *Dracula* and Sheridan Le Fanu's *Camilla*, were both written by Anglo-Irish men during the English occupation of Ireland, suggesting a direct link to English colonialism. In Western literature, the myth has traditionally been ascribed to Eastern Europeans, the racial Other, who posed a constant threat to Western Europe. In the African mentality, the vampire became the cultural Other, the white man. The figure of the white vampire in Africa was a symbol for the brutality of "the white man": "The name of the bloodsucker superstition is Mumiani. I understand the superstition is fairly widespread throughout Africa" (George Brown in a letter to Elspeth Huxley).[2] The use of the term "vampire" in Africa referred directly to the draining of African lands, peoples and even their blood by "white colonizers and slave traders; the blood of Africans was taken . . . for use by Medical Departments for the treatment of Europeans."[3]

The term "vampire" was then used by Africans to describe the police and even the fire brigade; each region had its own definition of vampire. The attribution of the term seems initially to have been a literal way of describing the abductions and massacres that occurred during slavery and colonialism and which developed into mythology and fictions. Each story was historically and reasonably situated and contextualized to identify the exploitation of Africans specific to that area.

Vampire stories are, then, confusions and misunderstanding of the best kind: they reveal the world of power and uncertainty in which Africans have lived in this century. Their very falseness is what gives them meaning; they are a way of talking that encourages a reassessment of everyday experience to address the workings of power and knowledge and how regimes use them.[4]

The use of the vampire myth in Africa also refers to the segregation of society. Vampires live outside normal society, beyond our rules, with powers beyond our comprehension. They move in exclusive groups, exploit others, are like us and yet not like us, and transgress boundaries.

Blackness has traditionally been associated with all things negative or evil. Whiteness, on the other hand was linked to purity and the light of God. Vampires complicate these binaries. They are white, but a white that is the absence of all color, a spiritual emptiness, a death (particularly when viewed in terms of colonialism). If whiteness is to symbolize Christianity, then vampires, like the Klu Klux Klan, Le Front National or the BNP, are, to quote Luise White, "a dreadful parody of Christ."[5]

The *Blade* films and *Queen of the Damned* could both be accused of attempting to erase large chunks of history by producing their absence. They are set in a world that seems to be our world (or possibly, in *Blade's* case, sometime in the near future) and yet is not our world. It is a world where color is present and yet treated as absent; and where gender is clearly an issue (e.g., see Deacon Frost's living quarters, which resemble a harem) and yet is ignored (it is treated as natural that men rule the world). The fact that race and gender are coded as incidental makes them more powerful visually. The unsaid becomes very powerful when it is acknowledged by all but never mentioned. For example, when Akasha enters an all-white vampire nightclub and is threatened with dismemberment and bleeding, one recalls segregation and the lynchings that occurred against those seen to transgress boundaries. Likewise, taunts against Blade that he is not a "pure-blood" recall the language of fascism. Within colonialist discourse, metaphors, tropes and allegorical motifs played a constitutive role in "figuring" European superiority: "The idea of race, for example, can be seen as less a reality than a trope."[6] The idea of race as a trope is concretized by the notion that race is carried in the blood, hence the "one drop rule" in America (one black ancestor could define you as black regardless of your actual skin color). Blood has been related to "religious affiliation (Jewish blood), class membership ('blue blood'), national appurtenance ('German blood') and race ('black blood')."[7] It has played a key element in the construction of racial ideology, as well as religious and class divides across the world.

Queering the Vampire: Gender and Sexuality

The "queered" attitude to the vampire applied to a subversive figure like the black vampire may serve to liberate the representation of blackness. As a male vampire, being "queer" can be self-empowering: Blade delights in his queerness and exploits it; it is his binary-defying, mixed-race identity (half-vampire and half-human; white vampire father and black human mother; dead and undead; devoid of emotion yet susceptible to emotion; artificial and organic; asexual and sexual; us and not-us) that gives him his power. It is this position in-between definitions that defines him only as "the chosen one," whose blood is sacred, a blood that when used in the correct rituals has immense power for the vampire world. His queerness, his non-categorizable identity, is his power.

In Akasha, queerness is the expression of her insanity, her evil, and it identifies the need for her destruction (though even her death—bitten by a white female vampire—is a lesbianized image). She is seductive in her interaction with both sexes, and she does not fit into a traditional view of femininity (she is depraved, violent and independent). She embodies the draining (Freudian), castrating power of the abject, that which collapses polarities. Polymorphous sexuality is deemed threatening in her representation; her penetrative power subjugates Lestat (an excessively white and queer/homo-erotic vampire) and results in genocide.

Blade seems to fulfill the stereotype of the "Buck," the excessively sexual, violent black male. But although he is portrayed as a male fantasy—tall, dark and handsome, strong and silent, his sexualized clothing (tight leather) being reminiscent of Batman—he is not actively sexual. Perhaps this is in order to struggle against the stereotype. Blade's sexuality is something of an anomaly. It is as ambiguous as every other area of his life. It is possible that the mystery of Blade's sexuality is a result of his comic-book character background, a side-problem of making a film about an inadequately developed character.

Blade has close female friends in both films: in *Blade*, a black female doctor Dr. Karen Jenson (N'Bushe Wright); in *Blade II*, Nyssa; and in *Blade: Trinity*, Whistler's daughter Abigail. However, as much as he risks his life to rescue and protect these women, he never clearly expresses anything more than platonic love for them (a passivity which suggests his homosexuality). At a crisis in *Blade*, though, Dr. Jenson allows him to feed from her. This is a very sexual moment which builds to a climax, clearly implying a deep sexual connection between them (after which Blade roars and moves like a beast as though a monster has been wakened in him, implying that black sexuality is monstrous). However, it is she who pursues him, while he is focused solely on his crusade.

In the same film, Blade has to avoid the incestuous urges of his mother and then kill her (it is interesting to note that he can kill her but not Whistler). His relationship to her is fantastical and bizarre: he idealizes and obsesses over her as one might a life-long love (which may prevent him from being able to love any other woman) and then decides that she is a monster whom he must destroy.

He falls in love with Nyssa in *Blade II*—he takes great risks to protect her and looks at her with great sentiment. When she is wounded he allows her to feed from him (stroking her hair gently as she does) in a tender (and rather animalistic) moment which saves her life and seems to parallel sex (she feels she must apologize to her father afterward for disgracing the family honor). And when she asks him to take her into the light to die (having received the reaper bite, she wants to die before the infection takes hold), it is a very romantically charged scene; he carries her in his arms, holds her face in his hand and looks into her eyes as she dies.

In *Blade*, Blade shares a sexually intense moment with Whistler; Whistler holds Blade's hand as the latter takes his antidote—to which he reacts with an extreme ferocity building to a shattering climax. Dr. Jenson comments on how much Blade loves him. Yet despite the obvious homo-erotic overtones, I see their relationship far more as one of trust and friendship. Perhaps they do share sexual gratification, but this is not clear from the film. What is clear is that they genuinely love each other, and in this way they form a queer family which emphasizes the value of love (in contrast to their loveless world). Their coupling could be seen as a father/son relationship (he is Blade's only father/parent figure), a homosexual union or an example of fraternal love (he is Blade's only friend). Their love is not stated as sexual, yet they cohabit, work together, rescue each other and appear to be life partners. At the start of *Blade II*, Blade states that his one aim is to find Whistler ("nothing will stop me"), albeit to destroy him. Whistler has been taken by the vampires and presumably "turned"—an action Blade was too sentimental to take in the first film. When he finds Whistler, he discovers that he loves him too much to kill him, and in a romantically charged scene carries him over his shoulder saying "let's go home." His affection pays off; Whistler is cured and ready to continue the war against vampires with Blade. Their alternative home life, in its defiance of sexual norms, elevates the queer family over the heterosexual couplings of the vampires as loving and constructive over disloyal and destructive.

Blade's inactive sexual aspect may be a reaction to the dominant culture's hypersexualization of the black male. It is quite possible that the filmmakers chose not to portray him as a sexual being in order to move away from such careless stereotyping. If this is an attempt to reconstruct black masculinity, it allows Blade to be self-determining and to develop his sexuality across the films rather than assuming his sexuality from the start. By not focusing on Blade's sexuality, the viewer is able to see Blade first and foremost as a human being and to recognize his ability to bond with others, black or white, male or female. Blade's nonaggressive sexuality reconstructs him as a friend and achiever who is aggressive in his job but not in his personal life. This moves the viewer away from the tendency to see all black males as aggressive with women or competitive with other men.

When considering Akasha's sexuality we must examine her in terms of her femininity and her ethnicity. Weiss notes that the lesbian vampire is said to merge "two kinds of sexual outlaws."[8] However, if this is true, then the black female vampire must be three kinds of outlaws (having a triple consciousness as black, woman and vampire), while the queer/lesbian black female vampire is so over-laden with deviancy that she must surely be the number one public enemy. The lesbian vampire is a male sexual fantasy but also a male fear; her predatory nature is dangerous to male supremacy. She is a negative stereotype as well as an object of desire, an image of death and of freedom, expression and hedonism. I draw the comparison between the black female vampire and the lesbian vampire to illustrate this position. Weiss claims that "outside of male pornography the lesbian vampire is the most persistent lesbian image in the history of the cinema."[9] The erotic power of the female vampire and the male fascination with lesbianism has meant that lesbianism is implied in nearly all representations of female vampires. If the lesbian vampire "provokes and articulates anxieties in the heterosexual male spectator,"[10] then Akasha must provoke an explosion of anxiety necessitating her destruction even more than theirs.

Akasha is portrayed as a beautiful, sophisticated cultural aristocrat. She is a queen from an ancient royal legacy but also a sexually aggressive, independent, perverse vampire. By contrast, Jesse is a working girl; she is inquisitive, unstable, passive, naive, confused, weak, flawed and plain looking. She is confused by her sexual desire for Lestat and waits for him to take her (sexually), whereas Akasha takes him. Jesse fulfills the traditional male expectations of a "good girl," whereas Akasha is a "vamp," defined as a serious threat in the early days of cinema: "Vamp: a beautiful woman whose sexual desire, if fulfilled would drain the life-blood of a man."[11] Akasha is Jesse's direct opposite, and although clearly (and perhaps in a self-conscious, witty way) fantastical in her seductive, unreal beauty, she is also inherently evil, which makes Jesse a sexually pure, virtuous example of humanity and femininity. On the representation of white femininity Dyer observes, "White women are constructed as the apotheosis of desirability, all that a man could want, yet nothing that can be had, nor anything that a woman can be . . . white representation in general has this everything—and nothing quality."[12]

Akasha, on the other hand is securely fixed as an obsessively sexual creature. She is so identified with sexuality that it is this that kills her; she dies after she allows Lestat to bite her, leaving herself vulnerable to attack, an attack which matches the violence she herself perpetrated. Jesse embodies the triumph of good over evil, the straight over the queer.

In *Queen of the Damned* Akasha engages in a sexual interracial relationship with Lestat but is punished with death very early on in the film. She is destroyed by white vampires in order to protect Jesse's "great family" and to save "the world as we know it," which in my opinion identifies her as a threat to whiteness. She is punished for daring to cross and blend boundaries, for asserting her will as a black woman and a vampire. In this way, Akasha could be seen as a reproduction of the "tragic mulatto" stereotype (a woman who tries to pass for white, falling in love with a white man but always ending in disaster).

Akasha is represented as an Oriental monarch through the cultural flattening of "Eastern" tropes that Hollywood filmmakers traditionally collapse into a single stereotypical figure. Hollywood has rarely taken great interest in being accurate in its representations of other races, and the image of the Eastern goddess is exemplary of its carelessness. The East was colonized and thus feminized in colonialist discourse (which defined Egypt as the East, or the Orient, along with Asia and the Middle East). The imagery of Akasha is a mixture of Eastern tropes in the Orientalist style: Arabic music, Egyptian headdress, African jewelry, Middle-Eastern dress and a bodice that is both revealing and war-like in its sexualized resemblance to armor. She speaks in a variety of accents: Caribbean, West and East African, Arabic and Eastern European. Her history is never discussed or contextualized. She awakes from what is presumably an extremely long sleep but mentions nothing about slavery or colonialism, nor even expresses any desire to return to rule her empire, Egypt.

The Psychosis of Akasha, the Black Queen

Akasha is named the mother of all vampires, the first vampire from which all others are descended. As a black woman, this is a powerful concept that subverts the (white) biblical story of Adam and Eve. This may remind the viewer of theories of Africa as the birthplace of humanity, and it is a very revolutionary statement, placing blackness as the norm rather than whiteness. In terms of America, this idea is very potent because, as a result of slavery, there are many white people with black ancestors (and vice versa). As with Blade, the image of Akasha (if taken in a positive light) attributes to a black person a degree of power usually denied to black people in society. She is a vision of individual mobility, regency and beauty that was destroyed and massacred by colonial rule and slavery, whose descendants are left with that terrible legacy. Yet problematically, the film does not explore the history that brought Africans from regency to slavery.

Akasha is a problematic figure as she, being sexually transgressive, emphasizes the "excessive, undomesticated femininity as a problem and source of anxiety for the hero."[13] Her feminine power disturbs and distorts male supremacy and the masculine selfhood (as embodied in Lestat's emasculation). Akasha's representation seems to excite a desire for the exotic, for the black female, in the white male. But she also represents a desire "to deny kinship and retain masculine power on the maintenance of racial difference."[14]

Akasha is a femme fatale: "the projection of those libidinous cravings, which, since they are forbidden, must always prove fatal."[15] She is one of many modern femme fatales whose downfall is their psychosis. Historically, uncontrolled feminine sexuality has been linked with psychosis, and it seems that in the sexually liberated female vampire, psychosis is set free. She is also a spectacle; an excessive masquerade of femininity which attempts to veil her psychosis. Late-19th-century art and literature constantly referenced the figure of the female as destroyer and delighted in exploring her wild sexuality while real women were strictly governed by men and denied any sexual freedom. Akasha repeats these strange practices, allowing the viewer to enjoy her ecstatic sadomasochism and candid, provocative queerness.

Akasha's presence and the overtly sensational display of her body betray an uneasiness about miscegenation and sexuality which seems to demand her execution. Her power, on the other hand, betrays the reality of black women's lack of power or influence, whilst her regency contrasts with the reality of widespread black poverty and limited social access and opportunity. Her "power" is a fantasy that bears little relation to reality: "No woman of color has ever symbolized citizenship in the United States history, only the denial of citizenship. Women of color were among the last group to achieve the right to vote and all the attendant rights of citizenship that flow from it."[16]

Akasha seems to have no capacity for growth, while the film's main concern is Lestat's self-growth and the role she plays in that. Following classic Hollywood narrative structures, he is the hero and it is his character arc which is centralized.

Akasha's power over fire (she can inflame objects at will) relates to racial fears of the supernatural power of black society and locates her as an embodiment of a "hot" (i.e., a climatically hot and sexually "in heat") na-tion. Fire is a powerful weapon, one of Mother Nature's greatest weapons, which makes Akasha a very traditional representation of the earthy, natural native (from a time before science, when fire was a great tool, and the abil-ity to create fire a divine mystery). Her power over fire is also significant in terms of her mystery as a black vampire (and by extension as a black woman). One is unsure what to make of Akasha; she is inhumane and pos-sessed of superhuman power yet her beauty, love and desire are human attributes. She speaks in a booming voice which is deep and masculine, and she walks more like a snake than a human, evoking thoughts of blackness as strange and animalistic: "Black magic, primitive mentality, animism, animal eroticism, it all floods over me."[17] Her control over Lestat appears to be a kind of spell in which she has trapped him. She is almost transsexual, a mys-tery who plays with fixed borders of femininity and masculinity, becoming both and neither. This is the nature of the horror genre, of the abject, a place where meaning, borders and order collapse, making Western knowledge and methods of understanding powerless.

Akasha evokes ideas of colonial travel literature—she sees the world as her own, and Lestat's initiatory bath with her could be associated with the trav-elogues of the Western discoverers who used the discourse of virginity and baptism to discuss their sea voyages and discoveries. It is she who chooses Lestat, she who makes him king, she who makes the world their garden. The trips she takes him on could also be likened to the trips the devil takes Jesus on to tempt him. She is certainly devilish, and it is her evil doings that make Lestat defy temptation and opt for the goodness of Jesse. Thus, even if we take Lestat as a Christ-figure and her as a Satan-figure, she is still an autonomous and immense power.

The representation of Akasha is very clearly that of the abject mother; as Queen of the Damned, she is the mother of all vampires, their goddess, and yet she lives in the open (never hiding her vampirism) and feeds on immor-tals (vampire taboos). So her relationship with Lestat is an incestuous union. Her love affair with Lestat is one of enforced sexuality, controlled by her, the sexual predator. However, she also gives him everything he has ever dreamt of, the power to rule the earth. Like Deacon Frost she desires the death of the human race which she views as food, as animals. When faced with this, Lestat sees only evil in her and his former dream and assists in her killing. With Lestat and Jesse's union, the film ends on a romantic but segregated note, as the two walk hand in hand into the night. They affirm conventional gender roles and form a union of heterosexual whiteness, which has excluded the evil of the queer black female vampire. Perversion is destroyed and the "natural order" restored. This leaves us with some serious questions. Does the black female vampire have any chance of equality on screen? What does the black female vampire have to do to have the freedom of a white vampire and move beyond cultural stereotyping and fears of blackness?

Akasha's perversion and demonic attitude could be read in the light of Fanon's theories on the collective trauma of colonization and the first encounters with the "discoveries" as psychosis caused by colonization. Like a mummy or an artifact, Akasha is revived or "discovered" by Lestat (in the tradition of colonial archeologists' effective robberies of other cultures' heritages). Technically speaking, she is awoken by his music, which locates her as a primitive responding to ancient rhythms before language (Africa and women were historically defined as pre-scientific/pre-linguistic). She awakes to find her empire gone, her people oppressed and her continent dying, which could explain her psychosis. Akasha's distorted representation underlines this psychotic image; the nature of her voice is more akin to that of a robot or a traditional monster than of a human. But this could also be an artistic device to differentiate her from the other characters; she is their god, after all.

Perhaps her strange, inhuman attitude relates to her rejection of the traditional feminine ideal in favor of revenge. Perhaps it was revenge that made her and her king drink the earth dry during their reign and that makes her come back to do it once again to her colonizers "who slashed and violated and spat on Africa to make the stripping of her easier."[18] She speaks about humans as food, in the same way black people were seen as chattel during slavery or Jews were seen as vermin by the Nazis. Akasha could be said to represent the horrors of fascism, but her color redefines this as a black story, a story of the struggle for equality and revenge for centuries of immense brutality. Césaire and Fanon both compare colonialism to a system of rape and revenge. In her psychosis, Akasha revisits the sins of the white forefathers on their children, using their traditions (e.g., burning and pillaging) against them.

Akasha embodies Freud's castration anxiety by "cannibalizing" Lestat's phallic power. The archaic mother symbolizes the fear of female genitalia as cannibalistic and empty (the womb as a black hole, castrated) which threatens to bear a monster. Akasha's incestuous union with Lestat starves him of autonomy or separation from her. He blends into a oneness with his vampire mother and is lost in her perversion. Such disintegration threatens the viewer, as we fear the monster may take our selfhood, and thus we too seek its destruction in order to save ourselves.

The maternal body is a site of conflicting desires, and in its mixture of fluidity and solidity it is considered abject; it disturbs identity, rules and binaries, ending in the ultimate disorder, the collapse of meaning. Akasha is necessarily presented as defiled, aggressive and polluted so that Jesse can be the feminine ideal: pure, vulnerable and subordinate. Akasha plays on three major white anxieties: immigration paranoia, black power paranoia and interracial sex. She confirms each anxiety, serving as a paradigm to exemplify the need for white control and segregation. However, although the whiteness of the family is represented as homogenous in the film, this homogeny ignores the real heterogeneity of whiteness, e.g., within the film some characters are American and others European, descendants of both colonizers and colonized, oppressors and oppressed, immigrants and natives.

In *Queen of the Damned*, it is the fearful threat that Akasha poses to the "pure blood" vampires that causes her marginalization and death. This fear of Akasha and desire to protect cultural homogeneity reflects Western cultures' socially constructed myths that races are pure and must be kept pure. In truth, hybridity is an essential part of our racial history. The white utopia portrayed at the end of *Queen of the Damned* is thus nothing more than a fiction, removed from reality.

Conclusion

Vampires are a source of the fantastic and what Freud called "the uncanny": that which is familiar but when repressed becomes abject to us (e.g., excretion, menstruation) and when reawakened provokes a feeling of the uncanny. Vampires destabilize fixed meaning and our understanding of reality, playing on "the fragility of the limit between matter and mind; the collapse of the limit between subject and object; and lastly, the transformation of time and space."[19] Blade, quite literally, bleeds these boundaries open in each of his films.

Fantasy takes the natural world and transforms it into something curious, a strange Other, an extreme inversion or expression of the human condition (and, in the case of the vampire, the aspects we normally hide). Fantasy allows for the dominant social politic to be de-centered and for the marginalized voices to be heard, and heard with authority. This is also the aim of the postmodern: to deconstruct the mainstream and uncover the forgotten histories, the unheard stories, and to incorporate the abnormal as it is discussed within the field of analysis. The fantastic thus uncovers lost peoples and realities, tracing "the unsaid and the unseen of culture: that which has been silenced, made invisible, covered over and made 'absent.'"[20] In this way a postmodernist approach undermines and/or deconstructs oppositional structures. It was my desire to provide a postmodernist account of these films to seek out their potential, to complicate and break down clear-cut binaries, ideologies, essentialism and other false assumptions. The most interesting character of these films is Blade, for his miscegenistic contradictory persona and for his double point of view: he is both the subject and the object of analysis, the vampire and the human. While he lacks the freedom of a white vampire, he is far more emancipated than Akasha, who remains subjugated by her race.

"Other people are raced, we are just white."[21] This quote exemplifies the problem of the white male cultural hegemony that dominates Hollywood, denying black people adequate voice. Dyer comments that whiteness has the power "to speak for the commonality of humanity. Raced people can't do that—they can only speak for their race."[22] This is what must change so that art may adequately mirror life.

Films (and popular culture as a whole) shape the way we relate to each other as they shape our views and identifications. These films are signposts of certain cultural assumptions about race and gender. By examining the origins of these distorted representations of race and gender, one may find the distortion in wider cultural representations, or even in one's own perspective.

Other Black Film Vampire Synopses

Beast of Morocco (Goode, 1966): A widower takes a job accompanying an archaeologist and his daughter on a North African tomb-hunting expedition. In Morocco they learn of legends regarding a Moorish vampire haunting a tomb. The widower is seduced by a mysterious woman whom he discovers is the evil black vampire.

Blacula (Cronin, 1972): A blaxploitation film, the 100th production of American International studios, it starred Shakespearean actor/singer William Marshall in the lead role as Prince Manuwalde, an 18th-century African prince who is turned into a vampire while visiting Transylvania. Two centuries later he rises from his coffin to wreak havoc in the Watts district of Los Angeles. He targets a woman whom he thinks is the reincarnation of his long lost lady love. He is pursued by a vampire hunter (a Van Helsing type).

Scream, Blacula, Scream (Kelljan, 1973): A blaxploitation sequel to *Blacula* that focuses on the revival of the black vampire Prince Manuwalde (played by William Marshall) by an American voodoo cult. He enslaves one of its members and then goes on a feeding spree. When he encounters Lisa (played by Pam Grier), a voodoo priestess, he believes she is his salvation.

The Vamp (Wenk, 1986): This vampire-stripper film begins with a group of fraternity boys looking for a stripper for their next party. The boys end up on the wrong side of the tracks, in a seedy vampire strip joint. Katrina (played by Grace Jones) performs an erotic dance painted in zebra stripes.

Vampire in Brooklyn (Craven, 1995): Eddie Murphy plays Maximillian, a black vampire who arrives in Brooklyn to find his vampire mate (the only other of his race, a half-vampire who thinks she's a human and lives in Brooklyn under the name Rita). Rita (played by Angela Bassett) is a policewoman who is tortured by dreams she does not understand and the feeling that something is missing from her life. To gain Rita's love, Maximillian enlists the help of Julius (played by Kadeem Hardison) whom he turns into a ghoul. He also deploys sinister magic and murder to hypnotize and destabilize her mind to a point where he can manipulate her to his desire. However, she is watched by her detective partner Justice (played by Allen Payne) who secretly loves her and eventually rescues her from Maximillian.

Notes

1. E. Shohat and R. Stam, *Unthinking Eurocentricism: Multiculturalism and the Media* (London: Routledge, 1994), 24.

2. G. Brown, "Letter to Elspeth Huxley," from Elspeth Huxley Papers, Rhodes House Oxford, RH MSS Afr. s. 782, Box 2/2, Kenya(1).

3. J. K. Wachanga, "The Swords of Kirinyaga: The Fight for Land and Freedom," *Kenya Literature Bureau*, R. Whittier, ed. (1975), 9.

4. L. White, *Speaking with Vampires: Rumor and History in Colonial Africa* (Berkeley: University of California Press, 2000), 43.

5. White, *Speaking with Vampires*, 28.

6. Shohat and Stam, *Unthinking Eurocentricism*, 137.

7. Shohat and Stam, *Unthinking Eurocentricism*, 137.

8. A. Weiss, *Vampires and Violets: Lesbians in the Cinema* (London: Jonathan Cape, 1992), 84.

9. Weiss, *Vampires and Violets*, 84.

10. Weiss, *Vampires and Violets*, 90.

11. Weiss, *Vampires and Violets*, 96.

12. R. Dyer, *White* (London: Routledge, 1997), 1.

13. R. Dyer, *The Matter of Images: Essays on Representations* (London: Routledge, 1993), 127.

14. M. Hammonds Evelynn, "New Technologies of Race," in *The Gendered Cyborg: A Reader*, ed. G. Kirkup, L. Janes, K. Woodward and F. Hovenden (London: Routledge, 2000), 317.

15. A. Carter, *Nothing Sacred* (London: Virago, 1978), 119.

16. Evelynn, "New Technologies of Race," 317.

17. F. Fanon, *Black Skin, White Masks* (New York: Grove Press, 1986), 126.

18. A. Césaire, Introduction to Victor Schoelcher, *Esclavage et Colonisation* (Paris: Presses Universitaires de France, 1948), 7.

19. Tzvetan Todorov, *The Fantastic: A Structural Approach to a Literary Genre* (Cleveland, OH: Case Western University Press, 1973), 25.

20. Rosemary Jackson, *Fantasy: The Literature of Subversion* (London: Methuen, 1981), 200.

21. Dyer, *White*, 1.

22. Dyer, *White*, 2.

9

She Would Be No Man's Property Ever Again": Vampirism, Slavery, and Black Female Heroism in Contemporary African American Women's Fiction

Marie-Luise Loeffler

H AVING LONG HELD A RATHER marginal and obscure status within the scholarship of the field, the works of African American women writers of vampire fiction, such as Jewelle Gomez's *The Gilda Stories* (1991) and Octavia Butler's *Fledgling* (2005), have only recently garnered more extensive academic interest, a trend that is also visible within anthologies such as *Dark Thirst* (2004) and *Dark Dreams* (2004). Yet contemporary African American women writers already began turning to the figure of the vampire as early as the 1990s, radically transforming conventional representations of this literary trope by centering their focus primarily on black female vampire protagonists. In so doing, they have not only inscribed the traditionally white male genre of vampire fiction with voices that were previously relegated to the margins. Even more so, they have also actively engaged with the historical past of the United States, using this Gothic trope to reimagine subject matters that have been frequently written out of (American) history. This holds particularly true for black women writers who have turned to the setting of slavery in their fiction. Their works profoundly illustrate the metaphoric potential of the vampire in unveiling the racial, sexual, and gendered mechanisms of oppression that undergirded this historical chapter and, going beyond this, empowering their black female protagonists to challenge and reconfigure the white master's narrative of "History."

Using the example of J. M. Jeffries's *Blood Lust* (2005), in this chapter I will exemplify black women authors' utilization of the trope of the vampire as a transgressive narrative strategy for the recovery of "things forgotten and the tragedy of forgetfulness,"[1] as well as for the reconceptualization of social and cultural hierarchies within historical settings. This is particularly visible when *Blood Lust* returns to and reimagines a subject that has been repeatedly written out of official histories: the enforced sexual relations between slave women and their white owners in the antebellum American South. It is here that vampirism comes to function as a signifier of resistance against dominant societal structures for the novel's protagonist, a slave mother named Mignon du Plessis. As I will argue, Jeffries's use of the trope of the vampire not only gives her black maternal character a voice but enables her to reclaim control over her children, her own life, and their future histories. This narrative trajectory, in constructing a black maternal vampire, clearly transcends comparative portrayals in black women's neo-slave narratives, as it entails a unique fictional framework for the destabilization of the white plantation-master's physical and discursive authority over the (procreative) bodies and families of black women.

Moreover, as both the slave mother protagonist and her white male antagonist continue to exist transhistorically as embodiments of the legacy of slavery in the novel, this depiction not only signifies the continuous impact of the past on the present (and future) within the United States but also sets the stage for an unprecedented image in black women's literature of slavery: a black maternal heroic figure with the power to seek retaliation for the historical injustices inflicted on slave women by white masters. In this way, *Blood Lust* echoes contemporary African American women's vampire fiction in general, as this unusual text celebrates the unique potential of the fantastic trope of the vampire to de(con)struct the very racial, gendered, and sexual ideological foundations of American politics and culture that remain pervasive to this day.

Before turning to a detailed analysis of *Blood Lust*, however, I will first contextualize the (sub-)genre of contemporary African American women's vampire fiction by tracing its origins and major influences. Besides locating black women's vampire fiction within larger feminist reconfigurations of the traditionally white male genre of vampire fiction that emerged within American women's fiction beginning in the 1970s, I will also place this body of texts within a larger spectrum of postmodern fantastic African American women's literature. As will be explicated—most notably by exploring contemporary black women's vampire literature's deep engagement with the historical past of the United States—this body of literature is preoccupied with underlying themes similar to comparable works by other contemporary black women writers. Turning to American history—that is, particularly slavery and its repercussions in the present—black women writers have brought a profound historical revision and an emphasis on cultural legacy to the traditionally

white male genre of vampire fiction as they challenge ideological constructions of racial hierarchies and give central importance to black female voices.

Contemporary African American Women's Vampire Literature

As Veronica Hollinger argues,[2] the wide popularity of the trope of the
vampire in recent decades reflects the nature of the vampire as an "inherently deconstructive figure" which thus poses a "real threat in any cultural
moment that invests heavily in assumptions about stable reality, essential
humanity, and clear-cut ideologies of good and evil."[3] Not surprisingly, a
large number of women writers have claimed and remodeled this traditionally white male genre since the late 1970s and early 1980s, turning female
vampires into subversive literary metaphors for the reconceptualization of
multiple patriarchal conventions. In this regard, late-20th-century literary
representations of female vampires take quite a different narrative trajectory from that of their female (and male) vampire predecessors in 19th-
century—predominantly white male—fiction, such as the ones featured in
the prototypical *Dracula* (1897) by Bram Stoker, who largely constituted
negative figures given a fatal ending.[4] In fact, postmodern writers have
embraced precisely those highly transgressive features of the vampire that
Victorian authors worked so hard to contain.[5]

   As works such as Jan Jennings's *Vampyr* (1981), Jody Scott's *I, Vampire*
(1984), and Sarah Smith's "When the Red Storms Come"[6] (1993) have
explicated, contemporary women's vampire fiction has ceased to portray
the subversive behavior of vampiric women characters as restrained and
smothered, but has instead reinvested it with positive meanings. Such redefinitions of the female vampire, as Carol Senf has pointed out, clearly reflect women's increasing equality and sexual liberation and the influence of
the women's liberation movement on American culture in general.[7] Indeed,
women writers of vampire fiction since the 1970s have frequently drawn
on the figure of the (female) vampire as a signifier for openly sensual eroticism and, in so doing, have celebrated this literary motif as a means to rebel
against restrictive societal scripts that continue to circumscribe women's
sexuality. As Gina Wisker concludes, "[t]he erotic, conventionally a site of
control and prohibition, [has] become a site for liberation and exploration
in contemporary women's vampire fiction."[8]

   These (feminist) redefinitions of traditional genre conventions of vampire literature were taken to a new level in a body of vampire fiction by
African American women writers that emerged in the early 1990s.[9] While

their works continue to be concerned with the exploration of gender-based oppression and resistance, these writers have complexified these issues in their fiction, unveiling and renegotiating the multifaceted intersections that emerge between the socially constructed categories of gender, sexuality, *and* race.[10] The vampire, in fact, can function as a prime strategy for this undertaking, not only because this figure's inherent fluidity unsettles clear gender boundaries, but also due to the vampire's location at the crossroads of gendered, sexual, and racialized discourses. This is especially prevalent in the vampire's bloodsucking abilities. As Brad Epps has pointed out, the mixing of bodily fluids between vampires and their hosts has simultaneously symbolized the mixing of gendered, sexual, and racial "identities, bodies, bloodlines and borders,"[11] making the vampire a prime figure to challenge and ultimately destabilize categories of race, gender, and sexuality that underlie hegemonic societal structures.[12]

While this destabilization has historically resulted in the projection of a number of racist, sexist, and homophobic anxieties onto the vampire, contemporary black women authors have reread this figure's sexual and racial Otherness as a site of both promise and subversion.[13] Their depictions of black women vampires have not only negotiated conceptions of monstrosity related to unconventional expressions of sexuality, a trend that Paulina Palmer has also identified in depictions of lesbian vampires.[14] They have also thrown back the curtain on constructions of the monstrous that have historically been associated with racial Otherness.[15] Going beyond this, these unusual black female vampire protagonists depart yet more radically from their (historical and contemporary) white male (vampiric) counterparts,[16] as it is their—previously marginalized—perspectives that represent the prime focus in African American women's vampire fiction.[17] As Kathy Davis Patterson notes further, in creating black female vampires who—due to their gendered, racial, sexual, and vampiric identities—are subject to multifaceted Othering mechanisms, black women writers of vampire fiction enable their protagonists to serve as "astute observers of . . . their own existence within yet always on the periphery of that society."[18]

This conception resonates with particular importance, as the genre of vampire fiction has long been dominated by white (male) writers, publishers, and readers—until very recently to the exclusion of black women writers themselves.[19] In their explorations of this genre, then, black women writers not only rewrite the textual conventions of vampire fiction. They also consciously inscribe their voices into the genre itself, "construct[ing] a more inclusive vision of those traditionally absent from literary discourses in general, and sf, horror, and especially vampire tales in particular."[20] In this way, these black women have injected the entire field with a political and social agenda: Through their works, the conspicuous absence of African Americans within the genre of vampire fiction is laid bare, openly criticized, and consciously amended.[21]

Moreover, in writing from the perspective of black female vampire protagonists, they also seize the trope of the vampire in order to actively recreate a historical past that has been frequently ignored or written out of the American imagination.[22] Through this shift to the viewpoint of the (former) object of history rather than its (white male) subject, that is, through a primary focus on black female perspectives, black women writers of vampire fiction have proposed a powerful critique of the continuous silencing of black voices in American history. This has allowed black women writers of vampire fiction to reveal the exploitative structures and underlying ideologies of both patriarchy and racism that have been behind the negation of the black (female) experience. Thus, as these texts utilize complex literary expressions to repeatedly question the ideological constructions underlying hegemonic and patriarchal societal structures, the trope of the vampire in the works of black women writers has become a powerful tool for protesting social injustice and renegotiating conventional power hierarchies in general.[23]

Within this context, it is especially important to consider black women writers' repeated emphasis on the cultural legacy of slavery within their vampire fiction. Indeed, similar to other fantastic fiction(s) by black women writers—such as Octavia Butler's *Kindred* (1979), Toni Morrison's *Beloved* (1987), and J. California Cooper's *Family* (1991)—which have merged depictions of the historical past of slavery with its seeming antithesis, the fantastic, black women writers of vampire fiction have also frequently turned to reimaginations of this period.[24] By deliberately shunning the laws of probability and verisimilitude in order to challenge dominant representations of the American past, African American women writers of both vampire fiction and fantastic literature in general have utilized this strategy of bringing into the open underlying ideologies of (white) writings of history. In this regard, black women writers of vampire fiction similarly render their black (female) characters as subjects and not as victims of history.[25]

Besides reconfiguring generic conventions of vampire fiction, black women writers have also harnessed its subversive possibilities. Vampires are not only boundary crossers, they also hold a substantial amount of power as they present, to use Jewelle Gomez's expression, "character[s] of larger-than-life proportions."[26] As such, they have become prime figures for the reconceptualization of a wide array of dominant racial and gendered hierarchies that have historically structured the societal order within the United States. Indeed, the use of the fantastic, and in particular the vampire, has presented black women writers with a productive vehicle for imagining a redistribution of power into the hands of a subject whose autonomy has historically been repeatedly abridged within dominant legal, political, and cultural contexts, allowing for the construction of unprecedented cultural and discursive positions. Even more so, these (primarily) black female vampires have generally allowed for the construction of fantastic realms in which contemporary African American women writers have proposed highly revisionary worlds— worlds, to use Anne Koenen's words, that hold the "possibility of alternative modes of being."[27] The following reading of *Blood Lust* and its explorations of the tangled intersections of race, gender, and sexuality within the specter of black female oppression, as well as its portrayal of a black maternal vampire's self-reclamation, will serve as a case in point.

African American Women's (Vampiric) Voices of Resistance: J. M. Jeffries's *Blood Lust*

Blood Lust, a vampire novel written by the interracial duo of writers Jacqueline Hamilton and Miriam Pace and published under the pseudonym J. M. Jeffries in 2005,[28] focuses on the quest of its black female protagonist, Mignon du Plessis, a (formerly enslaved) mother and vampire.[29] This unusual character undertakes a transhistorical and transnational journey from a plantation in Martinique in 1745 to a battlefield in South Carolina during the Civil War, to the roaring twenties in Berlin, and finally to vampire hunts in present-day Louisiana. Jeffries's text interleaves two thematically and stylistically disparate parts. The main plotline, based in contemporary New Orleans, focuses on Mignon's missions as a venator (executioner) of immoral vampires, whom she hunts and slays for the Praetorium, the head vampire council. Within this frame, the novel explores a developing romantic relationship between the black protagonist and a detective, Ryan Lattimore, drawing heavily on the genres of romance and detective fiction.

Yet this narrative trajectory is continuously disrupted by a second plotline consisting of multiple detailed flashbacks which explore the protagonist's past. These describe Mignon's experiences as a slave mother, her subsequent metamorphosis into a vampire, her escape to freedom, and the liberation of her children, as well as the continuing impact of her past under slavery on her present life in contemporary Louisiana. It is this plotline—a highly unusual take on the (African American) neo-slave narrative—that will present the primary focus of my analysis. In fact, the novel's prologue already highlights the centrality of returning to the past, as Jeffries draws the reader into the historical period of slavery—a time and place that was characterized by highly policed racial boundaries. In these initial pages of the novel, Jeffries furthermore turns to a subject that has long been suppressed within the annals of American history as she frames her text with the depiction of a coerced sexual relationship between an enslaved black mother and her slave master.

Set on a plantation in 18th-century Martinique—a French slave colony in the Caribbean[30]—*Blood Lust*'s very first paragraph encapsulates some of the major concerns of the novel as it interweaves the concepts of slavery, power, corporeal control, motherhood, and voice:

"You sold my children!" Mignon curled her hands around the edge of the blanket covering her nakedness . . . Candles lit the opulent bedroom, casting flickers of flames over his face, highlighting the evil twist of his lips and the shadows of his eyes. Charles Rabelais seemed to gloat. "Your brats were mine to dispose of as I chose." He stroked her cheek with long, pale fingers. She tried not to turn away as he traced her bottom lip with his thumb. Instead, she concentrated on his white skin showing stark against her duskiness. "Please give them back." Because he was her children's father, she had hoped they'd be safe from the slave blocks. Charles felt no kinship . . . "*Non*," he said. Agonizing pain knifed through her as his chilled fingers slid across her light brown cheeks. She steeled herself not to draw away no matter how she loathed his touch. Once before, she'd been foolish enough to defy him. The bite of the whip still echoed in her mind, as well as the piercing pain that had raced across her back . . . Her darlings were gone. They had been the only reason she had not taken her life as her mother had.[31]

Beyond foreshadowing the black mother's imminent rape—alluded to by Mignon's nudity and the master's touch—this scene evokes a long and traumatic history of sexual exploitation by the white plantation patriarch. To use Saidiya Hartman's famous phrase, this portrayal graphically constructs a prime "scene of subjugation"[32] by exposing the deeply interrelated historical narratives of violence, rape, and enforced reproduction perpetrated against black women by their white masters. By alluding to repeated instances of rape as well as to the black female protagonist's failed resistance against her owner's sexual violations (and the resulting violent punishment for her assertion of a glimpse of autonomy), Jeffries powerfully illuminates the position that female slaves frequently held in the social order of the antebellum South, as Mignon is trapped within circumstances that leave her little to no room to claim control over her body and her self.

The protagonist's lack of agency over her life is further explicated through the painful loss represented by the sale of her offspring. This absence graphically exemplifies both the limited maternal rights that slave mothers had over their children, as well as the slave mother's deprival—at the hands of white men—of the possibility for maternal nurturing. In so doing, Jeffries's portrayal connotes Mignon's motherhood as what Hortense Spillers has elsewhere referred to as an inescapable state of "unrelieved crisis"[33]—a notion that is even further emphasized as the novel traces black maternal violations through generations, epitomized in the reference to her own mother's desperation and suicide. This dynamic of highly disparate power relations between slave mothers and their white masters is also underlined by Mignon's pleading—a clear signifier of her helplessness—which is contrasted with the white master's short response, "*Non,*" an ultimate verdict over her children's lives made with incredible, almost impatient, ease. With this scene, the novel thus evokes a central underlying tenet of black women's writing about slavery in general: Echoing works ranging from Harriet Jacobs's slave narrative *Incidents in the Life of a Slave Girl* (1861) to Nobel Prize Laureate Toni Morrison's *Beloved* (1987), Jeffries inscribes herself into a black female literary tradition which has continuously explored the "unspeakable" horrors inflicted on black women under slavery.[34]

It is against this initial frame based on the physical and psychological vulnerability of the novel's black maternal character that *Blood Lust* soon embarks on a sharply contrasting narrative trajectory. This departure is closely tied to Jeffries's introduction of the element of the fantastic through the slave mother's transformation into a vampire. Although enforced by the slave master who is himself a vampire, Mignon's metamorphosis to vampirism nevertheless creates what Kathleen Brown has elsewhere referred to as a "shift in 'paradigm' or 'episteme' in which [a person's] way of understanding the world is radically altered,"[35] as her transformation from a mortal to an immortal being also encompasses a new construction of her self as an individual and as a mother.

Indeed, Jeffries repeatedly draws on vampirism within the novel's remaining chapters in order to imagine the slave mother's transition from voicelessness to voice, from powerlessness to power, and from the status of object to that of self-possessed subject—a shift that is also accompanied by a complex and unique destabilization of the social roles played by master and slave. Similar to other works by contemporary African American women writers of vampire fiction, *Blood Lust* thus signifies a narrative strategy that Teresa Goddu has so eloquently termed "haunting back" within African American literature in general.[36] As Goddu has argued, the reconfiguration of Gothic thematic and narrative conventions as a powerful means to dismantle dominant constructions of (racial) master-narratives has played a central role in literary works by African Americans since their beginnings:

> From Harriet Jacobs and Frederick Douglass to Charles Chesnutt, Richard Wright, and Toni Morrison, the gothic has served as a useful mode for African-American authors to resurrect and resist America's racial history. As the producers of terror instead of its text, African-American writers use the gothic to haunt back . . . to intervene in discourses that would otherwise demonize them.[37]

Following the prologue, *Blood Lust* features numerous instances that exemplify the powerful potential of the vampire for the resistance of marginalized groups dealing with white, hegemonic societal structures. Mignon's newfound powers enable her to escape from Martinique, defeat slave patrollers hired to return her, interfere in lynchings, and ensure a successful outcome of the Civil War for the North. Yet this theme is most forcefully explicated in Mignon's reclamation of her children, Angeline and Simon, rescuing them from a brothel in Charleston to which they had been sold by her master. As the novel makes clear, her successful search for both children through the Deep South—avoiding threats of recapture—relies on the protagonist's newly acquired vampiric abilities of "see[ing] as clearly at night as during the day" and her acute hearing with which she can "isolate and identify sounds and tell what direction they came from," paired with being "physically strong in a way she'd never been before."[38]

Moreover, Mignon's newfound status also propels her into a position in which she can (physically and figuratively) overcome her former state of maternal helplessness and instead actively claim her children. This is most prominently illustrated when the black female protagonist frees her daughter from the clutches of a white male client in the brothel:

> The man smiled lazily. He patted the bed next to him . . . "So you like little girls?" Rage filled [Mignon] and she clenched her hands and fought against the snarl that grew in the back of her throat. His smile faded and he shrank back from the fury in her voice. "Are you going to hurt me?" . . . She advanced toward him. "How can I, I'm just a woman." He eased off the bed and picked up a poker from the fireplace and took a swing at her. She grabbed the poker and bent it until it broke. His mouth fell open at the demonstration of her strength and he started to sidle toward the door, his gaze darting back and forth as though looking for another weapon. "I'm not going to hurt you." She dropped the broken poker on the floor. "I'm going to kill you."[39]

This portrayal marks a clear intervention in black women's sexual exploitation, reversing the white man's dominating power and assertion of control over black female bodies. While the client initially assumes her availability and submissiveness, his intentions are quickly thwarted by Mignon's unanticipated physical strength. This scenario is pushed even further, as the black woman not only exerts authority over the white patron by cornering him and breaking his "weapon," but—as the novel indicates—she eschews from killing him with his own instrument and instead chooses to "penetrate" her daughter's rapist with her own teeth, thus inscribing the formerly abused (black female) body onto the (white male) body of the abuser. In so doing, *Blood Lust*'s protagonist fundamentally disrupts the white, patriarchal order of the antebellum South: Besides regaining agency over her own body, Mignon extends her reclaimed corporeal integrity to her children, freeing her offspring not only from the brothel, but ultimately, as the novel makes clear, from the very object status they endured under slavery.

Moreover, the protagonist's vampiric identity grants her the ability to create her own alternative and highly empowering black maternal "her-story" by actively establishing an existence for her family outside the reach of her master's authority. By keeping her family under the protection of her supernatural powers, this black mother also seizes control over her family's discursive representation—her history—as her own and her children's bodies and voices encompass the "texts" that bespeak the atrocities of slavery as well as bear witness to their survival and resistance.[40] As Valérie Loichot has noted in the context of general post-slavery fiction, there is indeed a close correlation between claiming physical control and claiming discursive control over one's (enslaved) family. As she concludes, "Agency comes not only through the control of sexuality but also through the historical imagination. The shift marks the passage from surviving bodies to controlling subjects" and "amounts to an epistemic detour of the [white patriarchal] world."[41]

What is more, in her hybrid slave mother/vampire protagonist, Jeffries constructs a black female character who lives not only a powerful but also a transhistorical and diasporic existence through time, guarding her kin and their historical legacy across centuries. Throughout the novel, in fact, Mignon's primary drive revolves around the protection of subsequent generations of her family, with whom she retains a close bond throughout different chapters of American history, from Reconstruction, to the Harlem Renaissance, to the civil rights movement, and finally to the present day. This connection between Mignon and her transhistorical kin is best encapsulated in the novel's description of a cross-generational family portrait: "[S]he picked up an old daguerrotype from the sideboard. Her youthful face stared back at her. She clearly remembered the day the photographer had done the sitting . . . She had been seated on a bench with her great-grandson Jean Pierre, and her great-great grandson, Victor."[42]

While the idea of the strong interrelatedness of the past under slavery and the present also takes central stage in other neo-slave narratives by contemporary black women writers utilizing the fantastic, *Blood Lust* introduces a further layer to this concept. As not only the black female protagonist but also her vampiric white plantation master continue to live for centuries, the novel symbolically captures the struggle of black women against the oppression implied by slavery and its historical legacy, as both characters become embodiments of the repercussions of the past that echo to the present day. Furthermore, this transhistorical framework allows for a narrative trajectory unprecedented in the literature of slavery by black women: a black mother seeking active vengeance for her own and her children's (sexual) abuse.

In the last chapters of the novel Jeffries stages a climatic fight between "good" and "evil" in contemporary New Orleans. In contrast to conventional plot dynamics in vampire literature, however, Jeffries features a black female protagonist, the formerly Othered, fighting against the novel's epitome of evil, a white plantation patriarch, in order to seek retribution for the traumas of history. *Blood Lust* thus delivers catharsis in the form of the black mother's overcoming of the historical legacy of slavery when Mignon slays her former master by decapitation—a final power reversal between Charles Rabelais and the black female protagonist.[43] Besides presenting Mignon's final assertion of her own (and her children's) corporeal integrity, this portrayal graphically demonstrates the unique potential of the fantastic within the black female vampire, as Jeffries's protagonist becomes a powerful "tool"—to rephrase Audre Lorde's famous statement[44]—to eradicate the historical figure of the master and thus to dismantle the "master's house." In so doing, the novel's ending thus symbolically stages a de(con)struction of the very ideological manifestations of white patriarchy that not only historically formed the foundations of the traumatic chapter of slavery within U.S. history, but which—as Jeffries's transhistorical perspective exemplifies—continue to "haunt" the American cultural, political, and literary landscape to this day.

Thus J. M. Jeffries's *Blood Lust* graphically illustrates the multifaceted versatility that the (postmodern) vampire can embody. Within contemporary African American women's vampire fiction, this figure has particularly enabled the imagination of innovative reconceptualizations of (historical and contemporary) societal patterns of dominance and control circling around the intersection of race, gender, and sexuality. In putting this subject matter at the heart of these highly unusual fictional visions, black women writers not only give their works a profoundly political edge in critiquing the oppressive structures and underlying ideologies of both patriarchy and racism. Even more importantly, they advance revisionary alternatives for dominant racial, sexual, and gendered configurations of the past and present. In this way, contemporary African American women writers of vampire fiction resoundingly answer Toni Morrison's call to "avert the critical gaze from the racial object to the racial subject; from the described and imagined to the describers and imaginers; from the serving to the served."[45]

Notes

1. Nnedi Okorafor-Mbachu, "Of Course People Can Fly," in *Afro-Future Females: Black Writers Chart Science Fiction's Newest New Wave Trajectory*, ed. Marleen Barr (Columbus: Ohio State University Press, 2008), 131.

2. Veronica Hollinger, "Fantasies of Absence: The Postmodern Vampire," in *Blood Read: The Vampire as Metaphor in Contemporary Culture*, ed. Joan Gordon and Veronica Hollinger (Philadelphia: University of Pennsylvania Press, 2007), 199–212.

3. Hollinger, "Fantasies of Absence," 201.

4. See Gina Wisker, "Love Bites: Contemporary Women's Vampire Fiction," in *A Companion to the Gothic*, ed. David Punter (Malden, MA: Wiley-Blackwell, 2001), 167; and Brad Epps, "Vampires, Mestizas, Rouges, and Others: Figuring Queerness with Gloria Anzaldúa and Luis Zapata," in *Desde Aceras Opuestas: Literatura/Cultura Gay Y Lesbiana En Latinoamérica*, ed. Dieter Ingenschay (Frankfurt am Main: Vervuert, 2006), 93.

5. See also Margaret Carter, "Lust, Love, and the Literary Vampire," in *Strange Horizons*, www.strangehorizons.com/2002/20020722/vampire.shtml.

6. In Michele Slung, ed. *Shudder Again* (New York: Roc Books), 149–64.

7. Carol Senf, *The Vampire in Nineteenth-Century English Literature* (Bowling Green, OH: Bowling Green State University Popular Press, 1988), 155–61.

8. Wisker, "Love Bites," 175. Paulina Palmer has also argued that contemporary women writers of vampire fiction "problematiz[e] . . . hetero-patriarchal norms and structures," putting this issue "to the fore in the[ir] narratives." See "The Lesbian Vampire: Transgressive Sexuality," in *Horrifying Sex: Essays on Sexual Difference in Gothic Literature*, ed. Ruth Bienstock Anolik (Jefferson, NC: McFarland, 2007), 208. See also Anne Koenen, *Visions of Doom, Plots of Power: The Fantastic in Anglo-American Women's Literature* (Frankfurt am Main: Vervuert, 1999), 232.

9. There are multiple novels, short stories and poems by African American women writers that revolve around vampiric figures. These include Jewelle Gomez, *The Gilda Stories* (New York: Firebrand, 1991); Tananarive Due, *African Immortals* (a four-novel series, 1997–2011); Jemiah Jefferson, *Voice of the Blood* (a four-novel series, 2001–2007); Linda Addison, *Consumed, Reduced to Beautiful Grey Ashes*, 2001; Linda Addison, *Being Full of Light, Insubstantial*, 2007; L. A. Banks, *The Vampire Huntress Legends* (a twelve-novel series, 2003–2009); Octavia Butler, *Fledgling* (2005); Jewell Parker Rhode, *Yellow Moon* (2008); and numerous short stories by Angela Allen and Donna Hill.

10. For a similar assessment of black vampires in the realm of film, see also Frances Gateward, "Daywalkin' Night Stalkin' Bloodsuckas: Black Vampires in Contemporary Film," Genders 40, www.genders.org/g40/g40_ gateward.html.

11. Epps, "Vampires," 87.

12. See also Judith Johnson, "Women and Vampires: Nightmare or Utopia?" *Kenyon Review* 15 (1993): 76; and Shannon Winnubst, "Vampires, Anxieties, and Dreams: Race and Sex in the Contemporary United States," *Hypatia* 18 (2003): 7–9.

13. See also Winnubst, "Vampires, Anxieties, and Dreams," 2003, 7–9.

14. Palmer, "The Lesbian Vampire," 212.

15. For a more detailed discussion of reconceptualizations of the monstrous in Jewelle Gomez, *The Gilda Stories* (1991), see Kathy Davis Patterson, "'Haunting Back': Vampire Subjectivity in *The Gilda Stories*," *Femspec* 6 (2005).

16. As Miriam Jones has pointed out, the black female vampire "inverts the traditional figure of the vampire as landowner and master of serfs in *Dracula*, or more to the point, as Southern plantation owner as in Anne Rice's *Interview with the Vampire*." See Miriam Jones, "*The Gilda Stories*: Revealing the Monsters at the Margins,"

in *Blood Read: The Vampire as Metaphor in Contemporary Culture,* ed. Joan Gordon and Veronica Hollinger (Philadelphia: University of Pennsylvania Press, 1997), 157.

17. This assessment is also reflected in Miriam Jones's discussion of Jewelle Gomez, *The Gilda Stories* (1991). In reference to Gomez's black female protagonist, Jones has argued that "[i]nstead of from 'without,' the threat is now from those who have done without" (*"The Gilda Stories,* 153) in Gomez's novel. See also A. Timothy Spaulding. *Re-forming the Past: History, the Fantastic, and the Postmodern Slave Narrative* (Columbus, OH: Ohio State University Press, 2005), 105; and Patterson, "'Haunting Back,'" 35.

18. Patterson, "'Haunting Back,'" 36.

19. As African American writer Jewelle Gomez notes, one of the major reasons why she began working with the trope of the vampire was in order to "try to push boundaries outward" for (black) women and lesbian writers within this genre. See "Recasting the Mythology: Writing Vampire Fiction," in Gordon and Hollinger, eds., *Blood Read,* 85. In her overview of the genre of vampire fiction, she explicitly points to the dearth of minority and lesbian writers: "Prior to the 1990s, however, people of color and lesbians were rarely allowed to participate in these fantasies, either in fiction or in the movies" (88). See also Spaulding *Re-forming the Past,* 101; and Jones *"The Gilda Stories,"* 152.

20. Jones, *"The Gilda Stories,"* 154.

21. This assessment also holds true for a number of black male writers who have similarly turned to the vampire in their fiction, among them Brandon Massey (*Dark Corner,* 2004); Chris Hayden (*A Vampyre Blues: The Passion of Varnado,* 2004); and Javan Shepard (*Vampire of God,* 2008).

22. For a comprehensive analysis of reconceptualizations of white history in fantastic black women's fiction in general, see Koenen, *Visions of Doom,* 105–31.

23. As Spaulding argues in the context of Gomez's *The Gilda Stories,* "Vampires . . . are haunted and shaped by history . . . The vampire and the narrative genre as a whole become vehicles of history rather than an escape from it." See Spaulding, *Re-forming the Past,* 103. See also Patterson, "'Haunting Back,'" 35; and Jones *"The Gilda Stories,"* 157. For insightful discussions of contemporary black women's vampire fiction's unique blend of conventions found in American slave narratives with central characteristics of vampire fiction, see Spaulding, *Re-forming the Past*; and Ingrid Thaler, *Black Atlantic Speculative Fictions: Octavia E. Butler, Jewelle Gomez, and Nalo Hopkinson* (New York: Routledge, 2010).

24. Numerous African American writers of vampire fiction have either consciously engaged in exploring the historical past of slavery or have extensively referenced in their works the historical legacy of the violent exploitation of slaves. For fiction that is either set in or that references slavery and its repercussions, see, for example, Jewelle Gomez's *The Gilda Stories*; J. M. Jeffries's *Blood Lust* (2005); Tananarive Due's *My Soul to Keep* (1997); and Brandon Massey's *Dark Corner* (2004).

25. See also Koenen, *Visions of Doom,* 124. Nancy Rhyne's compilation of stories by former American slaves also makes clear that there is, in fact, a long tradition of vampiric figures in African American folklore. In particular, vampires called "hags"—

dead people who shed their skin during the night and seek "vengeance on the living" by sucking the blood of their victims—repeatedly surface in these accounts: N. Rhyne, *Slave Ghost Stories: Tales of Hags, Hants, Ghosts & Diamondback Rattlers* (Orangeburg, SC: Sandlapper Publishers, 2002), vi.

26. Jewelle Gomez, "Black Women Heroes: Here's Reality, Where's the Fiction?" *Black Scholar* 17 (1986): 2. See also Patterson, "'Haunting Back,'" 40.

27. Koenen, *Visions of Doom*, 307. There are also a number of works by contemporary black women writers outside of the United States that draw on the vampiric folklore trope of the "soucouyant." Examples include Caribbean-Canadian writer Nalo Hopkinson's *Brown Girl in the Ring* (1998), as well as British writer Helen Oyeyemi's *White Is for Witching* (2009). For a scholarly discussion of the vampire in their fiction, see especially Giselle Liza Anatol, "A Feminist Reading of Soucouyants in Nalo Hopkinson's *Brown Girl in the Ring* and *Skin Folk*," *Mosaic* 37 (2004): 33–50.

28. In the following, I will refer to the pair of authors simply as "J. M. Jeffries," and I will correspondingly use the singular pronoun "she."

29. While Gomez and Butler have successfully breached popular culture and academia, as their works are read both by non-academics and scholars alike, Jeffries's *Blood Lust* holds—even within American popular culture—a rather obscure niche status. Although Jacqueline Hamilton and Miriam Pace certainly have quite a number of (predominantly female) readers, *Blood Lust* is largely unknown, even among avid vampire fiction readers and scholars focusing on African American vampire fiction. Thus there is, to my knowledge, no existent scholarship on this novel as of this writing. This also holds true of its sequel *Blood Seduction* (2007).

30. As Valérie Loichot has noted in her comparative study of post-slavery American and Caribbean fiction, despite differing geographies as well as "economic, national, and linguistic positions, the Plantation structure created similar worldviews, and in particular yielded related ways of reconstructing history." See V. Loichot, *Orphan Narratives: The Postplantation Literature of Faulkner, Glissant, Morrison, and Saint-John Perse* (Charlottesville: University of Virginia Press, 2007).

31. J. M. Jeffries, *Blood Lust* (Greenville, SC: Genesis Press, 2005), 1.

32. Saidiya Hartman, *Scenes of Subjection: Terror, Slavery, and Self-Making in Nineteenth-Century America* (New York: Oxford University Press, 1997).

33. Hortense J. Spillers, "Mama's Baby, Papa's Maybe: An American Grammar Book," *Diacritics* 17 (1987): 76.

34. See also Thaler, *Black Atlantic*, for a detailed analysis of central conventions of the female slave narrative in Jewelle Gomez's *The Gilda Stories* (1991).

35. Kathleen Brown, *Good Wives, Nasty Wenches, and Anxious Patriarchs: Gender, Race, and Power in Colonial Virginia* (Chapel Hill: University of North Carolina Press, 1996), 5.

36. Teresa Goddu, "Vampire Gothic," *American Literary History* 11 (1999): 125–41. See, for example, Patterson, "'Haunting Back,'" 35, for a discussion of this concept in Jewelle Gomez's *The Gilda Stories*.

37. Goddu, "Vampire Gothic," 153.

38. Jeffries, *Blood Lust*, 27.

39. Jeffries, *Blood Lust*, 30.

40. This depiction is echoed in numerous other neo-slave narratives by black women writers, who "engage the theme of slavery . . . in order to bear witness to the 'unspeakable'" and rewrite history. See Angelyn Mitchell, *The Freedom to Remember: Narrative, Slavery, and Gender in Contemporary Black Women's Fiction* (New Brunswick, NJ: Rutgers University Press, 2002, 5). In this regard, children play a central role. One need only think of Sherley Anne William's famous novel *Dessa Rose* (New York: HarperCollins, 1986), in which the black female protagonist Dessa passes on her story to her children: "Well this the childrens have heard from our own lips. I hope they never have to pay what it cost us to own ourselves . . . Oh, we have paid for our children's place in the world again, and again" (236). See also Carol Henderson, *Scarring the Black Body: Race and Representation in African American Literature* (Columbia: University of Missouri Press, 2000), 100.

41. Loichot, *Orphan Narratives*, 35.

42. Jeffries, *Blood Lust*, 57.

43. This depiction echoes Koenen's *Visions of Doom* and her assessment of contemporary women's vampire literature in general as she argues that within these works, "the fantasy of power revolves around the reversal of traditional positions of victim and agent of terror when the vampires instill terror in men" (232). See also Jones "*The Gilda Stories*," 157; and Patterson, "'Haunting back,'" 40.

44. Audre Lorde, "The Master's Tools Will Never Dismantle the Master's House," in *Sister/Outsider: Essays and Speeches*, ed. Cheryl Clarke (New York: Random House, 2007), 110–23.

45. Toni Morrison, *Playing in the Dark: Whiteness and the Literary Imagination* (New York: Random House, 1993), 90.

III

NEW READINGS OF THE VAMPIRE

10

Blood-Abstinent Vampires and the Women Who Consume Them

Alaina Christensen

"WE CALL OURSELVES VEGETARIANS," Edward Cullen tells Bella Swan, with no small dose of irony.[1] The Cullen family of vampires chooses not to consume human blood, and instead to live off the blood of woodland animals; it is because of this abstinence that Edward is able to enter into a relationship with Bella in *The Twilight Saga*, Stephenie Meyer's best-selling series. However, just because Edward doesn't intend to take some surreptitious sips from the lovely Bella does not mean that no one is devoured in *The Twilight Saga*. Ironically enough, it is the Cullens, and the latest incarnation of the popular culture vampire, who are consumed. The Cullens are portrayed not only as desirable consumables within the novels but also for hoards of fans the world over. Texts like *The Twilight Saga*, which will be the primary discussion in this chapter, but also *True Blood*, *The Vampire Diaries*, and their predecessors, *Buffy the Vampire Slayer* and *Angel* are ushering in a new era for the vampire archetype: the vampire as a sexy consumer object. Applying the theories of Jean Baudrillard,[2] particularly his theories on sign value in a consumer society, we find contemporary vampire texts ripe with new and surprising examples of consumption. Baudrillard argues that sign value, or the signification of "worth" and desirability, drives our late-capitalist consumer economy; the term "consumption" then deals with not only economic purchasing, but also metaphorical consumption, including how members of Westernized society participate in society, in culture, and in other signification systems.

No longer scary monsters in the dark, vampires are now tortured heroes and boyfriends for a few lucky heroines like the women of recent vampire fictions. The vampires of recent pop-culture texts all feature similar male vampires as anti-heroes who are sensitive and have the emotional complexity typically reserved for humans. These new romantic human-vampire relationships have led to vampires as general characters coming out of the shadows (so to speak) to interact with human characters in ways far beyond predator and prey. Vampires have always been fascinating creatures in science fiction and fantasy genres: dangerous and with a variety of supernatural powers, these once-human-but-no-longer-living characters are isolated from, yet unable to live without, humans. If one looks at the typical vampire body, it is not difficult to discern why these creatures exemplify the desirable Other's[3] body. Whether beautiful or not, and strong ranging towards invincible, vampires retain enough humanity or human traits to be comparable to humans but never seem to suffer the many faults of human bodies. And by investing (whether time, money, or attention) in the prolific number of texts abounding today, audiences—in a process of "symbolic exchange"—are able to appropriate vampires' desirable attributes for themselves as they consume the text. In this way, these new vampires are not only designed to kill, they are designed to be desired or to be consumed by their own prey.

Baudrillard argues that Western society exists in a system of "consummativity," a process by which consumer or human needs are a "function induced (in the individual) by the internal logic of the system: more precisely, not as a consummative force liberated by the affluent society, but as a productive force required by the functioning of the system itself, by its process of reproduction and survival."[4] The desires we experience living in a consumer society, even those we determine to be needs, are actually tools within the consumer system, which is self-sustaining precisely because what it trains us to do is desire and consume. While individual examples of needs may be fulfilled, "need" itself is never fulfilled. The goods that will in theory discharge the needs experienced by consumers are chosen based on sign value, rather than use value. It is useful to think of the distinction as that between object and Object; a car is an object that one drives from point A to point B, but a Rolls-Royce is an Object that has many cultural associations attached to its perceived value beyond transportation. There may be a particular use, which may be of value to a consumer, in an object: however, the driving force in this system is the desirability of the Object, or in the case of a vampire narrative, the desirability of the Other.[5] If the goal is the achievement of recognition and acceptance by others in society, then consider the idea that the Lacanian subject can and would not be drawn towards appropriating a non-desirable Other, but would actively cling to difference from it if the Other's sign value was less than the subject's own. Baudrillard claims that "one can only speak of objects in terms other than themselves, in terms of social logic and strategy,"[6] meaning that our relationship to any given object is always determined by its and our relationship to society and to desirability. The Rolls-Royce is not a car: it is a symbol of prestige, wealth, and the owner's merit in society. The systems of consummativity and commodity fetishism divorce specific meaning, value, and use from any individual item in order to propagate a system of unfettered want in consumers.

This is demonstrated in both inanimate objects and bodies, which have come to take the historical place of the soul as the human characteristic of penultimate importance. As bodies are visible to others (whereas a soul would not be), the goal for consumers is now to possess bodies in which health, happiness, and beauty are demonstrable to an outside observer, regardless of whether the traits are "authentic." The difference between the reality of the subject and its appearance to others is key in a system emphasizing sign value over use value: a vampire may be undead, but he's still good looking. The concept of sign value creates the understanding that only what is desirable to others is worthwhile, a statute that exists for both inanimate objects and bodies and further drives home the primacy of importance of demonstrable desirability to others.

But what is a desirable body? The answer is far from simple, as there are a great many pressures, fears, and concerns in how members of Westernized society decide and define what bodies should or need to be. According to Susie Orbach in her book *Bodies*, "in the discourse about self-created identity, the body is central."[7] No longer the mere receptacle of the soul, bodies are instead the canvas by which the self is created; therefore, our bodies play the primary role not only functionally in our daily lives, but also in the creation of our understanding of self and place in society. Orbach claims that "our social and economic position [depends] on how our bodies are seen,"[8] a perceived merit that should determine their acceptability in society at large. Vampire bodies are particularly attractive because of what they offer for symbolic exchange: the vampire body is beautiful, indestructible, and permanent, all of which are traits human bodies are variously perceived or felt to lack. Vampires are also appealing because of the extreme beyond-the-norm they represent, while audiences, particularly young audiences, may feel themselves mired in appearances while lost in our late-capitalist society. With the body playing such a central role to our entire existence, it is not surprising that its physical health and appeal are given such emphasis and are such a site of envy and admiration in vampire texts.

While standards of desirability vary, it is easy to see the ways in which the Cullens embody the contemporary Westernized view, particularly (but not exclusively) for a young female audience. Bella says, "Physically, I'd never fit in anywhere. I should be tan, sporty, blond . . . I had always been slender, but soft somehow, obviously not an athlete."[9] Upon her first encountering them, her descriptions of the five Cullen teenagers are in direct opposition to this description of herself. She describes the males as "muscled like a serious weight lifter" and "taller, leaner, but still muscular."[10] Here Bella deftly demonstrates Baudrillard's notion that athleticism is for masculinity the tantamount desirable trait; and phryneism[11] is to be the goal all women must aspire to in order to be of consequence in society. Describing Rosalee, Bella explains, "[T]he tall one was statuesque. She had a beautiful figure, the kind you saw on the cover of the Sports Illustrated[12] swimsuit issue, the kind that made every girl around her take a hit on her self-esteem just by being in the same room."[13] Bella notices that none of these siblings look alike, but what strikes her about them is that despite their differences in hair color and height, "they [are] all exactly alike. Every one of them [is] chalky pale . . . they all [have] very dark eyes [and] their noses, all their features, [are] straight, perfect, angular."[14] However, beyond the pale skin, dark eyes, and perfect facial features, there is one more trait they all share which will be a constant point of fascination for Bella throughout *The Twilight Saga*: their universalized attractiveness.

This broadly recognizable or homogenous attractiveness is but one of the multiple attributes which the Cullen vampires, like so many other current pop-culture vampires, possess which are desirable to humans or audiences. Because of the many similarities between vampire bodies and human bodies, vampires are more effective vessels for articulating our cultural attitudes about desirability and bodies. Vampires, as transgressive-but-not-too-transgressive Others, are precisely called for in a culture where the subject constitutes itself by defining itself in opposition to an Other but also desires to be more and other than itself. Baudrillard makes a claim that the body has gained a specific sign value in our culture and now serves as "the finest consumer object."[15] Because the body has supplanted the soul, caring for—which is synonymous with making beautiful—the body is now a moral imperative in the way that spirituality and prayer were historically an imperative in caring for the soul. The ethics of beauty and the desirable norms of personal appearance allow only a select few to be special and desirable, or even to personify "normal." Orbach posits that "the visual nature of our world sucks out variety and replaces it with a vision that is narrow and limited as far as age, body type and ethnicity are concerned,"[16] implying a homogenized imagery of the body that must be fit, trim, and generic to be attractive.

Bella claims, "I stared because their faces . . . so similar, were all devastatingly, inhumanly beautiful . . . They were faces you never expected to see except perhaps on the airbrushed pages of a fashion magazine. Or painted by an old master as the face of an angel."[17] Bella refers to their beauty as "inhuman" and relates it to the images in magazines or artworks, rather than to people. The emphasis on their similarities in pallor, features, and beauty further isolates the Cullens from individuality by stressing what is homogenous among them. "It was hard to decide who was the most beautiful,"[18] ponders Bella. Their beauty is not in individuality, but in similarity to each other and to culturally desirable imagery. Their faces are so obviously different from those around them that they belong only in the world of altered advertising or religious aesthetic celebration. In both cases, the images are understood to have been altered or to have been purely created to express beauty, which is isolated from reality in an artificial two-dimensional image, rather than existing in a "whole" person or character. Despite the awareness on Bella's part that this beauty is unnatural or inhuman, she nevertheless aspires to it. Like any contemporary consumer, she desires the sort of calculated signifying beauty that the Cullens possess despite its unreality. Baudrillard claims that the ethics of beauty, and by association desirability, may be defined as the reduction of all concrete values—the "use-values" of the body (energetic, gestural, sexual)—to a single functional "exchange-value," which itself alone, in its abstraction, encapsulates the idea of the glorious, fulfilled body, the idea of desire and pleasure (*jouissance*), and which of course thereby also denies and forgets them in their reality and in the end simply peters out into an exchange of signs.[19] By continuous relation to inanimate objects or to exotic animals, the Cullens are reduced to an abstract but desirable idea of strength, speed, and beauty. They act as ideals or foils—signs of what Bella isn't—which are always contrasted against her thoughts on herself and her own desires and insecurities.

In this series, vampires' skin sparkles in direct sunlight. When Bella sees Edward in the sun for the first time, she is near dumbstruck by the sight; she states, "Edward in the sunlight was shocking . . . His skin . . . literally sparkled, like thousands of tiny diamonds were embedded in the surface . . . his shirt open over his sculpted, incandescent chest . . . A perfect statue, carved in some unknown stone, smooth like marble, glittering like crystal."[20] Relating Edward, who is, from her perspective, perfection, to diamonds—possibly the most desirable consumer good—seems appropriate for a Baudrillardian reading. If bodies and objects can "'show each other off' mutually,"[21] then what could be more perfect than relating one's love interest to a diamond, the rock of romance and the stone of forever, as engagement ring retailers will tell you? Edward's desirable body here is discovered in relation to desirable objects, as Baudrillard explains;[22] Bella sees him as both diamonds and a perfect sculpture. Both Bella and Edward later relate his body to diamonds when he gives her a diamond pendant. "I thought it was a good representation," he says, "it's hard and cold [and] it throws rainbows in the sunlight." "You forgot the most important similarity . . . It's beautiful," Bella tells him in reply.[23] Again

Edward's body is accessed and possessed by Bella through an object. By the objectification of the Cullens, Bella and audiences are attempting to salve their own insecurities and to possess and assimilate these desirable traits. But in so doing, paradoxically, Bella and audiences are made animate and active in contrast and have a certain agency that is not present in these desirable vampires as objects.

Throughout their early relationship, Edward distances himself from physical intimacy with Bella because he is so dangerous to her, but when he attempts to demonstrate this dangerousness to her by threatening behaviors and explanations of his vampire nature,[24] her reaction is probably not what he would have expected. "I'd never seen him so completely freed of that carefully cultivated facade. He'd never been less human . . . or more beautiful,"[25] claims Bella. It is when Edward is the least human that she desires him most. The controlled affectation that Edward and the Cullens use to blend into society is less attractive to Bella than that which makes them Other. Because she desires their abnormal or nonhuman traits most, it is those traits to which she is attracted, not those that would or could make them more relatably human.

Beyond beauty, there is another significant requirement to desirability: age, or more accurately, young age. A young age is of utmost importance as aging is associated with a loss of strength and vitality, key tenets in health and desirability. Deborah Lupton claims, "[T]he 'mask of ageing', the external signs of old age—sagging flesh, wrinkles, loss of muscle tone, overweight—are culturally stigmatized."[26] This stigma is one of many that encourage our constant reliance on the health and beauty industry: use of Botox, liposuction, face lifts, or any other alteration of our aging body is looked at as a means of escaping judgment—but also as a moral imperative for those who love themselves. Accepting aspects of one's body that diverge from the norm, including the inevitability of aging, is seen as lazy or defeatist.[27] The cultural narratives at work here have linked the signs of aging to death with such a firm grasp that even innocuous things like grey hair and wrinkles hold a cultural significance of imminent demise. Perhaps it is this fear of age—and inevitable death—that offers the most immediately accessible reason for the popularity of vampires in science fiction and fantasy genres. As creatures that remain the same bodily age (usually young) forever, vampires neatly avoid the issue of aging, while nevertheless continuing on to experience more "life" time. Vampires in fiction today, as the expression goes, "Die young, and leave a pretty corpse"—but they get to continue "living in it."

Bella's feelings of inferiority play a large role in her near-instantaneous desire to become a vampire after she discovers that this is what the Cullens are. Though the primary reason she expresses is to be with Edward forever, it is fairly apparent in her dialogue and her dreams throughout the novels that there are other motives at work in and upon Bella. Her anxiety about aging is acute and intense from the very beginning of their relationship, and she tells Edward, "I'm going to die sometime. Every minute of the day, I get closer. And I'm going to get old."[28] Here Bella's words seem to support Baudrillard's, Orbach's, and Lupton's proposed perspectives on young and beautiful bodies. For Bella, age has a "gravely" negative cultural value, though not due to age itself, as her boyfriend is over one hundred years old, but instead due to the appearance of aging; it is Lupton's "the mask of ageing"[29] that Bella despises, the idea of her face as "creased, and withered" that wakes her up in a cold sweat.[30]

Brian Massumi, in "Everywhere You Want to Be," writes, "[W]e know we are alive . . . as long as we are shopping. 'I buy therefore I am.' The commodity encounter not only specifies but actualizes the subject of the purchase. The subject of capitalism cannot be said to exist outside the commodity relation."[31] Bella feels incomplete without possession or assimilation of Edward and his desirable consumer object traits. The fear Massumi discusses, which permeates our late capitalist culture, is combated by consumption. What we consume identifies and validates us to our peers and insulates us against the inherent anxiety we feel at our impermanent subject positions. Similar to Massumi, Baudrillard claims, "[I]t is thwarted legitimacy (with respect to cultural, political, and professional life) which makes the middle classes invest in the private universe, in private property and the accumulation of objects with a dedication all the more fierce . . . trying to celebrate a victory, a true recognition which escapes them."[32] It is precisely that which is beyond Bella (and human beings) that is the most appealing about Edward throughout *The Twilight Saga*.

Bella's voracious pursuit of Edward, as well as her intense drive to become a vampire—to consume that identity—is her way of insulating herself against losing Edward, but also against imminent death. After an injury in the first novel, Bella begins attempting to convince Edward to turn her: "I may not die now . . . but I'm going to die sometime. Every minute of the day, I get closer."[33] Massumi claims, "[B]uying is preventions. It insures against death."[34] Here Massumi claims that consumers are offered permanence or immortality through the buying and possessing of objects. The consumer becomes a subject, a subject which is active and actively exists in its relationship with the purchased objects. The act of consumption creates an identity within society, that of consumer or participant which lasts beyond a human lifetime (i.e., heirlooms, inheritance, etc.). This message is more literally possible for Bella, who if she "buys" into vampirism is literally making death (nearly) impossible. And by this purchase or transformation, she ensures her place in society as not only a permanently living (so to speak) subject, but also as a desirable object; which is its own insurance in a system that thrives on sign value.

If Bella is attempting to better herself, and particularly her body, through becoming a vampire, then she is taking some of Orbach's and Lupton's ideas to an extreme. If the body is central to how we create our identity, then Bella is attempting to alter her body by death and supernatural transformation. Lupton claims that "if the fleshly body represents oneself, then it is imperative to ensure that the appearance of the body is as attractive and conforming to accepted norms as possible."[35] Rather than the steps usually taken by people in our culture, such as make-up, cosmetic surgery, dieting, exercise, and the like, Bella is going much further. If she becomes a vampire, she is assured athleticism, as well as beautification by the transformation. And though she would not entirely conform to human norms, she would cease to be the odd human in the Cullen vampire family. Thus she would be able to become both the homogenized ideal version of the desirable Other which the Cullens represent to humans and also an accepted and like member of the Cullen family.

Bella's motivations for becoming like Edward are consciously stated at times: she loves him and wants to be with him forever, and she doesn't want to die. But subconscious motivations can be read into her behavior as well. For instance, each time that Edward and Bella begin to become intimate, Bella escalates the encounter and Edward retreats. She explains, "As I had just that once before, I smelled his cool breath in my face. Sweet, delicious, the scent made my mouth water . . . Instinctively, unthinkingly, I leaned closer."[36] The relationship between Bella's sexual desire for Edward and hunger and/or consumption is obvious, as during a sexually intimate encounter she notices his delicious and mouth-watering smell, rather than other more overtly sexual attributes. Every time she advances, it is compulsive, instinctual, or out of her control; she is driven wild by his proximity,[37] and, in kissing, she attempts to take possession of him in some way (hand holding, wrapping her hands around his neck, climbing into his lap, etc.). In *A World Made Sexy*, Paul Rutherford notes that "the very form of the commodity [has] changed . . . the meaning and utility of that commodity [is] informed by an aura of sensual excitement or its role as an instrument of sexual desire or its function as a catalyst for some erotic narrative."[38]

Applying Rutherford's idea to the body and Baudrillard's claim that there is a distinction between a sexual body and "an eroticized" body, one could read Bella's sexual attraction to Edward as demonstrating "the generalized imbuing of the whole field of 'consumption' by eroticism,"[39] particularly when reading Edward's body as having consumer sign-value, given its relation to advertising materials, art works, and diamonds. Baudrillard claims, "The erotic is the reinscription of the erogenous in a homogenous system of signs (gestures, movements, emblems, body heraldry) whose goal is closure and logical perfection—to be sufficient unto itself."[40] Edward's body is certainly more self-sufficient than a human being's body, and the physical attributes of youth and beauty are frequently emphasized by Bella when discussing it, which implies that they are also a significant part of its appeal for her. In fact, many attributes of Edward's body are those that Bella would gain in her vampiric transformation, which she is actively pursuing in the novels. That being the case, one could argue that while she is attempting to possess Edward sexually in this relationship, as a consumer she is attempting to obtain that which he signifies. That it is his smell (an element of his vampire capital) that causes her to lose control over herself in their kiss could be read as her consumer drive going into overdrive due to his consumer object appeal, though that would likely be oversimplifying the issue if it were listed exclusively as the reason.

Edward believes himself to be a damned creature, without a soul, and this is why he does not want to turn Bella into a vampire.[41] However, in our contemporary culture, the bodily transformation that Bella seeks and inevitably gets from him is actually her salvation. Baudrillard claims, "The obsession with youth, elegance, virility/femininity, treatments and regimes, and the sacrificial practices attaching to it all bear witness to the fact that the body has today become an object of salvation. It has literally taken over that moral and ideological function from the soul."[42] In her transformation, then, is Bella's salvation: she becomes the object which she so desired by subsuming that identity from Edward. Her bodily revamping (pardon my pun) begins to allow Bella to identify her body as the special one, but still it is an objectified body, rather than a body that is understood by her as her own. She thinks,

> My first reaction was an unthinking pleasure. The alien creature in the glass was indisputably beautiful, every bit as beautiful as Alice or Esme. She was fluid even in stillness, and her flawless face was pale as the moon against the frame of her dark, heavy hair. Her limbs were smooth and strong, skin glistening subtly, luminous as a pearl.
>   My second reaction was horror.
>   Who was she? At first glance, I couldn't find my face anywhere in the smooth, perfect planes of her features . . .
>   All the while I studied and reacted, her face was perfectly composed, a carving of a goddess.[43]

She is unable to identify herself within the body reflected in the mirror, insisting that whatever the thing in the mirror is—it is better than she.

Baudrillard posits that "the sign object is neither given nor exchanged: it is appropriated, withheld and manipulated by the individual subjects as a sign."[44] This can be seen in the way that Bella's perspectives on vampirism change with her access to it. She seeks vampirism rapaciously, but once she "achieves" it, the attributes, which were formerly so awe-inspiring, quickly become normal or even lesser, and she begins to undermine their significance as she pursues more. She demonstrates this by her disappointment that she did not become a vampire with a bonus superpower (as some of the Cullens possess). What the sign of vampire means is still contingent on what she determines it to be, and how she values it is still linked to further want.

Baudrillard's commodity fetishism is a power that is "transferred to beings, objects, and agencies, it is universal and diffuse, but it crystallizes at strategic points so that its flux can be regulated and diverted by certain groups or individuals for their own benefit."[45] The contemporary cultural fixation on the vampire can and should be read as demonstrating this crystallized power at work, commanding youth, beauty, and vitality of its audience at times at the cost of their very "humanity," metaphorically speaking, of course, as human characters and audiences almost vampirically devour these vampires and vampire fictions. In *The Twilight Saga*, and other contemporary examples, we can see the vampire as a figure whose hunger can be far less insatiable than its human counterparts. While Edward quickly learns to resist Bella's blood, though it smells to him like "exactly my brand of heroin,"[46] Bella is never finished consuming him, and neither are audiences, who are currently consuming everything *Twilight*, whether it be novels, films, or merchandise.

Applying a Baudrillardian reading to the ironic role reversal of humans and vampires allows for a close examination of Bella's relationship to these vampire bodies, as well as that of the legions of female fans relating to her. Bella is not alone in consuming these vampires—audiences everywhere are doing the same thing, and for the same metaphorical reasons. Vampire bodies have become a desirable and consumable site where readers can enact consumption in order to obtain a bolstered sense of identity, or at the very least, enact the insecurities that drive them to desire it. Rob Latham, in *Consuming Youth: Vampires, Cyborgs, and the Culture of Consumption*, claims that vampire texts "not only depict youthful consumers, they also interrogate the fetishization of youth as a desired/desiring substance at play within the collective activity of consumption."[47] By being forever young (at least in external appearances), vampires have what might be the ultimate visual capital for our body-conscious consumer society. They have the youth, which implies the athleticism and the phryneism, and they have a variety of special attributes beyond those of which humans are capable, and they get to keep them forever. Perhaps it is fundamentally that core notion of achieving and maintaining specialness forever that makes the vampire such a ripe metaphoric character. While human beings seem doomed to want forever, these new vampires have everything a person could need, and they cannot lose it to the wear and tear of time. For Lacan, the opposite of subjectivity is death, at least symbolically. Vampires in immortality have what would seem to be a permanent subject position, which contemporary consumers are striving for in their pursuit of anything at all with positive sign value and permanent signifying worth, so their subjectivity will remain despite their mortality.

These new vampires are driven by their nature to consume the women with whom they interact. It is never in question within the texts that these women are desirable both sexually and in a more epicurean sense, but the vampires choose not to partake. The question now might be why not? If one considers the motivating drives to consume that have been examined here, then perhaps it is the vampires' exclusion from those motivations that makes them immune to (or at least able to resist) the drive to consume their lady loves. Perhaps it all comes down to their permanence. The vampires cannot drastically alter their physical appearance, so they cannot supplement it, nor do they have any need to put effort into maintaining it: their looks will not fade with age. Without the fear of age and death that Massumi discusses, the vampires do not need the commodity encounter in order to "actualize" themselves. Their permanent youth and beauty legitimize and even elevate them by the standards of the norm.[48] The vampire is a figure who has and maintains that perfection without the work: hence they have achieved by their own nature what human consumers are supposed to strive for.

Though such an examination is not within the scope of this chapter, perhaps there is a case to be made for vampire consumption still active within the texts. Though the vampires in these new fictions actively attempt not to physically devour the women with whom they fall in love, maybe the attraction they feel for these women demonstrates their own feelings of insecurity or lack. Though the novels' audiences read Bella as an average teenager, Edward continuously identifies her as special and beautiful. Bella's most defining attribute from Edward's perspective is perhaps her fragility (both physical and in the temporal sense); that being so, maybe what Edward is most attracted to about Bella is that which is unattainable to him. Edward resents and is depressed by his belief that he is damned for eternity, and his permanence as well as vampiric tendencies are factors in that, so an argument could be made that it is her humanity and not her blood that appeals to him most of all. Or consider another text, the HBO series, *True Blood*.[49] Early in their courtship, vampire Bill tells Sookie that he "can smell the sunshine on [her] skin."[50] He says this with noticeable bittersweet sadness, which one can assume implies the loss he feels of sunlight, among other things. He then goes on to kiss her very passionately, implying the appeal which she and, by extension, the sunshine on her skin, have for him. The traditional understanding is that vampires cannot live without humans for the nourishment that human blood supplies, but perhaps it is the underlying human soul as well, and the fragile and faulty human body and life, that are now tying the vampires to mortal love interests. It might be that these lady loves are just as desirable consumer objects, and it is another metaphorical consumption at work in these novels (though paradoxical to the one previously discussed in this chapter) when the vampires enter into a relationship with a human character who possesses the humanity the vampire finds unattainable. This is a fairly interesting idea for further analysis, but it is a discussion for another time and place.

It likely surprises no one that any given vampire text is so full of consumption. However, this contemporary phenomenon of the abstaining (from drinking, not other things) vampire is a new and interesting cultural trend. The vampires of *The Twilight Saga, True Blood, The Vampire Diaries*, and even *Buffy the Vampire Slayer* are finding themselves the subjects of the unquenchable appetites of their human female counterparts. Because of their uniquely similar—but different—relationship to human bodies, vampire bodies are an extraordinarily effective site to interrogate the relationship of people to their bodies. At work in the creation of these perfect creatures, one can read the ideals and desires of the texts' authors but also, and especially, their devoted fans. *The Twilight Saga* has become extraordinarily popular with people of many demographics, but especially with females of all ages. These girls and women are also the demographic most likely to deal with body and beauty issues. Watching Bella's relationship to Edward and the Cullens throughout the series, it is easy to read Bella's interest as beyond that of romantic love. Her absolutely reverential views on the Cullens' appearance and her intense need to become one of them can and should be read as demonstrating more than just true love. She cannot be happy until she possesses that which she admires, and though she does achieve vampirism, there are hints that the transformation is not the end of this consummativity cycle.[51] Likewise, audiences continue to devour series material with incredible enthusiasm; the books have and are being adapted to film; an interlude novella has been published; and even the small town of Forks, Washington, in which the novels are set, has become a tourist destination. When discussing his role in the movie adaptation of *The Twilight Saga*, Robert Pattinson, who plays Edward, says, "You know what? I've never felt so objectified in my life."[52] Kristen Stewart, who plays Bella, claims, "Seriously, it's a trip to sit back and look at the sexual objectification of these dudes. I've never been asked to do any of this stuff,"[53] referring to the amount of time that her male costars spend topless on screen, or having their hair worked on.

The drive to consume, which motivates Bella as well as the huge audience of contemporary vampire fans, can be linked to a variety of motivating desires, fears, and other factors in our contemporary cultural milieu. The vampire as a site for consumption is obvious in light of their perfect bodies and permanence, but they are also perfectly unachievable. In Lacanian terms, lack can never be fulfilled as it is that recognition of other and difference that defines and gives subjectivity to us. However, the drive is still obviously present in the relationship of audiences to these texts. A Baudrillardian reading of the consumer relationship to sign value, particularly as it relates to bodies, complicates any readings of these texts that would regard these vampires as the monstrous consumers of the text. Perhaps authors and audiences, by humanizing the vampire, are humanizing their own compulsive consumption.

Notes

1. Stephenie Meyer, *Twilight* (New York: Little, Brown and Company, 2005), 188.

2. Since the 1980s, Foucault-influenced critical historicism has often circumvented psychoanalysis to such an extent that it has been difficult for critics to describe processes of exchange and identification that occur between cultural artifacts, discourses, and images and the people who receive and invest in them. Over the past fifteen years, because of Slavoj Zizek and others, critics have developed new uses for psychoanalysis within models that remain broadly historicist, while largely deriving from Lacan's theories of identity-formation. Zizek's work, in particular, explains how ideology operates as a support for fantasy (the "ideologies" I address are those we find in the various "vampire" discourses my project examines). I think, however, that Baudrillard's early work on symbolic exchange can supplement Lacan's theory of identification in terms that are more materialist then we find in most Lacanian revisionism. The scope of such a meta-critique is beyond what I can accomplish in this analysis, but my use of Baudrillard is intended to prepare the way for further materialist research that attempts to conjoin Baudrillard on symbolic exchange with Lacan on psychic identification. Since the 1980s, Foucault-influenced critical historicism has often circumvented psychoanalysis to such an extent that it has been difficult for critics to describe processes of exchange and identification that occur between cultural artifacts, discourses, and images and the people who receive and invest in them. Over the past 15 years, because of Slavoj Zizek and others, critics have developed new uses for psychoanalysis within models that remain broadly historicist, while largely deriving from Lacan's theories of identity-formation. Zizek's work, in particular, explains how ideology operates as a support for fantasy (the "ideologies" I address are those we find in the various "vampire" discourses my project examines). I think, however, that Baudrillard's early work on symbolic exchange can supplement Lacan's theory of identification in terms that are more materialist then we find in most Lacanian revisionism. The scope of such a meta-critique is beyond what I can accomplish in this analysis, but my use of Baudrillard is intended to prepare the way for further materialist research that attempts to conjoin Baudrillard on symbolic exchange with Lacan on psychic identification.

3. According to Jacques Lacan, the subject (a human being) realizes during the "mirror stage" that there is something outside of the "self"—what will be referred to

in this chapter as the Other. This understanding creates the concepts of difference and of lack. The subject will then spend its life seeking to achieve completion by fulfilling that lack. As the "self" can never reintegrate into an understanding of being one with that which is outside, the myth of or desire for self-completion is impossible to achieve. A subject lacks what is different, but negating difference would negate the subject of difference, in that a subject position is contingent on the existence of something that or someone who is other, that is, existing outside the self. In the case of these vampire texts, the audience may desire to achieve the desirability and permanence of the vampire, however it is obviously impossible, these being fictitious creatures after all, and therefore difference and the human subject positions remain. That being the case, vampire bodies serve as the perfect Other, in that they are unattainable, but similar enough to be attractive.

4. Jean Baudrillard, *For a Critique of the Political Economy of the Sign*, trans. Charles Levin (St. Louis, MO: Telos Press, 1981), 82 (hereafter cited as *Critique*).

5. Other and object are effectively synonyms here: vampires as animate fictional characters are an Other. However, in the framework of this argument they also serve as Objects, which are passive, and consumable.

6. Baudrillard, *Critique*, 36.

7. Susie Orbach, *Bodies* (New York: Picador, 2009), 167.

8. Orbach, *Bodies*, 165.

9. Meyer, *Twilight*, 10.

10. Meyer, *Twilight*, 18.

11. "[P]hryneism being defined roughly as the woman of Elle and the fashion magazines" (132, 136): Jean Baudrillard, "The Finest Consumer Object: The Body," in Jean Baudrillard, *The Consumer Society: Myths and Structures* (London: Sage), 1998.

12. This is another obvious example of the combination of athleticism, phryneism, and sexuality. It also, references to the Cullen bodies as advertising images or artificial imagery of the body once again.

13. Meyer, *Twilight*, 18.

14. Meyer, *Twilight*, 18.

15. Baudrillard, *The Consumer Society*, 129.

16. Orbach, *Bodies*, 167.

17. Meyer, *Twilight*, 19.

18. Meyer, *Twilight*, 19.

19. Baudrillard, *The Consumer Society*, 132.

20. Meyer, *Twilight*, 260.

21. Baudrillard, *The Consumer Society*, 134.

22. Baudrillard, *The Consumer Society*, 133.

23. Stephenie Meyer, *Eclipse* (New York: Little, Brown and Company, 2007), 439.

24. Meyer, *Twilight*, 264.

25. Meyer, *Twilight*, 264.

26. Deborah Lupton, *Medicine as Culture*, 2nd ed. (London: Sage, 2003), 42.

27. While large claims of this kind are problematic in light of today's postmodern notion of the constructed rather than the purely necessary, I think it is a fair statement given the recent trend of celebrity openness about cosmetic enhancement and

the aligning of procedures like Botox injections with a healthy concern about oneself. Consider a recent article from *USA Today* which discussed the rise of plastic surgery for adolescents: "'The kids I see, their desire is almost uniformly to be normal, non-deviant. Kids don't want to stand out in a negative way,' says Gerald Pitman, a plastic surgeon in New York City," in Mary B. Marcus, "Cosmetic Surgeries: What Children Will Do to Look 'Normal,'" *USA Today*, March 30, 2010, http://usatoday30.usatoday .com/news/health/2009-06-24-cosmetic-surgery-kids_N.htm?csp=usat.me. Marcus also brings up the role of celebrity and media in the changing perspectives on body modification, saying,

"There's less of a taboo about plastic surgery than ever before because of reality shows focusing on it and more celebrities who acknowledge they have had it," [Donn Chatham, president of the American Academy of Facial Plastic and Reconstructive Surgery,] says, "so children know it's an option. And today's parents are more willing to consider it for their kids."

28. Meyer, *Twilight*, 476.

29. Lupton, *Medicine as Culture*, 41.

30. Stephenie Meyer, *New Moon* (New York: Little, Brown and Company, 2006), 5.

31. Brian Massumi, "Everywhere You Want to Be: Introduction to Fear," in *The Politics of Everyday Fear*, ed. Brian Massumi (Minneapolis: University of Minnesota Press, 1993), 7.

32. Baudrillard, *Critique*, 40.

33. Meyer, *Twilight*, 476.

34. Massumi, "Everywhere You Want to Be," 9.

35. Lupton, *Medicine as Culture*, 41.

36. Meyer, *Twilight*, 263.

37. Meyer, *Twilight*, 263, 282.

38. Paul A. Rutherford, *A World Made Sexy: Freud to Madonna* (Toronto: University of Toronto Press, 2007), 6.

39. Baudrillard, *The Consumer Society*, 134.

40. Baudrillard, *Critique*, 94.

41. Meyer, *Twilight*, 37, 476.

42. Baudrillard, *The Consumer Society*, 129.

43. Stephenie Meyer, *Breaking Dawn* (New York: Little, Brown and Company, 2008), 403.

44. Baudrillard, *Critique*, 65.

45. Baudrillard, *Critique*, 89.

46. Meyer, *Twilight*, 268.

47. Rob Latham, *Consuming Youth: Vampires, Cyborgs, and the Culture of Consumption* (Chicago: University of Chicago Press, 2002), 5.

48. The norm here being humans, as we've established that all of these new vampires are interacting regularly with a population of human beings rather than other vampires.

49. *True Blood*, created and produced by Alan Ball, is based on *The Southern Vampire Mysteries* by Charlaine Harris. The series follows the residents of fictional Bon Temps, Louisiana, as they endeavor to coexist with vampires, werewolves, and other supernatural creatures.

50. "The First Taste," in *True Blood: The Complete First Season on DVD*. Alan Ball. HBO, 2009.

51. Consider Bella's potentially foreshadowing comment about her daughter, Reneesme, and a diamond necklace: "She could play with it if she wished; she liked sparkly things" (Meyer, *Breaking Dawn*, 752). Reneesme does not sparkle like her vampire parents, and she is drawn to it (523), much as Bella was when still human.

52. Karen Valby, "Blood Buddies," *Entertainment Weekly* 1076, November 20, 2009, 35.

53. Valby, "Blood Buddies," 35.

11

"Exactly My Brand of Heroin": Contexts and the Creation of the *Twilight* Phenomenon

Ben Murnane

ELENA KAGAN'S SENATE CONFIRMATION hearings were by all accounts uneventful. Wrote the *Economist* of Barack Obama's second Supreme Court nominee and her appearances before the Senate Judiciary Committee in June 2010: "The public knew little about Ms Kagan prior to this week's hearings, and they've learned little new about her during her three days of testimony, at least when it comes to how she might act as a justice."[1] One issue on which the public may have learned Justice Kagan's attitude—or, at least, an issue on which Senator Amy Klobuchar (D-Minn.) attempted to elicit Kagan's opinion—was the pressing case of "Edward versus Jacob."[2]

> Sen. Klobuchar: Solicitor General Kagan, you did, had [*sic*] an incredibly grueling day yesterday and did incredibly well, but I guess that means you missed the midnight debut of the third *Twilight* movie last night. We did not miss it in our household and it culminated in three fifteen-year-old girls sleeping over at 3 a.m. . . . I keep wanting to ask you about the famous case of Edward versus Jacob or the vampire versus the werewolf, but—
>
> Kagan: I wish you wouldn't.[3]

Several months before, in April 2010, a New York City police detective was accused of sexually harassing a subordinate via *Twilight*-themed text messages:

> Detective Dawn DelValle-Sanchez said Deputy Chief Michael Gabriel, the head of Bronx detectives, made the squad room a hostile workplace with obsessive behavior.

"I ask for ur forgiveness and another chance (Think Bella forgiving Jacob),"
Gabriel wrote in a text DelValle-Sanchez showed to the Daily News . . .

In another text message from an NYPD-issued BlackBerry, the chief asked for
forgiveness: "I will accept any penalty; hard labor, probation, a time out . . . Do
werewolves kill humans just like vampires?"[4]

On Friday July 30, 2010, on Ireland's *RTÉ* Radio 1, the regular *Today with Pat Kenny* programme was being presented by Myles Dungan. Dungan was discussing the news stories of the week with Dearbhail McDonald, legal affairs editor of the *Irish Independent*; Frank McDonald, environment editor of the *Irish Times*; and PR consultant Paddy Duffy. The group was debating an exchange of insults between Dermot Ahern, justice minister in the governing Fianna Fáil–Green Party coalition, and opposition (Fine Gael) finance spokesperson Michael Noonan. Duffy remarked, "Michael Noonan is like James in *Twilight*, he's out for blood . . . Fianna Fáil blood, Green blood, even Labour [Party] blood if they get in his way." None of the panelists seemed to view as odd the comparison between a seasoned politician and a character in a popular teen vampire novel.

Identifying a Phenomenon

There are two identifying factors of a literary phenomenon: sales, and a book's or series' impact on the broader culture. The former influences the latter, and vice versa. By either standard, the *Twilight* saga by Stephenie Meyer has become a literary-cultural phenomenon, a hugely popular creation. Of particular note is the series' acknowledged appeal to older women, those outside the target teenage demographic. Countless websites and forums have been set up by and for adult *Twilight* readers, including TwilightMOMS (www.twilightmoms.com), and the Facebook group Confessions of an Adult *Twilight* Fan. "[Y]ou are *exactly* my brand of heroin," vampire Edward tells Bella in *Twilight*.[5] It seems that, for multitudes, Meyer's creation is exactly their kind of literary fix.

The series—incorporating *Twilight* (2005), *New Moon* (2006), *Eclipse* (2007), and *Breaking Dawn* (2008), plus the novella *The Short Second Life of Bree Tanner* (2010)—has sold some 116 million copies worldwide, placing it firmly among the bestselling novel series of all time; translation rights have been sold in almost fifty countries. The series has spent more than two hundred weeks on the *New York Times* Best Seller list. Meyer's novels have won numerous awards and accolades. *Twilight* was named one of *Publishers Weekly*'s Best Children's Books of 2005, a *New York Times* Editors' Choice, and one of Amazon.com's "Best Books of the Decade . . . . So Far." *New Moon* won the Young Reader's Choice Award, Senior Division from the Pacific Northwest Library Association in 2009. At the 2009 Children's Choice Book Awards in the United States, *Breaking Dawn* was named the year's Teen Choice, and Meyer was named Author of the Year. And then there are the movie adaptations, which have collectively grossed over $2.5 billion at the box office worldwide. An unofficial parody film, *Vampires Suck*, premiered in summer 2010.

The publishing industry has been scrambling to produce products associated—even if only marginally—with *Twilight*, with a raft of unofficial biographies of Meyer and the movie series' stars hitting stores, along with unofficial "guides" and much more. *New Moan: The First Book in the Twishite Saga* by "Stephfordy Mayo" is a parody published in 2009. *In My Sky at Twilight: Poems of Eternal Love* is a 2010 selection chosen by Gaby Morgan; ostensibly named after a Pablo Neruda poem, it features a Gothic *Twilight*-style cover and title in similar font, and it is dedicated to Robert Pattinson, the actor who plays "good" vampire Edward Cullen in the films. Young adult novels with similar themes to *Twilight*, such as L. J. Smith's *Vampire Diaries*, have been reissued with *Twilight*-esque covers. First published in 1991, a 2009 reissuing of the first two books in Smith's series, *The Awakening* and *The Struggle*, sports a red-and-black color scheme and a plump apple on the cover, *à la Twilight*. The *Vampire Diaries* has also been developed into a television series in the wake of *Twilight*'s success, premiering on the teen-oriented CW network in the United States in 2009. *Wuthering Heights* has even been republished by HarperCollins in two *Twilight*-themed covers, one for the American market and the other for the United Kingdom. The British version is branded "Bella & Edward's Favourite Book."

The proliferation of official and unofficial merchandise, and products aligning themselves with the phenomenon, has included everything from vocabulary workbooks using *Twilight* to a vampire-inspired dildo that sparkles in sunlight.[6] An iTunes and DVD documentary on the real town where the series is set is called *Twilight in Forks: The Saga of a Real Town*. The Native American reservation Meyer features in her books has also become involved. The Quileute Nation established an exhibition at the Seattle Art Museum entitled "Behind the Scenes: The Real Story of Quileute Wolves," which ran from August 2010 to August 2011, with the aim of raising "important issues of identity and cultural appropriation" and creating "a public forum for clarifying misconceptions resulting from the popular *Twilight* books and films."[7] The exhibition ran at the Smithsonian in 2012. Hugely diverse cultural elements are all converging on this one point: *Twilight*.

Openings: From a Wizard to a Vampire

In accounting for the popularity of *Twilight*, it is important to acknowledge at the outset that it is in many ways not an outlier, merely the culmination or latest incarnation of trends and traditions that have been in train and popular for a long time. Meyer's series gives us a family of vampires, creatures which have been firmly embedded in popular culture since the 19th century, gaining multimedia mega-stardom in the 20th. From Polidori to *Varney the Vampire* to Stoker to *Nosferatu* to Anne Rice to more *Dracula* recreations to *The Lost Boys* to *Buffy* to Charlaine Harris, vampires have always found appeal with the public. Vampires appeal to two of the only constants in life: sex and death, mirrored with inhuman pleasures and eternal life.

Vampires reflect their societies. Hence, the vampire as aimed at young women is not a new phenomenon. This trend grew during the 20th century as youth became the culture's ideal state and women's and teenagers' power in the marketplace expanded. The teenage vampire, the vampire in a high-school setting, was well established—with the likes of Smith's *Vampire Diaries* and TV's *Buffy the Vampire Slayer* (1997–2003)—before the arrival of *Twilight*. Women's vampire fandom has tended to revolve around texts such as Anne Rice's, where the vampire is a sympathetic hero in the Byronic style, rather than works in the *Dracula* vein.[8] Angel in *Buffy* surely fits this Byronic template, as does Edward Cullen.

On a broader level, the supernatural, the fantastic, and the paranormal—the unknown, unseen, and mysterious—have always fascinated, stretching back into mythology. They have enthralled children and teens, boys and girls, in particular. R. L. Stine's *Goosebumps* series of scary stories aimed at children, for example, is one of the world's bestselling novel series; also among the world's bestselling books are such fantasy/supernatural fare as the Harry Potter stories, *The Lord of the Rings*, *The Chronicles of Narnia*, and now, the *Twilight* saga. Children's and teens' developing sense of material and ethical reality may play a part in their interest in these stories. O'Quinn writes that, for teens, there is no privileged reality because "no reality can be claimed as fixed and stable."[9] The facing of fears has long been associated with adolescent transition and rites of passage.[10] In an age when religion's overt influence in the West has waned, stories of the supernatural and paranormal allow for a continuing fascination with something beyond human life, a seemingly constant curiosity of the human soul.

Though its moral emphasis is different, as explored below, *Twilight* still follows in a tradition of popular fantastical novels—exemplified in two different generations by Tolkien and Rowling—grounded in conservative, mythically "eternal" values: love, family and fighting for one's own or what's right. Such narratives have appealed to adults and children. These fantasies create what Bloom terms "a parallel 'world' which can be 'lived' by a group of readers."[11] Readership conflation, adults enjoying books intended for children and teen-agers, has been a trend throughout the 20th and early 21st century. According to O'Keefe, "We are circling back to the early custom whereby readers of all ages read the same narratives"; "[t]he genres of adults' and children's fantasies are collapsing together: both adults and children are now reading Harry Pot-ter and Philip Pullman, just as both have been reading J. R. R. Tolkien and C. S. Lewis for the past fifty years."[12] As with Disney movies, made for both children and their parents, these fantasy narratives pull in both children and "grownups." The trials of modern life can leave adults looking for an "out," a way back to imagined simplicity. At the same time, as the world has become more "wildly open, unmanageable, unfathomable," "children came to have more uncertainty, more choices, more contact with clashing social groups; more confusing, buzzing information; and more jarring, violent, sexual im-ages in their heads, than ever before."[13] And so adults have become more childish in their tastes, and children have grown more like adults.[14]

The apotheosis of the readership conflation trend is surely J. K. Rowling's seven Harry Potter novels. Rowling is the first author to make a billion dol-lars. Her books have become the bestselling series in the world, with around 450 million copies sold. They were also the first novels to be marketed dif-ferently to adults and children at the same time, with the same content pack-aged in both "kids" and "adult" covers. The global Harry Potter phenomenon became a point of reference throughout all aspects of popular culture and a multibillion-dollar industry across publishing, movies, toys, and videogames.

In a culture obsessed with instant celebrity, or "the next big thing," media and business interests have become interested in the replicability of the Harry Potter phenomenon. Susan Gunelius's book *Harry Potter: The Story of a Global Business Phenomenon*, for instance, devotes some space to the question of whether Rowling's success can be repeated, identifying possible future literary phenomena. Although Gunelius's book was published in 2008, *Twilight* is not listed among the contenders; demonstrating, perhaps, the in-definable quality of the bestseller: its unpredictable nature. As with the Potter books, *Twilight*'s success grew initially as word spread among readers and in critical circles before the series exploded into a global brand.

America's Next Top Model–like when it first began to accrue noticeable success, the *Twilight* saga was described in the media as "the next Harry Pot-ter" and Stephenie Meyer as the next J. K. Rowling. The similarities, though superficial, were too juicy not to be remarked upon: a previously unheard-of female author becomes a multimillionaire, and both series feature magical/ mythical worlds attached to our own. Harry Potter, as well as whipping up

interest in what could be called "the next Harry Potter," is credited with creating a generation of young readers (and, indeed, adult readers) interested in
similar material. *Twilight* has become that something similar. Meyer herself
credits Rowling with opening the way for her; children now don't mind reading big books, and adults read books for children.[15]

Nevertheless, the fundamental psychological and narrative appeal of *Twilight* is quite different from that of Harry Potter. *Twilight* does not possess the
layered, intricate story and plot twists of Rowling's wizarding world. While
there are the noted superficial similarities, and the Potter novels may have
created a generation receptive to reading "the next big young adult thing,"
Twilight is in essence a romance, and so it has come to be identified with a
generation of girls and women. Although its Gothic, erotic and fantasy tropes
mark its difference, and it is perhaps intended for a slightly older audience,
Twilight in some ways follows in the tradition of the hugely popular *Sweet
Valley High* (1983–2003) and *Baby-sitters Club* (1986–2000) series for pre-
teen/teen girls, which also extolled the pleasures of chaste relationships and
idealized boys. For older women, the *Twilight* novels provide pleasures familiar to readers of popular (Nora Roberts–style) romance: erotic intensity and
an idealized male fantasy-figure.

Twilight's form of fiction and the forms of fantasy found therein are not
new. In the early 1970s, Joanna Russ identified the same escapist pleasures
with a type of romance-adventure she terms the Modern Gothic, whose primary consumers were middle-class female homemakers. The plot of Meyer's
series matches in important respects Russ's elements of the Modern Gothic.
The heroine "is shy and inexperienced. She is attractive, sometimes even
beautiful, but she does not know it." She has often spent time looking after
ineffectual parents (Bella's parents are divorced, and she moves from being
the "sensible" one in her relationship with her mother to looking after her
father, whose parenting skills are somewhat inept).[16] After some preamble,
the heroine, "whose reaction to people and places tends toward emotional
extremes," forms a connection "with an older man, a dark, magnetic, powerful brooding, sardonic *Super-Male*, who treats her brusquely, derogates her,
scolds her, and otherwise shows anger or contempt for her" (initially Bella
cannot understand why Edward appears to hate the very sight of her—it is
because he is so tempted by her blood).[17] The heroine is "*of extraordinary
interest to everyone*," though "ordinary, characterless and usually very haz-
ily delineated, being (as one might suspect) a stand-in for the reader"; she is
"rewarded with love" simply for being who she is, without ever seeming to
particularly deserve or have earned it.[18]

For Russ, the mid-20th-century Modern Gothic "is a means of enabling
a conventionally feminine heroine to have adventures at all."[19] The plots

of the novels are marked by the heroine's "extraordinary passivity": she cannot participate effectively in any action that is required.[20] The same is remarkably true of Bella, at least until her conversion to a vampire in *Breaking Dawn*, and Meyer's own view of her character and her stories seems to converge with Russ's notion of the Modern Gothic heroine: "We can't all be slayers."[21] For the traditionally feminine woman, *Twilight* allows a fantasy of both adventure and love.

"Paranormal romance," which is perhaps the best generic label for Meyer's series, was a subgenre on the rise throughout the 1990s and 2000s before *Twilight*'s arrival, its allocation in many bookshops growing to at least that of the traditional horror section, which has been primarily frequented by men.[22] Paranormal romance editor Paula Guran defines the romance genre as centering around "a love relationship between two people (usually one male and one female) [with] a positive satisfying ending in which the reader is assured the couple will remain together"; the subgenre "paranormal romance" must add to this some element of the supernatural, be it magic, the occult or beings such as vampires or angels.[23] This definition, states Guran, relies on the expectations of readers who come to the genre, and within paranormal romance, vampires have been among the most popular and frequent participants.[24] While "men's" adventure stories such as the exploits of James Bond tend to be about taking out the bad guys and having sex without commitment, women's adventures—including paranormal romance—often involve finding one's soul mate through adventure, "And, yes, adventure can even be found in one's own neighbourhood."[25] These descriptions of "women's adventure" and paranormal romance fit well with the *Twilight* series narrative.

Also noting the "virtual deluge" of vampire romance since 2000, Bloom describes one of the primary aspects of these works as vampires who are "caring and sad and are miserable and lonely until brought out of their self-defensive shell by the woman they have searched for over the centuries"; "these vampire books repeat the mantra of female desire" dating back through decades of fiction, where the woman allows herself to be mastered when she also feels loved.[26] Again, *Twilight* checks with this.

While on the subject of *Twilight*'s place among its pop-fiction peers, the question of its literary merit should be briefly addressed. Reviews have been critical of Meyer's writing style, with Elizabeth Spires of the *New York Times* describing it as "amateurish"—too much telling and not enough showing.[27] The books are full of long, rambling passages and repetition, and read in some respects like undisciplined first drafts. Nevertheless, it is a truism that the quality of the writing (or lack thereof, a subjective test anyway) is not a barrier to popular enjoyment of novels. On the contrary, readers often perceive literary merit to be inversely related to their own reading pleasure.[28] Meyer's series exemplifies the qualities Gelder identifies with popular fiction, the kind of fiction with "a large number of readers."[29] *Twilight* is "simple" in terms of language, theme and plot, whereas Literature with a capital L is complex. Meyer's novels appeal to fantasy while Literature appeals to life; her books are sensuous, with danger and intrigue at every turn; they are emotionally "excessive" and "exciting," with plots including the heroine's kidnapping and a rampaging horde of vampires that must be stopped. These are all facets common to popular fiction and its mass industry, in Gelder's terms.[30] The contexts explored in this chapter may play their part in explaining *Twilight*'s distinct popularity, but were the books not an "easy read," they likely would not have gained such popularity in the first place.

The Vampire: From Edge to Center

The vampire has fascinated in Western culture since it first appeared in fiction. Meyer has commented on the vampire's "dual nature" and our attraction to it from this standpoint—the vampire is terrifying, yet often rich, beautiful, and cultured.[31] The primary reason cited by scholars for reader identification with the vampire in recent decades, is identification with the outsider. As Williamson puts it, "The vampire offers a way of inhabiting difference with pride, for embracing defiantly an identity that the world at large sees as 'other.'"[32] Feminist scholars in particular have used reasons such as this to explain the growth in women's vampire fandom throughout the second half of the 20th century, and the proliferation of "sympathetic vampires" as epitomized by, and begun with, Anne Rice's novels. "[T]o me at least," writes Nina Auerbach, vampires "promised protection against a destiny of girdles, spike heels, and approval"; "a secret talisman against a nice girl's life."[33] Analysing the work of Rice, Sherry Gottlieb, and others—and using Auerbach as a starting point—Gina Wisker describes how late-20th-century vampire fictions by women offer "protection against conventional representations and constraints of femininity, conformity and domestic bliss: the 'happily ever after' of romantic fictional promises for 'real life.'"[34] Wisker concludes that the vampire is the most transgressive figure in late-20th-century fiction by women.[35]

In the first decade of the 21st century, *Twilight* castrates this feminist vampire. Meyer's series has been the subject of huge controversy and criticism from a feminist viewpoint, with 17-year-old Bella described as setting a poor example for young women, and her relationship with 104-year-old (but frozen at 17) vampire Edward, characterized as abusive. Most of the series is told from Bella's first-person perspective; thus, it is presumably intended that the reader will identify with this "average" teen girl. Bella appears helpless outside the domestic sphere and defines herself in relation to men. She dutifully takes over the cooking and laundry when she moves in with her father. She is psychologically paralyzed in the wake of Edward's departure in the second novel and does not begin to feel happiness again until she falls under "the gaze of a virile werewolf," Jacob Black.[36] A significant proportion of the plot of the series involves Bella being saved by either Edward or Jacob. The Internet is packed with articles on the abusive nature of Bella's relationship with Edward, and the mainstream press has picked up on this too. Edward is exceedingly controlling and seeks to make all the decisions about whom Bella sees and what she does; the first time they have sex she ends up covered in bruises. A master's student in Connecticut, Katie Cushman, has written a curriculum that uses extracts from the novels "to get young girls beginning at about age 12 to start thinking about healthy and unhealthy relationships."[37]

Regardless of whether Bella and Edward's relationship is abusive or romantic (or both), it is the case that—in its account of vampirism—*Twilight* represents the ultimate mainstreaming of a fantasy which heretofore was almost always portrayed as "on the edge": the desire to become a vampire. Bella expresses this wish from the end of the first book and the beginning of her relationship with Edward. In past vampire texts popular with women and celebrated by feminist critics, such as those by Rice and Gottlieb, the reader's desire to be/be with the vampire, as identified by Wisker and Williamson, has been a fantasy of existing outside mainstream society, in a romanticized parallel and underground life, away from the "normal" responsibilities of being a wife/mother/woman.[38] These texts have been popular, Wisker, Williamson, and others implicitly and explicitly argue, precisely because they exercise this fantasy.

Twilight reverses the fantasy: the desire to be with the vampire is the desire to enter the mainstream. Bella Swan comes to Forks as an outsider and falls in obsessive love—a normal teenage experience. Coming from a broken home, Bella is welcomed into her boyfriend's vampire family, a surrogate for the nuclear original. The Cullens live an idyllic, wealthy existence off the stock market, thanks to Edward's sister Alice's convenient ability to glimpse the future. As middle-class vampires eager to exist within, not outside, mainstream human society, the Cullens hunt animals, not people. Edward's "father," Carlisle, is an accomplished and respected doctor at the local hospital; his adopted children all attend high school and, although looked on a little suspiciously, still hold parties for their schoolmates at their large, beautiful home. Through her relationship with Edward, Bella gives up her reluctance to get married and learns to love motherhood. Bella's final conversion to vampirism in *Breaking Dawn* is her ultimate acceptance into these mainstream, middle-class, establishment, conservative ideals. She has no wish to pursue her own career, having given up the idea of going to college in favor of more time with her "true love," and she will live happily ever after with Edward and their child, presumably provided for by Alice's stock-market predictions.

While earlier women's vampire fictions and *Twilight* are in some senses both about the alienated "finding a place," they accomplish this in markedly different ways. The "average" (i.e., Bella), as any teenager will know, is just another form of the alienated, outside the elite ideal. ("Mainstream" and "average" are far from the same thing; the middle classes, after all, are the privileged classes.) Yet rather than celebrate the outsider, as previous "sympathetic vampire" texts have done, *Twilight*, by means of a vampire story, gives us a fantasy of the outsider becoming the insider. Turning Williamson's hypothesis on its head, the "Other" comes to inhabit the mainstream with pride.

The *Twilight* vampire is born of ignorance of vampires. Stephenie Meyer has said that the idea for Edward and Bella's relationship simply came to her in a dream one night, that she had read "maybe one" vampire novel before she wrote *Twilight* and that she doesn't remember ever seeing a vampire movie.[39] Meyer remarks that she prefers superheroes to vampires and that, in her stories, vampires are more like superheroes: "I am much more drawn to superheroes than I am to vampires. I really think there's a closer connection with my vampires and superheroes than with traditional vampires and who they are."[40]

George Beahm compares the traditional, *Nosferatu*-esque vampire to those in *Twilight*. The traditional vampire is ugly; is allergic to garlic, holy water, and crucifixes; can be killed by a stake; has long fangs and drinks human blood; sleeps in a coffin and bursts into flames in the sun; can only enter a house by invitation and "presumably cannot have human relations (i.e. sex)."[41] While later vampire tales have done away with many of these tropes, key features are always retained so we know the vampire is a vampire. Buffy slays with a stake to the heart, while the vampires in the HBO series *True Blood* (2008–present), based on Charlaine Harris's *Southern Vampire Mysteries*, must sleep during the day and cannot enter a home without invitation. There is an acknowledgement in both of what the vampire *has been* throughout its fictional history. There is no such acknowledgement in *Twilight*, except when it is pointed out that what we thought we knew about vampires—what Bella thought she knew—is not true.[42] The *Twilight* vampire has no fangs and is preternaturally beautiful; is unaffected by garlic, holy water, crucifixes, invitations and stakes; has no blood and resembles marble; and believes not drinking human blood is a desirable lifestyle choice (though Meyer's are far from the first vampires to survive on animal blood; those in Rice and the work of other writers have done it too). Most interestingly, Meyer's vampires are not even "(un)dead" in any traditional vampiric sense: there is no requirement for them to hide from the light or sleep in coffins. Daylight, rather than revealing Edward's true (dead) nature by causing his destruction, reveals his status as sparkling god:

> Edward in the sunlight was shocking. I couldn't get used to it, though I'd been staring at him all afternoon. His skin, white despite the faint flush from yesterday's hunting trip, literally sparkled, like thousands of tiny diamonds were embedded in the surface. He lay perfectly still in the grass, his shirt open over his sculpted, incandescent chest, his scintillating arms bare. His glistening, pale lavender lids were shut, though of course he didn't sleep. A perfect statue, carved in some unknown stone, smooth like marble, glittering like crystal.[43]

With *Twilight*'s vampire, the subhuman becomes the superhuman. The outsider becomes the ultimate insider: celebrity-like object of worship and the gaze. A creature of the edge becomes the centre of mainstream fantasy.

Vamps for Genme

The individual's desires lie at the heart of *Twilight*'s appeal, yet its success is also a product of current generations. The saga presents the trope of true love—a value found in fantastical narratives from Tolkien to Rowling—as a thing much more acutely focused on the self. Drawing on Jean M. Twenge's *Generation Me*, which analyzes "a shift in the social 'ethos' . . . of people born in the 1970s through the 1990s," Housel argues that Bella represents the epitome of "GenMe," a generation "unapologetically about the self."[44] For GenMe, the prevailing attitude is not, to use Housel's example, "I'm good at writing because I worked at it and then got published in a national magazine" but "I'm good at writing because I'm special"; divorce rates increase as abstract duties and commitments become less important than personal happiness.[45]

> When she learns that Edward has been watching her sleep at night and following her around in secret, she is flattered—Edward's actions feed in to Bella's GenMe narcissistic tendencies and focus . . . There is no thought of duty to family, of how others may feel, of how certain decisions will irreparably alter the lives of people Bella supposedly loves. Bella's singular thought is how to get whom she wants (Edward) and how to get what she wants (to stay with Edward forever). In her pursuit of immortality, a privilege Bella feels entitled to simply because she wants it, Bella justifies her desires through her belief that her death will only increase her specialness.[46]

Twilight's politics of personal gratification manifest in another way as well. The finale of *Breaking Dawn* involves the Cullens' gathering of vampires from around the world, to bear witness to—and possibly fight to defend—the fact that Bella and Edward's newborn child Renesmee is not an infant vampire but a "naturally conceived" vampire-human baby (the penalty for turning a child into a vampire in the vampire world is severe; not because it is immoral, but because of child-vampires' rampantly destructive behavior). Despite abstaining from human blood themselves, the Cullens take no position on the fact that, by bringing vampires to Forks to "bear witness" for them before the Volturi (the "vampire police"), they are at least indirectly responsible for the deaths of innocent people in the areas surrounding Forks, as the other vampires they have summoned hunt and kill humans. The realpolitik—one's own is always what matters first—is encapsulated in a single paragraph: "Jacob was even more upset. The werewolves existed to prevent the loss of human life, and here was rampant murder being condoned barely outside the packs' borders. But under these circumstances, with Renesmee in acute danger, he kept his mouth shut and glared at the floor rather than the vampires."[47]

Meyer's casual disregard for fictional human life to meet the ends of a story is a curious feature in a teen novel. Of course, morally questionable behavior is not new in young adult fiction. However, it is the lack of engagement with "issues" here which is surprising, a GenMe renunciation of the value of principles and, indeed, life itself, when they do not contribute to one's own completeness. The Cullens' actions are presented not so much as heroic but necessary, practical—after all, they are saving their family. The question is never implied, but arises nonetheless: would we all not do the same? The realpolitik is complete when the corrupt Volturi—the main antagonists and principle threat-source throughout the series—are allowed to remain in power to avoid a battle that might lead to casualties. Unlike in texts such as *Buffy* and the Harry Potter series, there is no sense that there are things larger than oneself/one's lover/one's family worth fighting for. *Twilight* is a vampiric fantasy of eternal youth and happiness writ large.

Notes

1. "The Kagan Hearings," *Economist*, June 30, 2010, www.economist.com/blogs/democracyinamerica/2010/06/elena_kagan_hearings.

2. I would like sincerely to thank Dr. Bernice Murphy, Trinity College Dublin, for her advice on *Twilight*, vampires, and popular literature.

3. "Senator Amy Klobuchar Talks *Twilight* with Elena Kagan," YouTube video, from a C-SPAN 3 broadcast, posted by "tpmtv," June 30, 2010, www.youtube.com/watch?v=YBp1BzAD0vQ&feature=player_embedded (my transcript).

4. John Marzuilli, "Bronx NYPD Commander Is a Wolf in Cop's Clothes: Detective Accuses Boss of *Twilight* Harassment," *New York Daily News*, April 18, 2010, http://

articles.nydailynews.com/2010-04-18/news/27062036_1_forgiveness-text-messages-christmas-party (second ellipsis in original).

5. Stephenie Meyer, *Twilight* (London: Atom, 2007), 235 (italics in original).

6. "The Vamp," Tantus, http://tantusinc.com/catalog/Dildos/The-Vamp.

7. "Seattle Art Museum Presents *Behind the Scenes: The Real Story of Quileute Wolves*," Quileute Nation, www.quileutenation.org/qtc/sam-quileuteexhibition.pdf.

8. Milly Williamson, *The Lure of the Vampire: Gender, Fiction and Fandom from Bram Stoker to Buffy* (London: Wallflower, 2005), 57.

9. Elaine J. O'Quinn, "Vampires, Changelings, and Radical Mutant Teens: What the Demons, Freaks, and Other Abominations of Young Adult Literature Can Teach Us about Youth," *Alan Review 31* (2004), http://scholar.lib.vt.edu/ejournals/ALAN/v31n3/oquinn.html.

10. Lynn Schofield Clark, *From Angels to Aliens: Teenagers, the Media, and the Supernatural* (Oxford: Oxford University Press, 2003), 6.

11. Clive Bloom, *Bestsellers: Popular Fiction since 1900*, 2nd ed. (Basingstoke, UK: Palgrave Macmillan, 2008), 129.

12. *Deborah O'Keefe,* Readers in Wonderland: The Liberating Worlds of Fantasy Fiction, from Dorothy to Harry Potter *(New York: Continuum, 2004), 13.*

13. *O'Keefe, Readers* in Wonderland, 14.

14. *O'Keefe,* Readers in Wonderland*, 14.*

15. Lev Grossman, "Stephenie Meyer: A New J. K. Rowling?," *Time*, April 24, 2008, www.time.com/time/magazine/article/0,9171,1734838-2,00.html.

16. Joanna Russ, "Somebody's Trying to Kill Me and I Think It's My Husband: The Modern Gothic," *Journal of Popular Culture* 6 (1973): 667–68.

17. Russ, "Somebody's Trying to Kill Me," 668 (italics in original).

18. Russ, "Somebody's Trying to Kill Me," 671, 678 (italics in original).

19. Russ, "Somebody's Trying to Kill Me," 686.

20. Russ, "Somebody's Trying to Kill Me," 679, 686.

21. Stephenie Meyer, "The Story behind the Writing of *New Moon*," www.stepheniemeyer.com/nm_thestory.html.

22. Kevin Jackson, *Bite: A Vampire Handbook* (London: Portobello Books, 2009), 179.

23. Paula Guran, "Introduction," in *Best New Paranormal Romance*, ed. Paula Guran (Juno Books, 2007), 7.

24. Guran, "Introduction," 8, 10.

25. Guran, "Introduction," 14.

26. Bloom, *Bestsellers*, 7, 9.

27. Elizabeth Spires, review of *Enthusiasm*, by Polly Shulman, and *Twilight*, by Stephenie Meyer, *New York Times*, www.nytimes.com/2006/02/12/books/review/12spires.html.

28. Victor Nell, *"The Psychology of Reading for Pleasure: Needs and Gratifications," Reading Research Quarterly 23 (1988): 20–21.*

29. Ken Gelder, *Popular Fiction: The Logics and Practices of a Literary Field* (Abingdon, UK: Routledge, 2004), 20.

30. Gelder, *Popular Fiction*, 19.

31. Stephenie Meyer, quoted in George Beahm, *Bedazzled: Stephenie Meyer and the* Twilight *Phenomenon* (London: J. R. Books, 2009), 137.

32. Williamson, *The Lure of the Vampire*, 1.

33. Nina Auerbach, *Our Vampires, Ourselves* (Chicago: University of Chicago Press, 1995), 4.

34. Gina Wisker, "If Looks Could Kill: Contemporary Women's Vampire Fictions," in *Fatal Attractions: Re-scripting Romance in Contemporary Literature and Film,* ed. *Lynne Pearce and Gina Wisker (London: Pluto, 1998), 51.*

35. Wisker, "If Looks Could Kill," 52.

36. Bonnie Mann, "Vampire Love: The Second Sex Negotiates the Twenty-First Century," in Twilight *and Philosophy: Vampires, Vegetarians, and the Pursuit of Immortality,* ed. Rebecca Housel and J. Jeremy Wisnewski (Hoboken, NJ: John Wiley & Sons, 2009), 136.

37. Pamela McLoughlin. "Blood Feud: Student Thesis Claims *Twilight* Vampire Tales Are Sexist," *New Haven Register,* December 6, 2009, www.nhregister.com/articles/2009/12/06/news/new_haven/doc4b1b0d6f22fde151077853.txt.

38. Williamson, *The Lure of the Vampire,* 1; Wisker, "If Looks Could Kill," 51–52.

39. Stephenie Meyer, quoted in James Blasingame, "Interview with Stephenie Meyer," *Journal of Adolescent & Adult Literacy* 49 (2006): 630.

40. Stephenie Meyer, quoted in Beahm, *Bedazzled,* 142.

41. Beahm, *Bedazzled,* 49.

42. Meyer, *Twilight,* 161–62.

43. Meyer, *Twilight,* 228.

44. Rebecca Housel, "The 'Real' Danger: Fact vs. Fiction for the Girl Audience," in Housel and Wisnewski, Twilight *and Philosophy,* 182.

45. Housel, "The 'Real' Danger,"183.

46. Housel, "The 'Real' Danger," 184.

47. Stephenie Meyer, *Breaking Dawn* (London: Atom, 2008), 563.

12

Disciplinary Lessons: Myth, Female Desire, and the Monstrous Maternal in Stephenie Meyer's *Twilight* Series

Hope Jennings and Christine Wilson

*T*WILIGHT HAS BECOME ONE OF "the most popular teen-girl novels of all time,"[1] and as such, it is potentially one of the largest cultural influences on young women coming of age during the early 21st century. Caitlin Flanagan argues that *Twilight* is so appealing because "within it is *the* true story, the original one . . . [It] centers on a boy who loves a girl so much that he refuses to defile her, and on a girl who loves him so dearly that she is desperate for him to do just that, even if the wages of the act are expulsion . . . from everything she has ever known." If this is the "true story" of "What Girls Want" (the title of Flanagan's review), then it seems the female sex is as masochistic and self-abnegating as Freud once proposed when he attempted to solve the age-old question "What do women want?" Indeed, Flanagan claims the "riveting" thrill of the erotic relationship sustained throughout the series derives from "Bella's fervent hope . . . that Edward will ravage her, and . . . the harrowing pain that is said to be the victim's lot at the time of consummation means nothing to her . . . This is sex and romance fully—ecstatically, dangerously—engaged with each other. At last, at last." Flanagan is on the verge of ecstatically, dangerously forgetting that regardless if, in her estimation, *Twilight* "perfectly encapsulates . . . the rapture—and the menace—that inherently accompany romance and sex for [teenage girls]," this is not necessarily what mothers want for their adolescent daughters, and the books themselves stress the menace of sex far more than its rapture.

As popular romance, *Twilight* offers a heroine with whom many female readers identify: Bella, to all appearances, crosses conventional gender boundaries and is able to produce her own desiring gaze through her often aggressive pursuit of Edward. Accordingly, the novels allow for a degree of power located in the desiring female gaze; yet when considering the over-all arc of the series, particularly in light of its concluding novel, *Breaking Dawn*, we find that the representation of female desire in these texts prob-lematically situates women's bodies and desires within the boundaries of patriarchal, and yes, Freudian, myths of femininity. The popular appeal of *Twilight* becomes quite troubling when we consider the extent to which it holds readers' imaginations hostage to an oppressive—and seductive—ro-mance in which female desire must be contained within the "traditional" enclosures of motherhood and family.

Twilight also clearly aspires to present a new mythology within the tradi-tion of vampire literature, yet it engages in a dangerous form of myth-making that fails to consider its ideological premises. Overall, Stephenie Meyer em-ploys the vampire genre as a medium for rewriting the Genesis myth, with the apparent intention of offering an alternative version of female desire and motherhood that is productive and liberating for young women. Her myth-making, however, reinscribes the gender dynamics that inform the Genesis myth and its subsequent structuring of sociocultural discourses often aimed at repressing the disruptive threat of female desire when it ranges outside the parameters of patriarchal control. Bella is emblematic of a transgressive, sexu-ally disruptive Eve who is eventually redeemed by her role of self-sacrificing mother; yet if Meyer's task is to convince teenage girls to trade the risks of sex for the safeties of motherhood, as if sex and motherhood were irreconcilable, then Meyer's representation of female desire and maternity end up trapping women within the same oppressive ideologies and gender hierarchies her rewriting of myth superficially resists. Thus, what we find both exciting and disconcerting in the *Twilight* series are the ways in which Meyer plays with myth while demonstrating a lack of understanding of how myth works or its effect on the very readers she is attempting to reach.

Myth functions as a language that communicates the seductive lie of universal truths.[2] The seduction lies in the fact that myths "do not present themselves neutrally but in codes that are always and already political," and their danger derives from "their accessibility and dissemination [which] means that they can be more . . . influential than state laws in educating, unifying, and perpetuating a society and its cultural conventions and ex-pectations."[3] As Flanagan correctly notes, *Twilight* does tell the "original story," which is concerned with disciplining and controlling female desire. In her epigraph to the first novel, Meyer signals her use of the Genesis myth as a framework for her own narrative of forbidden desire and its danger-ous consequences: "But of the tree of the knowledge of good and evil, thou shalt not eat of it; for in the day that thou eatest thereof thou shalt surely die" (Genesis 2:17). Of course, the threat of death directly links to Meyer's vampire mythology, but it also subtly highlights the inherent tensions the series sets up between sex and death.

In the *Twilight* novels, sex is represented as something menacing and dangerous. Bella insists on having sexual intercourse before she becomes a vampire and "trade[s] in [her] warm, breakable, pheromone-riddled body for something beautiful, strong . . . and unknown."[4] However, Bella's longing to fulfill her sexual desires also indicates the relentless pursuit of her own death, at least according to the narrative mechanism Meyer employs to explain why Bella and Edward are unable to consummate their erotic relationship: sex is so dangerous (for Bella) because Edward is so strong that he might accidentally tear her apart. Not only is this atypical within the vampiric literature, but the implication here is that sex is a time when one can no longer retain control in even the slightest manner; it is mythologized as an activity removed from ordinary life and emotions, and the physicality of it is, of course, absent, even when it does occur. For young female readers who are already subject to a wide array of conflicting cultural myths surrounding sex, Meyers adds yet another confusing and misleading spin on consensual sexual relationships.

When Edward and (the still human) Bella actually do have sex, she ends up covered with bruises and is made to feel ashamed for taking uninhibited pleasure in the sexual act. If Meyer were simply preaching sexual abstinence before marriage then this would not come off as so odd, but Bella and Edward have sex *after* becoming married. Furthermore, the following morning Bella is afraid to open her eyes, which is justifiable since the first thing she sees is an infuriated Edward. Bella's response underscores her profound sense of shame: "My first instinct, the product of a lifetime of insecurities, was to wonder what I had done wrong."[5] Although Bella reassures Edward that she had enjoyed herself, he informs her in patronizing tones, "That doesn't change the fact that it was wrong. Even if it were possible that you really did feel that way."[6] Regardless if Bella insists her experience of sex is "better" than her "happiest memories,"[7] Edward decides it is "wrong" and dismisses her feelings as insignificant, if not delusional.

Edward's insistence on protecting Bella at all costs depends on him remaining in perfect, rational control of his desires, which leads him to displace his guilt onto Bella. He blames her for seducing him and accuses her for taking pleasure in an act that he insists almost killed her. According to this scenario, Bella's desire is dangerous not simply because she is unable to control it, but because she tempts Edward into losing control of his own actions. Bella becomes the "Guilty One," a positioning enforced upon women, as theorized by Hélène Cixous and Catherine Clément, when their desires threaten masculine self-control over the integrity of the male body/phallus.[8] This positioning is

constructed by the gender dynamics underlying the Genesis text where it en-
codes women's bodies as the site of primal, regressive desires focused purely
on the pursuit of pleasure, while masculine powers of rationality are set up
as the authoritative word or law that ensures the progress of civilization and
culture through the repression of (female) flesh.[9] Although the *Twilight* series
articulates the romantic appeal of transgressing forbidden desires, it seems
more concerned with reiterating the dangers of temptation (and sex), especially as they exist for the female subject. In this way Meyer reinforces those
patriarchal myths in which female desire is represented as rampant, disruptive, and most of all shameful because it transgresses or circulates outside
the rationale of male inscribed boundaries, thus justifying the need for male
authority/control over female bodies and desires.

Bella's all-too-human lack of self-control and unrepressed sensual appetite
brings us to Meyer's unusual employment of the vampire trope. Though
Meyer is ostensibly writing within the genre of vampire novels, the vampire
has a much more specific function here that goes beyond generic convention.
Imagine, for a moment, what the *Twilight* series would look like without the
supernatural vampire. A much older man becomes interested in a vulnerable
teenage girl who has just moved into town; he commences upon a complicated series of games in which he acts as if he despises her, which triggers her
insecurity and desire to be liked. Secretly, though, he is so overwhelmingly
attracted to her that he is afraid he will be unable to restrain himself in her
presence. So he resorts to stalking her, and after he has rescued her from a
number of menacing situations, she feels indebted to him; they profess their
mutual attraction and become a couple. His almost obsessive worry often
translates into possessiveness; he forbids her to be friends with those he finds
dangerous, even though, by his own admission, he is the most dangerous
one of all, leading him to abandon her, supposedly for her own good. She
nearly dies of heartbreak, but he returns to save her, yet again, from her own
reckless, suicidal actions. Eventually he pressures her to get married at the
age of eighteen, against all of her misgivings and reticence. While on their
honeymoon, she insists they consummate their marriage; he resists, gives in,
and then blames her for making him hurt her. From that one sexual act, she
becomes pregnant; his response is to call their child a monster and try to force
her to have an abortion. In many respects, this sounds like a 19th-century
instruction manual warning girls away from a predatory and abusive lover.

With the insertion of the vampire, the story transforms. The age gap does
not implicate Edward within a pedophilic framework; instead, it demonstrates how long he has waited to meet his soul mate, thus testifying to his
supreme patience and the inevitability of their union (since Edward is an old-
fashioned Edwardian, for whom marriage is the only honorable thing to do if

they are going to consummate their mutual desire). Edward being a vampire, it's the intoxicating smell of Bella's blood that Edward can't resist, and so what looked like sadistic game-playing becomes a display of his admirable willpower and unwavering devotion, thus sacrificing his own monstrous impulses for Bella's well-being as well as deterring Bella from her own death-wish. All the same, in what seems to be the most culturally potent love story of our time, the lesson to be learned is that girls need to be protected, both from the outside world and themselves; and what girls really want is to find this protective father figure, especially if he is cloaked in the disguise of a sexy stranger with the proverbial heart of gold. More problematically, the *Twilight* series preaches abstinence while endorsing teenage motherhood, and for this confusing message alone it would have probably fallen into the abyss of contemporary teenage romance, yet with the addition of vampires, the novels seem much sexier, for lack of a better term.

Vampires have been nearly irresistible romantic figures in popular culture; they "evoke a marginal world of darkness, secrecy, vulnerability, excess, and horror. Whatever they are, it is positively Other."[10] This "Otherness" makes the vampire a potent love interest, and Meyer draws on many of the popular tropes of the vampire myth, but with a little tweaking. Her vampires drink blood and cannot eat food; they are not affected by garlic, crucifixes, or churches; and though the sun affects them in strange ways, it does not kill them—to be killed, they must be burned. Like many contemporary vampires, the *Twilight* vampires are immortal, refined, affluent, and beautiful. More importantly, Meyer capitalizes on the seductive sense of transgression inherent in the figure of the vampire, as Margaret Carter explains:

> Where the vampire's otherness posed a terrifying threat for the original readers of *Dracula* . . . today that same alien quality is often perceived as an attraction. As rebellious outsider, as persecuted minority, as endangered species, and as a member of a different "race" that legend portrays as sexually omnicompetent, the vampire makes a fitting hero for late twentieth-century popular fiction.[11]

What we also now have, especially in the young adult fiction market, is the "nice" vampire male, who is seductive and dangerous, while still holding on to a core of morality (often figured as humanity), thus making him an ideal figure of lust for the teenage American girl.

Ultimately, Meyer removes all traces of subversion and excess that traditionally attracted humans to vampires in the first place, though the *Twilight* vampires are certainly not unique in this regard. Jules Zanger, for example, delineates a number of relevant characteristics of "new vampires," which are no longer figures of the "Anti-Christ" or mere "social deviants."[12] We now have "good" vampires who live in families or communities, rather than alone.

They are often portrayed as possessing "secret sources of wealth" and an abundance of sexual appeal and sophistication, and they seem more human than monstrous, indicating an increasing domestication and "demytholigiz[ation] of the vampire."[13] Although Meyer is not concerned with demythologizing the vampire, she domesticates the Cullens to the point that they are *more* tame, *more* humane, and *more* disciplined than the humans in the texts. Furthermore, and oddly enough, Meyer does not want her novels to be read as vampire novels, much less as part of the genre of horror. Her books instruct us to read them, rather, as "harmless" fairy tales: "Edward had always thought that he belonged to the world of horror stories . . . It was obvious that he belonged *here*. In a fairy tale."[14] For Bella, at least, Edward is not monstrous, and the desired happy ending is achieved through the domestication of (her) desire through Edward's mediating control, since he is the only one capable of constraining her "raging" teenage hormones.

Again, Meyer seems minimally aware of how her texts inadvertently articulate the ambivalent pleasures afforded by the genre(s) in which she is working to the point where horror and fairy tale are shown to have more in common than realized. One of the chief pleasures of vampire tales is hedonism, or the indulgence in carnal pleasures. Likewise, fairy tales are often imbued with elements of horror in their symbolic staging of violent, unsanctioned desires, thus allowing readers the opportunity to release unconscious drives or fears by exploring taboo or repressed impulses. On the other hand, fairy tales are constructed in a way that ultimately impresses upon readers the safety of conforming to social norms and expectations of behavior that insist on the repression of desires.[15] The reward for doing so is the conventional happily ever after, and it seems the increasing domestication of the vampire story and all its powers of horror is in many ways rooted within the fairy tale.

Repression of carnality (and its attendant rewards) is one of the chief characteristics that mark the Cullens as "unusual" vampires. Through their choice to live a "vegetarian" lifestyle, they practice supreme self-control, resisting their natural appetites. Previous vampires, to be sure, have resisted drinking human blood—Anne Rice's Louis, for example, subsists on small animals instead of humans. In fact, this refusal to drink human blood is "at the heart of [Louis's] eventual domestication."[16] In Charlaine Harris's more recent Sookie Stackhouse novels, on which HBO's *True Blood* is based, the Japanese create a synthetic blood, which allows vampires to survive without killing humans or animals. However, in Rice's and Harris's novels, the vampires do sometimes drink human blood, whether for nourishment or sexual pleasure. The most significant difference between the *Twilight* vampires and their predecessors, or contemporaries, is that in "traditional" vampire stories, abstaining from human blood makes the vampire weaker. For the Cullens, such abstinence makes them stronger, smarter, and capable of "form[ing] true bonds of love."[17] They are extraordinary because they are so good at keeping their bodily desires under control, and throughout the *Twilight* series, rationality and its implicit companion, self-discipline, are valued above all else. Shortly behind them, for Bella at least, comes self-sacrifice.

These values reiterate those found in fairy tales and the Genesis myth, and in this way, Meyer's attempt to rewrite Genesis in order to make it more favorable to and for women proves unsuccessful. She may allow the sinful Eve/Bella a powerful redemption, but only because Bella reforms by embracing the culturally sanctioned role of motherhood. In the process, Meyer creates a seductive series of books that is (unintentionally) damaging in its influence on young women because it promotes and normalizes a hatred and fear of the female body. Just as Eve is punished with suffering in childbirth for her act of transgression and temptation, so too is Bella; her sexual desire is more or less the desire for a dangerous knowledge that culminates in an explicitly monstrous pregnancy, which we would argue is the most genuinely monstrous, terrifying aspect of the *Twilight* series (and the 2011 film adaptation of *Breaking Dawn*).

Indeed, the physical consummation of Bella's desire and her pleasure in the sexual act is answered—if not repudiated—by her becoming immediately impregnated with a hybrid, parasitic fetus gestating at such a rapid rate that her body turns against her, transforming her into a swollen, disfigured, and literally drained receptacle for the "*thing* that's sucking the life from her."[18] Edward tries to persuade Bella to have an abortion, but for once Bella resists Edward's authoritative control and insists upon continuing the pregnancy. She suffers at an inordinately horrific level for that decision, and Meyer seems almost sadistic in the punishment she inflicts upon Bella for engaging in some good, old-fashioned sex with her husband; or Meyer's view of pregnancy seems terribly conflicted and ambivalent, as her heroine morphs into a monstrous maternal figure bearing a blood-sucking, alien fetus that attempts to chew its way out of her womb (the imagery of the *Alien* horror films immediately comes to mind, and if one is going to scare teenage girls away from sex this is certainly the way to accomplish it).

Meyer's gruesome depiction of pregnancy may seem surprising, given the text's overall investment in promoting motherhood. However, it is not as contradictory as one might think, since *Breaking Dawn* supports a widely accepted view of pregnancy and mothering as two entirely separate endeavors. Sara Ruddick explains:

> Mothering and birthgiving, as experienced and practiced, are quite unlike each other. Mothering is a set of ongoing organized activities requiring discipline and attention. By contrast, pregnancy can appear as a condition, a physical

state of being. Whereas mothering requires deliberative thought, pregnancy may appear to require only the rational capacities that Aristotle attributed to slaves: the ability to understand and obey [doctor's] orders. Mothering is moral—a relational work that involves at least two separately and willfully embodied persons. A birthgiver seems to take care of her fetus by taking care of herself. Seen from a temporal perspective of the life of a mothered child, pregnancy and birth are but moments; birthgiving is a dramatic physical event soon out of sight or in the footnotes.[19]

In other words, mothering is cultural work—it is "moral," requires careful thinking, and "discipline and attention." Pregnancy, in contrast, requires only that the body function at its biological optimum, and all the woman needs to do to gestate a baby successfully is take care of her body; preserving the fetus simply involves self-preservation from this point of view. Meyer sets up a similar division between biology and culture, but she takes the distinction a step further, emphasizing that the female subject cannot exist in both realms of the physical and cultural but is categorically placed in one or the other: the "Bad" biological mother (since the pregnant female body has a "mind" of its own) or the "Good" culturally regulated mother. That which is physical in this text, Bella's pregnancy, is thus positioned as horrifying and "unnatural."

Furthermore, we are not allowed insight into Bella's subjective experience of her pregnancy; she is rendered passive (and mute) not only by her own body and the protective, oppressive guardianship of the Cullens, but also by the narrative device of shifting to the first-person perspective of Jacob. This switch is an oddly disruptive choice since it's the first and only time in the series that we are not given Bella's first-person point of view, yet it is a telling choice, revealing the text's attitudes toward the maternal body. Jacob, like Edward, expresses revulsion, fear, and confusion in reaction to Bella's gross physicality and her even more disturbing attachment to the "thing" growing inside of her. Through Jacob's eyes, Bella is reduced (or inflated) to a monstrous, aberrant object of loathing, describing her "torso" as "swollen . . . in a strange, sick way . . . like the big bulge had grown out of what it had sucked from her. It took me a second to realize what the deformed part was—I didn't understand until she folded her hands tenderly over her bloated stomach . . . Like she was cradling it."[20] Bella is presented here as a grotesque maternal body—unruly, excessive, and threatening—even while protecting her unborn child, yet Jacob's lack of "understand[ing]" provides insight into why Bella's pregnancy is viewed so negatively.

The pregnant body exists outside of male desire, knowledge, or power, and precisely because of "the one aspect of child care that men cannot undertake. The (hitherto) ineradicable inequality in women's ability and men's inability to give birth—the bodily potentiality, vulnerability, and power that is women's alone—evokes guilt, envy, and resentment."[21] Jacob, Edward, and Carlisle are unable to control Bella's pregnancy and are forced into becoming helpless spectators. This seems almost commonplace, or clichéd, but Meyer intensifies this lack of (male) understanding and marginalization of pregnancy, even for her female readers, by making Bella's thoughts during pregnancy inaccessible and, by implication, insignificant. It is as if Bella can only do one thing at a time—make a baby. She is the nonspeaking, unspeakable subject since in order to become "a speaking subject and/or subject to the [paternal] Law," one must become distinctly removed from the maternal body.[22]

That said, her pregnancy is the one time Bella takes some control over her own (human) body, subverting the wishes (or law) of the text's protective father figures; it is the only instance when Bella rejects Edward's desires and guidance by following her own "instincts." Her primary concern for protecting the child leads us to conclude, however, that the assertion of Bella's autonomy is permissible only because it is not about saving herself but the "fetus." Thus the value of the fetus over the mother is clearly at play within the reproductive politics of the novel. Moreover, even if desire is supposed to be the impetus for the subject to assert herself, Bella's desires are nullified by her desire *not* to assert herself: her desire is, first, for Edward to desire *her*, and second, to protect (i.e., mother) everyone around her, and always at the risk of her own safety, since she repeatedly states her willingness to die for those she loves. Jacob identifies Bella's penchant for self-sacrifice as one of the characteristics that make her "so *Bella*," observing that she is willing to "die for the monster spawn."[23]

In some ways, the representation of Bella's pregnancy is a reassuring myth. If we use Bella as a model, all of this can happen—during a pregnancy our bodies can rebel, and we can feel utterly terrible—yet we still love the child that is making us feel so awful, and we can still fulfill the role of "Good Mother." At the same time, Meyer's representation of pregnancy is quite insidious, particularly for young women, because a loathing and distrust of the female body and its reproductive capabilities is evident. Pregnancy is presented as a diseased state that must be managed, rather than as a natural condition, and the fear of death through childbearing, which is rare in industrialized countries, is insinuated as a likely outcome. The contradictory message Meyer offers here is that motherhood is the one function women are born to fulfill, yet the process of becoming a mother is a trial that just may result in disfigurement or death. Nevertheless, young women should take on this risk because, well, being a mother is the only path to asserting and gaining genuine identity, agency, and power. As Luce Irigaray argues, because women are granted little to no autonomous positioning within a patriarchal society, then children become their only form of currency "in exchange for a market status for *themselves*," and to the point where motherhood "gets wrapped up in some weird kind of holiness."[24]

Bella certainly insists on playing the "martyr" for her child,[25] and she does indeed die when giving birth, but it is only her human body that dies, since Edward is there, as always, to save her. Upon her initiation into vampirism (and motherhood) Bella is ironically no longer monstrous but "gifted" with perfect control over all hungers and desires; as Edward observes, "You shouldn't be so . . . rational."[26] Of course, Bella's self-discipline only occurs after she is rid of the chaotic maternal body and consigned to the traditional role of "Good Mother." All disruptive desires are neutralized the very moment her "pheromone-riddled" body literally dies, and at this point in the narrative, her voice is conveniently returned to her. She is no longer an unsettling force, and there is no longer any need to keep her body and desires safely contained (or silenced) because Edward has regained control by giving birth to *her* (as a "newly born" vampire).

This ultimately adds the phallus back into the equation of reproduction, something that adheres, and problematically so, to the typical representation of vampire reproduction. Sandra Tomc explains how traditional maternity is thrown over by vampires: "When Louis and Lestat [of Anne Rice's *The Vampire Chronicles*] make a vampire out of Claudia, they do so quite literally over her mother's dead body . . . This violent demystification of maternal power [is] centered . . . on the mother's body as something dead and obsolete."[27] Vampires do not need women to reproduce, nor do they need sex. They can simply create a vampire by exchanging fluids. In *Twilight*, producing a child through traditional vampiric means, as discussed below, is forbidden, yet Edward, as Bella's savior, lover, and metaphorical father, coopts the act of childbirth, as he simultaneously delivers Renesmee and Bella (who remains unconscious and powerless during the "ordeal" of labor). The phallus is thus represented here as the only acceptable (symbolic) mode of reproduction, severing all connection to the flesh of the maternal body.[28]

In the mythology of the text, then, Meyer redeems the "terrible flesh" of Bella with the combination of transforming her into a vampire and a mother, ultimately granting her a sense of coherent power: "It was like I had been born to be a vampire . . . I had found my true place in the world, the place I fit, the place I shined."[29] Bella discovers her greatest power is the ability to create a "shield" that protects those she loves, which becomes especially useful since Edward and Bella have violated the most sacred of vampire taboos. According to the myth Meyer has created, making a child into a vampire inevitably brings a death sentence to its creator. The logic behind this prohibition is that toddler vampires have no self-control and are apt to bring too much attention to themselves, breaking the cardinal rule of the vampire community: hide from humans.[30] The enforcer of vampire law is the Volturi (a corrupt group of vampires), and as soon as they hear reports about a child vampire living with the Cullens, they assume the worst and set out to destroy it. Since the Cullens will die to defend the child, their paradise is set to be destroyed—alluding to the expulsion from Paradise in the myth of Genesis. Bella, after all, has tasted the fruit of the tree of knowledge, and though she managed to escape immediate death during the act of sexual intercourse, this death is only delayed; she dies during childbirth to be reborn as a vampire only to face a more permanent death at the hands of the Volturi. Thus Bella's carnal lust, her one act of selfishness, even within the sanctioned bond of marriage, threatens the imminent destruction of everyone she loves. When the Volturi show up to punish the Cullens, however, Bella redeems herself by shielding her loved ones—and most importantly, her child—with an invisible, all-encompassing, and impenetrable bubble; their psychic powers rendered impotent against this gigantic metaphorical womb, the Volturi are forced to leave.

Through the power of maternal love, Bella conquers even the most omnipotent of forces. As a woman, her sexual desires threaten everyone, including herself. Fulfilling the archetype of the "Good Mother," she channels personal desire into the need (and ability) to protect those around her. Ironically, becoming a vampire, a figure that is supposed to embody decadence and unrepressed appetite, grants Bella the self-discipline that eludes her when she is human. This further demonstrates how the *Twilight* series reverses everything we have come to expect from the vampire genre: rather than the vampires existing as the dangerous other, representative of the return of the repressed, they are the norm, as not only the Cullens but nearly all the vampire groups, including the Volturi, conform to the patriarchal family structure. Vampires are typically boundary crossers, the epitome of a hybrid. Meyer inverts this and privileges stability over fluidity. It is Bella the human, with all of her messy human desires, her lack of a stable family, her ability to traverse boundaries (between the communities of werewolves, vampires, and humans), which makes her the dangerous other in the text, and no more so than when she is monstrously pregnant with her hybrid fetus—all of which, again, becomes safely contained the moment she gives birth, which is simultaneous to the moment her body dies.

This leaves us with the same metaphor/myth: motherhood equals the death of female desire, and in the world of *Twilight*, this is a positive thing, which makes its conclusion (and premise) so disturbing. Moreover, because the taboo of vampire reproduction is founded on the assumption that when children are "turned" they become enormously strong desiring machines, far too biologically driven to be controlled, and since creating a vampire child is the worst offense in Meyer's vampire culture, we might read this as an implicit critique of feminine-maternal desires. That is, because vampires cannot reproduce "naturally," and the most illicit thing a vampire can do is desire a child enough to make one into a vampire, then this seems to be a way of regulating the unruly female body, which Meyer's texts suggest is necessary for the survival of society. As such, *Twilight* remains faithful to the Genesis text; if read as maturation myths, or even fairy tales, the didactic message of both narratives asserts that the female subject cannot engage in unsanctioned or transgressive desires without disciplinary regulation and punishment. Pleasure is denied, and can only lead to shame, even within the socioculturally scripted confines of normative, heterosexual marriage and motherhood.

Lastly, once Bella becomes a vampire there is no threat of punishment/ death as a consequence of sexual desire, and she and Edward can have sex as much as they like (which they do). Rather, all the attendant dangers or risks of erotic love are subtracted. Love inevitably entails risking oneself in relation to the other,[31] yet Meyer indicates that the ideal is to remove all risk, that desire can only be satisfactorily experienced once its dangers are negated, thus elevating sex to an activity that has nothing to do with women's lived realities. Bella is the perfect Freudian masochist—a self-sacrificing (somewhat sexless) mother, more at place in the 19th century rather than a positive or realistic role model for 21st-century girls. The most detrimental aspect of the myth that Meyer promotes is that what is "natural" about motherhood is to place the value of the child over the value of the mother/self, and that every girl should want a father/lover who controls and effaces her desires. If anything, like most fairy tales, *Twilight* demonstrates how girls are shown great rewards for adhering to a system that endeavors to discipline their desires. Bella certainly receives her "happily ever after," as she and Edward "continued blissfully into this small but perfect piece of . . . forever,"[32] yet Meyer's romance merely offers a sanitized and unsatisfying utopia.

Notes

1. Caitlin Flanagan, "What Girls Want," *Atlantic Monthly*, December 2008, www.theatlantic.com/doc/200812/twilight-vampires.

2. Roland Barthes, *Mythologies* (London: Vintage, 1993).

3. Maria Aristodemou, *Law and Literature: Journeys from Her to Eternity* (Oxford: Oxford University Press, 2000), 182, 29.

4. Stephanie Meyer, *Breaking Dawn* (New York: Little, Brown, and Company, 2008), 22.

5. Meyer, *Breaking Dawn*, 87.

6. Meyer, *Breaking Dawn*, 93.

7. Meyer, *Breaking Dawn*, 94.

8. Hélène Cixous and Catherine Clément, *The Newly Born Woman*, trans. Betsy Wing (Manchester, UK: Manchester University Press, 1986).

9. Cixous and Clément, *The Newly Born Woman*, 28–30; Julia Kristeva, "About Chinese Women," in *The Kristeva Reader*, ed. Toril Moi (Oxford: Blackwell, 1986), 140.

10. Sarah Sceats, "Oral Sex: Vampiric Transgression and the Writing of Angela Carter," *Tulsa Studies in Women's Literature* 20 (2001): 107.

11. Margaret L. Carter, "The Vampire as Alien in Contemporary Fiction," in *Blood Read: The Vampire as Metaphor in Contemporary Culture*, ed. Joan Gordon and Veronica Hollinger (Philadelphia: University of Pennsylvania Press, 1997), 29.

12. Jules Zanger, "Metaphor into Metonymy: The Vampire Next Door," in Gordon and Hollinger, *Blood Read*, 17.

13. Zanger, "Metaphor into Metonymy," 18–19.

14. Meyer, *Breaking Dawn*, 479.

15. Bruno Bettelheim, "The Struggle for Meaning," in *The Classic Fairy Tales*, ed. Maria Tatar (New York: W.W. Norton & Company, 2009).

16. Sandra Tomc, "Dieting and Damnation: Anne Rice's *Interview with the Vampire*," in Gordon and Hollinger, *Blood Read*, 105.

17. Meyer, *Breaking Dawn*, 603.

18. Meyer, *Breaking Dawn*, 181.

19. Sara Ruddick, "Thinking Mothers/Conceiving Birth," in *Representations of Motherhood*, ed. Donna Bassin, Margaret Honey, and Meryle Mahrer Kaplan (New Haven, CT: Yale University Press), 35–36.

20. Meyer, *Breaking Dawn*, 174.

21. Ruddick, "Thinking Mothers/Conceiving Birth," 36.

22. Julia Kristeva, *Powers of Horror: An Essay on Abjection*, trans. Leon S. Roudiez (New York: Columbia University Press, 1982), 94.

23. Meyer, *Breaking Dawn*, 177.

24. Luce Irigaray, *Sexes and Genealogies*, trans. Gillian C. Gill (New York: Columbia University Press, 1993), 84.

25. Meyer, *Breaking Dawn*, 187.

26. Meyer, *Breaking Dawn*, 420.

27. Tomc, "Dieting and Damnation," 78, 98.

28. Irigaray, *Sexes and Genealogies*, 11, 14.

29. Meyer, *Breaking Dawn*, 524.

30. Meyer, *Breaking Dawn*, 34–35.

31. Hélène Cixous, "The Laugh of the Medusa," in *New French Feminisms*, ed. Elaine Marks and Isabelle de Courtivron (Brighton, UK: Harvester, 1981), 262–64.

32. Meyer, *Breaking Dawn*, 754.

13

Vampire Vogue and Female Fashion: Dressing Skin and Dressing-Up in the Sookie Stackhouse and *Twilight* Series

Sarah Heaton

G OD *HATES FANGS* MAY BE SHOWING at the movies in Bon Temps, Louisiana, and the vampires of Bon Temps and Forks, Washington, may have
an ambivalent relationship with television and the movies, but *we* seemingly
cannot get enough of vampires and the humans who hang out with them
looking great on screen. The success of both the *Twilight* franchise and HBO's
True Blood series has extended the novels' audience from teen females to the
whole family, whether they are the sincere "Twihards" and "Twilight Moms,"
the HBO diehards, or the fans who see all the flaws in both the novel and film
texts but love them anyway . . . with a slight sense of irony to validate the pleasure they derive.[1] These texts are all about pleasure; once on screen it is visual
pleasure. The first *Twilight* film opens submerged in the moisture-infused
green coniferous forests of Forks and a sun-bleached Phoenix: a visual delight
that, through camera work and soundtrack, sets up an indie-style mise-en-
scene. *True Blood*'s opening credits powerfully place the text not only in the
Southern Gothic but also call to mind the openings for other HBO series such
as *The Sopranos* and *Deadwood*, positioning the Sookie Stackhouse tales in
their aesthetically transgressive style. Both the *Twilight* movies and the *True
Blood* HBO series reposition contemporary vampire novels in a visual excess
that relies on youth and subcultural modes of expression through camera
work, soundtrack and, in particular, clothing.

In the *Twilight* series and the Sookie Stackhouse novels, both Bella and
Sookie avowedly refute any capability of dressing well. This denial feeds into
anxieties about their bodies, skin and femininity, yet they have nothing to
hide but themselves, whilst the vampires who have everything to hide, es-

pecially in daylight or sunlight, all dress well. In the written texts there is a clear division between the perception of human and vampire dress sense. In the transition to film, both television series and movie, there is a clear vamping up of the dress codes, which means that not only the vampires' but also Bella's and Sookie's dress becomes powerfully seductive even when it is still sweats and a waitress outfit. Not underestimating the power and seduction of clothing and adornment prior to HBO launching the first series, a *True Blood* jewellery range was released, and Bella's Carolina Herrera wedding dress is available to buy as an official copy at more than half the price by Alfred Angelo. Fashion is so important to these film texts not just because of the visual effects and the lucrative add-ons for sale but crucially because fashion is at the heart of female bodily desires and anxieties. Arguably these desires and anxieties are played out through clothing in the human and the vampire as well as the attraction for the audience.

The contemporary vampires in the Sookie Stackhouse and *Twilight* novels and film texts are style conscious, and it is precisely this which makes them more human. Contemporary vampire texts are infused with an underlying sensuality, which is what makes them unique in the world of the monstrous and in/unhuman: being bitten by a vampire in the modern world is more sexual than frightening. For a predominantly female audience, it is not just the desire to be on the receiving end of Edward's, Bill's or Eric's attentions; their gaze is attracted to positioning themselves as the females in the text. Integral to the desires both within and without the texts is clothing: "[F]ashion is more than a language. True, it communicates. It is also tactile, visual, it is about touching, surfaces, colours, shapes. It embodies culture."[2] Significantly, the vampires' everyday clothing is a "situated bodily practice" which hides the skin that they are in, hides their true selves, embodying a human culture, making them even more desirable.[3] No longer dangerous, the vampires are made more reachable through recognizable dress codes. Although not specifically part of the vampire's glamoring repertoire, clothes are certainly part not only of their othering in their success with fashion but also their attraction. Clothes are used by the vampires to exert their power.

> [C]lothes act as an extension of the self and body; in a very immediate way they represent culture; they will necessarily represent the dominant values of the culture . . . yet this dominance will itself open the way to a counter-discourse, to reinterpretation . . . The field of dress codes is a site of struggle for control of the power to define situations and ourselves; to create meaning. We can still acknowledge that dress is a powerful weapon of control and dominance, while widening our view to encompass understanding of its *simultaneously* subversive qualities.[4]

Initially Bella does not notice the Cullens' clothing, but when she does, she is struck by their level of fashion and style which sets them apart. "I hadn't noticed their clothes before—I'd been too mesmerized by their faces. Now I looked, it was obvious that they were all dressed exceptionally well; simply, but in clothes that subtly hinted of their designer origins."[5] In both the novel and film text, whatever the nuance of dress, the important thing is that they dress well and expensively. The vampire's ability to dress well comes from a transhistorical access to fashion and a high economic leverage. Clothing works for the Cullens in a peculiar way in that it is used to ensure they "fit" in a human environment, yet it simultaneously marks them out. They represent the "dominant value" of both their own and the human culture, so opening up a "counter-discourse."[6] The clothing of vampires is a complex amalgam of their power, representing their dominance in human and vampire culture simultaneously through codes which can and cannot be read. Through their clothing, contemporary vampires are making new meanings of their position in contemporary culture.

Just as when Bella first sees Edward, it is the body rather than the clothing which strikes Sookie about Bill when he first enters Merlotte's; no one else seems to notice Bill the Vampire, despite the glow his skin emits. She is struck by his Byzantine nose and his "curiously old-fashioned" sideburns.[7] Bill's transhistoricity is written on his body and is easy to read in his facial hair; he comments that "that was the fashion . . . It's lucky for me I didn't wear a beard as so many men did, or I'd have it for eternity."[8] Bill is no longer able to adjust his body according to fashion as he is his dress. Indeed in all cultures the body itself is difficult to radically modify as any diet or exercise regime will attest to: "Yet dress and adornment in virtually all cultures have been used to do precisely this: from tattooing and neck rings to the dyeing and curling of hair and the use of high heels, both women and men have worked hard to produce a 'different' body."[9] For Bill even clothing remains at times locked in the past, in particular his sense of female fashion: "It's hard for me to get used to young ladies with so few clothes on . . . I liked long skirts . . . I liked the underthings women wore. The petticoats."[10] In his clothing there is a sense of the traditional, in the conservative sense rather than historical which remains everyday rather than stand-out. His all-American jeans, which Sookie sees when he kneels to save her, make him more Marlboro Man than designer-fashion icon. The suggestive link to the Marlboro Man goes some way to intimate the vampire's relationship to nature: when the Marlboro Man's "masculine ego masquerades as being at one with nature, its true intention is to dominate nature. The world is presented as a natural dimension there only to be mastered. In the image, civilized man confronts untamed nature and takes up its challenge and invitation,"[11] although by *Club Dead*, Bill is no longer a jeans man when they have become the defining signifier for Eric's attractiveness.

Jeans are a mobile signifier because, in a democratic turn, they embody simultaneously their workwear origins, their contemporary associations with the myth of the cowboy, as well as their now designer pedigree.

> As a component of the fashion system, jeans have been adapted to different occasions, statuses and habituses. The humble origins of jeans reinforce the point that fashion does not automatically emanate from elite groups but may often reflect the establishment of distinct identities and lifestyles among everyday or subcultural groups. In the case of jeans, the process of prestigious imitation occurred last among elite groups, and even then amidst resistance.[12]

Many of the men in Bon Temps dress in workwear or as cowboys: Mike Spencer has a "fondness for cowboy boots and string ties," and Rene Lenier is usually in workwear.[13] The clothes link the men to the double American mythologies of American workwear turned fashion and the cowboy. Yet there is a queering of these mythologies: both Mike and Rene are clearly linked to the monstrous other in the human whereas in the inhuman vampire Bill, the mythology is upheld—the gentleman hero of the Civil War saving Sookie. Arguably this suggests that the dominant contemporary society which cannot accept the other or marginalised group distorts the mythologies on which America is founded upon whilst in cultural consciousness those mythologies still have a clear, untainted link to their originary moments. As Wilson suggests, in the social codes of dress there is a "struggle for control over the power to define situations and [them]selves," and clothes which are worn well can be a powerful tool of dominance as well as subversion.[14] Certainly with Mike and Rene there is the clear suggestion that they do not wear their clothes well, whilst it is Eric at Fangtasia who excels at the all-American jeans uniform: "The vampire he'd indicated was handsome, in fact, radiant; blond blue-eyed, tall and broad shouldered. He was wearing boots, jeans, and a vest. Period."[15] It appears that Eric's seduction of Sookie is written in the jeans, particularly as Bill gets out of his jeans and into his conservative "khaki Dockers and a green-and-brown striped golfing shirt, polished loafers, and thin brown socks."[16] Tellingly it is an outfit similar to that of the "conservative" Gabe who attacks and attempts to rape Sookie in *Living Dead in Dallas*. Even in a suit Eric outperforms Bill, who only wears one because Sookie's Gran suggests it. The transition to screen sees a slight reconfiguring of the dress codes: gone are the golf shirts and in comes a uniform of black jeans and shirts for Bill whilst Eric sports a still slicker version: the boy-next-door versus the designer-wearing entrepreneur. Whom are you going to choose, Sookie?

The vampire males all dress well, whether it is the cutting-edge designer fashion of the Cullens or the all-American jeans and T-shirts of the Sookie Stackhouse vampires. In both texts the vampires dress in human style akin to the vampires of the Romantic period: both Byron's Darvell and Polidori's Ruthven dress as the sophisticated male traveller on the Grand Tour. In the *Twilight* series, the Hollywood vampire dress code of long black cape made fashionable by Lugosi's vampire is the dress choice for the ancient, traditional Volturis who live separately from humans and for the humans dressing up at the vampire carnival. In a similarly carnivalesque environment, it is the fang-bangers and tourists in the Sookie Stackhouse series who wear

> [T]he traditional capes and tuxes for the men to many Morticia Adams rip-offs among the females. The clothes ranged from reproductions of those worn by Brad Pitt and Tom Cruise in *Interview with the Vampire* to some modern out-fits which I thought were influenced by *The Hunger*. Some of the fang-bangers were wearing false fangs, some had painted trickles of blood from the corners of their mouths or puncture marks on their necks. They were extraordinary, and extraordinarily pathetic.[17]

These burlesques reproduce a Hollywood-endorsed vampire dress code, and rather than marking out the fang-bangers as dangerous and rebellious, they render them as powerless. As Wilson suggests, when "we dress in the prevailing fashion, we are both trying to conform, yet simultaneously try-ing to individualise ourselves."[18] In the bar the tourists all wear black as do many of the vampires—living up to some level of expectation. In the film text even Bill and Eric dress up in black in Fangtasia. The capes and tuxedos are avowedly mainstream, coming directly out of Hollywood—not even the vampire made safe by the hegemonic forces of capitalism but rather capitalism's visual creation of the vampire. Trudi, a fang-banger Sookie meets at Stan's party, is less clichéd Hollywood representation and more youth subcultural expression of an alternative scene: "spectacular youth cultures convert the fact of being under surveillance into the pleasure of being watched."[19] But again it is a look that we have seen before; it has been coopted, reproduced and made safe by the media and capitalism over time since its first subcultural manifestations. Hebdige argues that whilst there is a power to subvert there is also the process of assimilation, of making safe, through incorporation in which subculture becomes a mass-marketed style which erodes and dilutes the challenge of subcultural style.

> Trudi had hair done in deep red spikes, a pierced nose and tongue, and maca-bre makeup, including black lipstick. She told me proudly its color was called

Grave Rot. Her jeans were so low I wondered how she got up and down in them. Maybe she wore them so low-cut to show off her navel ring. Her knit top was cropped very short . . . she wasn't as bizarre as her appearance led you to believe. Trudi was a college student. I discovered, through absolutely legitimate listening, that she believed herself to be waving the red flag at the bull, by dating Joseph. The bull was her parents, I gathered.[20]

That you can buy a black lipstick called Grave Rot on the local high street reinforces that this is just another mass-marketed look; no longer dangerous, the clothes do not stand for a subcultural movement. Neither are the clothes gendered; in fact, they go a long way to deny gender, and whilst a lot of flesh is on show, it is not seductive flesh. The clothes seemingly stand for the work-place—representing her status as student and her sexual preferences. Her clothes do not mark out a dominance or subversion but rather become a re-dundant gesture similar to the dressing up by the tourists who visit Fangtasia.

In the *Twilight* series, human clothing as youth subcultural style only re-ally becomes manifest in the adaptations for screen. In the novels the clothes remain "conservative," whilst on film they take on a grunge aesthetic, and there is a homological fit between the Forks scenery, the clothing and the soundtrack which feeds into a history of the Seattle-based grunge movement. Whilst for the humans this is manifestly a step away from mainstream capi-talist consumption, in Edward it is the apotheosis of capitalist style. Edward's may be a grunge style that is a move away from the tan, leather blouson and ivory turtleneck of the first novel, but it is still an expensively bought look. Bella, without the capital behind her, is in regular sweats except when Alice dresses her. Yet increasingly, tan leather jackets are coming back into fashion, and Bella's designer grunge Belstaff jacket in *Breaking Dawn* would certainly need economic leverage to afford the look when "'[g]runge' [has] moved swiftly from the margins to couture collections"—less subcultural youth style and more designer aesthetic.[21]

Alice and Rosalie in both the novel text and film text dress extremely well and expensively. "Alice was striking in a black satin dress with geometric cut outs that bared large triangles of her snowy white skin. [Rosalie's] scarlet dress was backless, tight to her cleaves where it flared into a wide ruffled train, with a neckline that plunged to her waist. I pitied every girl in the room, myself included."[22] Laura Mulvey, in her seminal essay, argued that the typical movie objectifies the woman as object of the male gaze so women are fetishized as they play out the desires of the male spectator. However the predominantly female *Twilight* audience position themselves with Bella and not being able to dress well, and through Bella's eyes they desire the dress sense and style of the two female vampires even whilst Bella attests to "rejecting" it, as well as Bella's own designer-led dressing down.

[T]he aesthetics of fashion are not primarily sexual in nature, nor are they designed, necessarily, to attract the male gaze. Rather, "fashionable" dress is a complex lexicon where the intention of sexual enticement may be absent altogether, or, if present, be unimportant in comparison with other criteria. Women, it is often observed, dress "for each other"; this colloquial observation contains, compressed within it, a number of important truths which include an awareness of the rituals of shopping, dressing up, adolescent identity parades, masquerade, and the concept of same-sex looking.[23]

When Alice dresses Bella for the ball and her wedding as well as packs her marriage trousseau, it is the ultimate female transfiguration dream, but it also reproduces the intimate female rituals of fashion: "The collective ritual nature of so much fashion-related behaviour—women shopping together, trying on clothes together, painting each other's faces and nails, doing each other's hair, in private and public spaces."[24] Whilst Bella succumbs momentarily to dressing up, she quickly reverts to dressing down. As with all humans, it is all very well looking great for your wedding day but far too hard to keep it up every day. Yet "[w]hether women follow current trends, ignore them and create their own style, are relatively uninterested in 'fashion' as such, or have little, if any, money to spend on clothes, they nevertheless, by the simple act of getting dressed in the morning, participate in the processes of fashion," and it is perhaps because of this, because of the importance of the rituals of fashion and dressing up and despite the narrative holding the vampires, Alice and Rosalie, and the human Bella as opposites in the signifying system of fashion, that, in fact, there is no difference between them at all.[25] Yet the female vampires do dress well every day, and so does Bella on film, and the watching audience "tries on" all the different outfits.

Sookie, like Bella has an anxiety about fashion and is happiest in her waitress outfits, and she knows she looks "good in the warm weather waitress outfit Sam picked for us: black shorts, white T, white socks, black Nikes" and her sleepwear.[26] For Sookie these clothes become a uniform to hide behind with a clear sense of identity and a body consciousness that is not sexual. "I turned on my own light and shut the door and began taking off my clothes. I had at least five pairs of black shorts and many, many white T-shirts, since those tended to get stained easily. No telling how many pairs of white socks were rolled up in my drawer . . . I crawled into bed in my favorite Mickey Mouse sleep T-shirt, which came almost to my knees."[27] There is a sense of security in the repetition and routine, her work clothes and their clear demarcation. There is a sense of regimented control: not only has she been told what to wear, but because it is part of her work, it is legitimised. Unlike Bella, there is a clear sense of her physical body in her first reflective description of herself. "And it's not because I'm not pretty. I am. I'm blond and blue-eyed and twenty-five, and my legs are strong and my bosom is substantial, and I have a waspy waistline."[28] So she is comfortable with her body although she is happier that her favourite two-piece bikini is a "little roomier than last year."[29] She is, to all intents and purposes, a contemporary Southern belle, and she does not shy away from describing herself as such. When she meets the "Geeky" vampire Stan in *Living Dead in Dallas*, she needs to persuade Bethany, the threatened bar girl, to trust her so she can read her mind. She comments on herself: "I look exactly like the girl you'd see in a low-paying job any place in any town in the South: blond and bosomy and tan and young. Possibly I don't look very bright. But I think it's more that people (and vampires) assume that if you are pretty and blond and have a low-paying job, you are ipso facto dumb."[30] Here she is clothing herself in the stereotype as a mask to enable her "disability," her individuality. Yet just moments earlier she has succumbed to the same stereotyping when describing Bethany: "I knew right away she was stupid. After all, what could I do against a room full of vampires?"[31] This is one of many seemingly "innocent" slips in terms of self-recognition, in awareness and in her relationships to other women and the contradictory desires of female fashion and friendship: "Fashion—a performance art—acts as vehicle for this ambivalence; the daring of fashion speaks dread as well as desire; the shell of chic, the aura of glamour, always hide a wound . . . of contradictory desire."[32] For Sookie, many of the females in the texts are her enemies. Even with her friends at Merlotte's there is an anxious "truce" because of her telepathic powers, and Tara appears as a friend only in the third novel although she is key to the television series from the outset. Yet she does dress for her Gran, who is killed off early on: "[I] wore a dress, since I knew Gran would have a fit if I didn't. It was a little blue cotton-knit dress with tiny daisies all over it, and it was tighter than Gran liked and shorter than Jason deemed proper in his sister. I'd heard that the first time I'd worn it."[33] Despite the pattern of small flower sprigs which is the innocent pastoral palate that she is often associated with and wears when she is not in Merlotte's hotpants or her bikinis, there is still an underlying sexualisation to her clothing which many who look at her disapprove. Sookie does seem to dress for men rather than the female gaze, whether it is Sam's hot-pants uniform or Bill asking her to "do me proud."[34] When she is going to Fangtasia for the first time she anxiously picks out an outfit:

> I wasn't tall enough or bony enough to dress in the sort of spandex outfit the Vampire Diane had worn. Finally I pulled a dress from the back of my closet, one I'd had little occasion to wear. It was Nice Date dress, if you wanted the personal interest of whoever was your escort. It was cut square and low in the neck and it was sleeveless. It was tight and white. The fabric was thinly scattered with bright red flowers and long green stems. My tan glowed and

my boobs showed. I wore red enamel earrings and red high-heeled screw-me shoes. I had a little red straw purse. I put on light makeup and wore my wavy hair loose down my back.[35]

An outfit of varying degrees of success, it appeals to Bill and Eric, but she certainly does not blend in, suggesting an anxiety with fashion as a performance. Repeatedly Sookie assumes Bill thinks she has dressed inappropriately. A similar scene is repeated throughout the series when Sookie gets "dressed" for an occasion, whether it is looking professional in a suit under Bill's orders for a "business" meeting or a disguise she adopts to do some "research." She is picking and mixing outfits according to her audience whether it is Bill, Eric, Gran, Jason, Sam or anyone else who is "just looking."[36] There is a complexity to her getting dressed in which the anxiety plays less around her body exposing itself and more around the conflicting interests the different audiences have in the way she dresses. Yet whilst at one level there is a sense of uncertainty to the autonomy or authority over her clothes, at another there is a sense of ownership and play in her clothing choices: "Those are . . . would that be a . . . thong?" Bill seemed a little preoccupied all of a sudden. "It would. I didn't see the need to be professional down to the skin."[37] There is also a pleasure in dressing up, and she is aware of how clothes operate not only as performance art but as a boundary with the skin; just as she is very aware of her own physical assets, she is aware of the layering effect of clothing,

For Bella, her avowed discomfort with clothes and fashion is more pronounced than Sookie's. Bella hides in her clothes. Often in the first film she seems to shrink into them with the familiar gestures of the body-anxious female teenager: she shrugs her cuffs over her hands and remains fully covered. She wears a "uniform" of jeans, T-shirts and parkas, staving off any gender identification through what she wears. From the outset of the first text her choice of clothes is functional and it responds to conditions: "It was seventy-five degrees in Phoenix, the sky a perfect, cloudless blue. I was wearing my favorite shirt—sleeveless, white eyelet lace; I was wearing it as a farewell gesture. My carry-on item was a parka."[38] There is no mention of her body and her physical attributes. For the audience of the movies, Bella's clothes are less obviously about body panic and anxiety and more about an appealing grunge aesthetic and vintage-style tomboy which allows the audience to position themselves as Bella. Few of us have the Southern belle aesthetic of Sookie, yet most of us can recognise if not the body shape of Bella, the female anxieties that align themselves with such a fashion consciousness—who doesn't own a pair of jeans, T-shirt and jacket? Clearly by *Breaking Dawn* it is a look which has been perfected as not only one we recognise but also one which has become aspirational as the audience can identify the precise style and brand to replicate the dress codes in their own lives: 7 for all Mankind jeans, an

American Eagle military henley, a Belstaff jacket and Wesley skater shoes. But
to some extent both Bella and Sookie are still girls next door, they are just at
opposite ends of America. And the attractively clothed male vampires are the
youth cultural icon which we've been falling for for years from *Rebel without
a Cause* through *Footloose* and on.

Sookie, despite some anxiety, appears to enjoy dressing up as different
identities in a pick-and-mix style, and in both series there are humans dressing up to enjoy themselves, whether it is the tourists at Fangtasia or at the
carnival in Italy. Yet for Bella, being dressed up by Alice and Rosalie is fraught
with anxiety and a discomfort in everything she wears, despite her recognis-
ing the importance of dressing up amongst friends. So whilst at one level
there is a nice feminist inversion in the usual gosling-turned-swan narrative
(when the male sends the ideal dress for the first date) because it is Alice
who sends the dresses, there is an uneasy sense that she is doing so for her
brother, that Alice is manipulating Bella's body for his desires. Bella's strong
reaction against this dressing up stands against both the sexualisation of herself, through the wearing of gendered and body-focused clothing but also the
sexualising of Edward. Core to the texts' success is, until Edward and Bella are
married, the chasteness. At the outset most of the erotic tension is around the
fact that they not only cannot have sex, but even to kiss for more than a brief
moment is dangerous. It is this continually displaced desire both for Bella
and Edward as well as the audience which is so appealing when played out
against the background of the formation of female sexual identity, whereas in
the Sookie Stackhouse texts much of the erotic tension is through the veiling
and unveiling of the skin.

In both the *Twilight* and Sookie Stackhouse texts there is a complex
relationship between clothing and the skin for both the human and the
vampire: "In Western clothing the fabric is cut to the bodyline and sewn.
The form of the attire is modelled after the body, with a shell similar to
the shape of the body thus being created. In so doing, the space between
the two is eliminated."[39] Clothing in vampire texts is fascinating because
rather than merely suggesting a character's social, economic and cultural
background, dress transmits social codes at the boundary, the marginal site
where the tensions between being human and anti-human or post-human
are played out. Increasingly in contemporary vampire dress codes there is
a move away from capes, which suggested the space between the body, the
skin and the clothing. The everyday clothes of the contemporary vampire
hide the gap but inversely increase the sense of space, the relationship between the clothing and the skin. It has already been pointed out that it is
initially the "glow" of the skin which marks out the vampires in both texts.
Such a glow transgresses the boundaries of the skin and clothing as does

glamoring. Even more dramatic are the shapeshifters' trans-morphing skin and the vampiric puncturing of the skin, but even Sookie's mind-reading suggests a fluid, transgressive body with neither the skin nor the clothes able to contain the body. Yet the vampires' skin is repeatedly referred to as intransigent, hard and glittering, not the soft, warm, more malleable human skin. So perhaps their clothes are retaining and restraining something else: their inhumanity. Arguably for the teenage girl and young woman it is the threat of the more mobile human flesh over-spilling which clothes are designed to restrain. Repeatedly at moments of threat and crisis it is Sookie's bra which comes under attack and breaks. In Fangtasia when she is sitting in Eric's shirt after the Maenad has attacked, she is worried about her bra-less state, perceiving the most voluptuous and mobile part of her body as the most potentially threatening to herself. Unrestrained, her breasts make her vulnerable as others can read her body despite its being clothed. Throughout the Sookie Stackhouse series, flesh is continually exposed or about to be exposed with varying degrees of anxiety, whether it is the "rebellious" dress codes of Trudi, the state of undress at the sex party in Bon Temps, the vampires at Bill's house when Sookie first visits or Sookie herself who is seemingly always getting dressed or undressed.

Whilst at some level both Bella and Sookie are constrained by and constraining in their clothes choices, they still remain, along with Edward, Bill and Eric, free thinkers who traverse boundaries. To some extent Sookie achieves such traversing in her clothing choice in her ability to pick and mix with some degree of success according to the narrative she is about to play out. She is also seemingly comfortable in her own skin—in particular in her bikinis, which she is still wearing in *Dead in the Family* despite the fact that the focus on clothing so predominant in the earlier texts has died down. But there is still an anxiety surrounding skin and the "wound of contradictory desires."[40] Erotically there is too much around at the vampire and human parties, and when she meets Eric half-naked and mad, she covers him with an afghan. Her own skin is under threat from vampire bites, being licked, uninvited groping or being attacked and threatened with rape. Time and again her skin is bruised all over and broken. Time and again her skin is saved by vampires through their strength or by her ingesting their blood. Although she is body confident, her skin is under attack and threatened. In a peculiar Freudian return, a letter from her grandfather arrives written on the skin of the sprite which drowned her parents.

> "This letter is written on the skin of one of the water sprites who drowned your parents."
>
> "Ick!" I cried, and dropped the letter on the kitchen table.

Claude was by my side in a flash. "What's wrong?" he asked, looking around the kitchen as if he expected to see a Troll pop up.

"This is skin! Skin!"[41]

Although this skin has been cleansed for Sookie as a human, there is still an issue with it, an underlying anxiety and sense of abjection.

Similarly for Bella there is an anxiety surrounding the skin. Her skin is ruptured and broken when she comes under attack, by accident and rather disturbingly when she makes love to Edward, whilst she is pregnant and when she gives birth. At these moments in the text, anxieties surrounding the female body go beyond teenage anxieties and the potential balm that clothing can promise. Most worryingly, it is precisely at the moments when the female body is in essentialist terms most clearly expressing its femininity: love making and giving birth. When Bella's body is at its most feminine in social constructionist's terms, the wedding and the ball, clothing directly born out of female community and ritual restores a "glow" to her skin even though she is still body conscious in terms of movement: "Her skin was cream and roses, her eyes were huge with excitement and framed with thick lashes. The narrow sheath of the shimmering white dress flared subtly at the train almost like an inverted lily, cut so skillfully that her body looked elegant and graceful—whilst it was motionless at least."[42] In the film the intricate lace-back panel to her Carolina Herrera wedding dress means her skin, and clothing become one, and Bella is clearly body confident enough to not need underwear. But when she makes love she is left bruised, and when she is pregnant her body is rendered, in the film, shockingly anorexic. Just as Sookie's anxieties are most pronounced when she is bra-less, it is the female body itself which disturbs the characters the most. For both Sookie and Bella, part of the appeal of the vampires is their skin, the coldness of it, the hardness of it. For Sookie, she is constantly attracted to the "imperceptible glow of Bill's skin. Whilst Bella is astonished by Edward's skin: "Edward in the sunlight was shocking. I couldn't get used to it, though I'd been staring at him all afternoon. His skin, white despite the faint flush from yesterday's hunting trip, literally sparkled, like thousands of tiny diamonds were embedded in the surface."[43] Even when she sees herself in reflection in her wedding dress, her skin is part of the appeal even as she does not recognise it as her own. The window her skin is reflected in works as a screen ironing out imperfections. And it is getting to know her own hard glittering vampire skin which allows her to throw the "silver satin shoes"[44] and to rip the "[t]ightly fitted ice-blue silk"[45] dress—"exerting the tiniest amount of pressure possible I ripped the dress open to the top of my thigh"[46]—which Alice has dressed her in. No longer body conscious, she is able to move freely.

The camera eye, like clothing, filters the skin and the body, allowing them to be veiled, transfigured even, like so many of the characters in the texts who literally trans-morph into what one desires. Just as clothing always has an audience—and is always on show whether it is a pair of sweatpants, a date dress or a wedding dress, continually communicating and filtering the complex link between the self, identity and society—the camera, which makes the fashion of the written-text spectacle, filters the skin, giving it a "glow" for all those on film and not just the vampires, even when a cinema-verité or dirty-realism aesthetic is applied. With the adaptation to film, these texts, with the use of the hand-held camera and the continually referenced motif of the camera and video camera, suggest a desire in both the vampire and the human to perfect the image of the self. In the film texts there is not just a complex tension around the anxiety of the female body as it is increasingly subject to the gaze during the period in which it attains sexual identity but also the complexity of the desire in the "just looking" of both the male and the female gaze at the spectacle and, as they are vampire texts, the spectrealised. Guy Debord in "The Society of the Spectacle" suggests the spectacle conceals the real conditions of existence; here it is the real conditions of the skin and the vampires.[47] Whilst clothing veils the skin and reshapes the body to iron out the imperfections, the camera eye has a similar effect on the skin: "Odourless and textureless, these skins nevertheless acquaint us with a kind of higher touching, an immaculate, intactile, imperishable touch of the eye. Whenever we look at a poster or a projection on an impersonal surface, we are looking at such an idealised, generalised human skin."[48] It appears that the appeal of the vampires' skin for Bella and Sookie is exactly the kind of appeal we as audience find in skin and the body on film in all its odourless idealisation. Bella says, "They looked more like a scene from a movie,"[49] and "He looked like he'd just finished shooting a commercial";[50] and for Sookie, "He wears jeans and T-shirts, mostly, but I've seen him in a suit. GQ missed a good thing when Eric decided his talents lay in building a business empire rather than modeling. Tonight he was shirtless, sparse dark gold hair trailing down to the waist of his jeans and gleaming against his pallor."[51] It is exactly the allure, the glamoring and the spectacle through the vamping up of the clothing and the camera eye which is the appeal of these vampire texts.

Notes

1. Francesca Haig, "Guilty Pleasures: *Twilight*, Snark and Ironic Fandom" in *Screening* Twilight: *Critical Approaches to a Cinematic Phenomenon*, ed. Wickham Clayton and Sarah Harmon (London: I.B. Tauris, forthcoming).

2. Elizabeth Wilson, "Fashion and the Postmodern Body," in *Chic Thrills*, ed. Juliet Ash et al. (London: Pandora, 1992), 14.

3. Joanne Enwistle, *The Fashioned Body: Fashion Dress and Modern Social Theory* (Cambridge: Polity, 2002), 11.

4. Wilson, "Fashion," 12–14.

5. Meyer, *Twilight* (London: Atom, 2009), 27.

6. Wilson, "Fashion," 14.

7. Charlaine Harris, *Dead until Dark* (London: Orion Gollancz, 2009), 2.

8. Harris, *Dead until Dark*, 64.

9. Wilson, "Fashion," 10.

10. Harris, *Dead until Dark*, 62.

11. Anthony Easthope, *What a Man's Gotta Do: Masculine Myth in Popular Culture* (London: Routledge, 1992), 47.

12. Jennifer Craik, *The Face of Fashion: Cultural Studies in Fashion* (London: Routledge, 1993), 215.

13. Harris, *Dead until Dark*, 44.

14. Wilson, "Fashion," 12–14.

15. Harris, *Dead until Dark*, 119.

16. Harris, *Dead until Dark*, 52.

17. Harris, *Dead until Dark*, 115.

18. Wilson, "Fashion," 6.

19. Dick Hebdige, *Hiding in the Light* (London: Routledge, 1989), 80.

20. Charlaine Harris, *Living Dead in Dallas* (London: Orion Gollancz, 2009), 198.

21. Pamela Church Gibson, "Redressing the Balance," in *Fashion Cultures: Theories, Explorations and Analysis*, ed. Stella Bruzzi et al. (London: Routledge, 2000), 358.

22. Meyer, *Twilight*, 424.

23. Gibson, "Redressing the Balance," 350.

24. Gibson, "Redressing the Balance," 360.

25. Gibson, "Redressing the Balance," 353.

26. Harris, *Dead until Dark*, 1.

27. Harris, *Dead until Dark*, 18.

28. Harris, *Dead until Dark*, 1.

29. Harris, *Dead until Dark*, 19.

30. Harris, *Living Dead in Dallas*, 81.

31. Harris, *Living Dead in Dallas*, 80.

32. Wilson, "Feminism and Fashion," in *The Fashion Reader*, ed. Linda Welters et al. (Oxford: Berg, 2011), 331.

33. Harris, *Dead until Dark*, 50.

34. Harris, *Dead until Dark*, 108.

35. Harris, *Dead until Dark*, 108.

36. Rachel Bowlby, *Just Looking: Consumer Culture in Dreiser, Gissing and Zola* (London: Routledge, 2009)

37. Harris, *Living Dead in Dallas*, 75.

38. Meyer, *Twilight*, 3.

39. A. Isozki, "What Are Clothes? . . . A Fundamental Question," in *Issey Miyake, East meets West* (Tokyo: Heibonsha, 1978), 55–56.

40. Wilson, "Feminism and Fashion," 331.

41. Charlaine Harris, *Dead in the Family* (London: Orion Gollancz, 2010), 56.

42. Meyer, *Breaking Dawn*, 52.

43. Meyer, *Twilight*, 228.

44. Meyer, *Breaking Dawn,* 378.

45. Meyer, *Breaking Dawn,* 377.

46. Meyer, *Breaking Dawn,* 379.

47. Guy Debord, The Society of Spectacle (1967), tr. Black + Red, 1977, Chapter 1, "Spectacle Perfected," accessed July 28, 2013, http://www.marxists.org/reference/archive/debord/society.htm.

48. Steven Connor, *The Book of Skin* (London: Reaktion, 2003), 60.

49. Meyer, *Twilight*, 35.

50. Meyer, *Twilight*, 37.

51. Harris, *Dead in the Family*, 75.

Filmography

Breaking Dawn, part 1, directed by Bill Condon (2011).
Eclipse, directed by David Slade (2010).
New Moon, directed by Charles Weitz (2009).
True Blood, season 1 (HBO, 2008).
True Blood, season 2 (HBO, 2009).
True Blood, season 3 (HBO, 2010).
Twilight, Catherine Hardwicke (2008).

14

The Politics of Reproduction in Stephanie Meyer's *Twilight* Saga

Batia Boe Stolar

T HE NEW BREED OF LITERARY and cinematic vampires departs from its predecessors largely by eradicating the ambivalence that traditionally characterized this enigmatic figure. By 2007, the polarization between the horrific monstrous and the romantic ideal was epitomized by the release of David Slade's *30 Days of Night* and the growing popularity of Stephanie Meyer's *Twilight Saga* with the publication of a third volume, *Eclipse*. In Meyer's saga, vampires are described as "devastatingly, inhumanly beautiful,"[1] sporting fangless, "perfect, ultrawhite teeth,"[2] "marble" skin,[3] that "literally sparkle[s]" in direct sunlight,[4] and facial features "chiseled from stone"[5] resembling depictions of Greek and Roman gods in art;[6] and although they can be destroyed, they are nevertheless referred to as immortal.[7] As the "good vampires"[8] strive to pass for human, to "blend in,"[9] they are rendered superheroes working behind-the-scenes, running "around saving people's lives"[10] to the point that readers bemoan the fact that Meyer's vampires "are not real."[11] In contrast, Slade's vampires pay homage to Count Orlok[12] and his descendants; they are stylized savage killers with an insatiable thirst for human blood and no redeeming qualities (other than providing an antithesis to Meyer's vamps). The polarization into camp Jekyll and camp Hyde, into sparkly superheroes and fangish ghouls, begs rephrasing Nina Auerbach's often-quoted statement, Why are these the vampires our age needs?[13] Since, as Judith E. Johnson notes, "the inherent metaphorical material in society's dreams of vampire narratives is social and involves questions of social justice, power, exploitation, race, and class, as well as the more obvious gender conflict,"[14] what societal anxieties do the polarized vamps, devoid of ambiguity, represent?

Most of the popular vampire narratives of the late 20th and early 21st century feature strong, active, female protagonists who, while human, often become involved in heterosexual relationships with young-looking but significantly older male vampires whose sexual performance is more in keeping with outdated notions of masculinity that teeter between romanticized chivalry and disturbing stalking/abuse. What is troubling these girl-fronted texts has been addressed largely by focusing on the protagonists' feminist credentials. As they take charge over their brooding sexual objects of desire rather than being seduced by them, they continue the "contradictory gender portrayals and diverse depictions of sexuality" characteristic of vampire narratives.[15] But as the human woman takes on the leading role, it is her body, rather than the vampire's, that is the subject of scrutiny and objectifies her. In Meyer's saga, this tension is evident in Bella's pregnancy and her desire to become a vampire. Although she is "consistently depicted as the damsel in distress forever in need of rescue by a male,"[16] her objection to Edward's over-protectiveness suggests a form of gender-bending self-assertion, and ambition: "I can't always be Lois Lane . . . I want to be Superman, too."[17] These contradictory elements have less to do with Bella's status as a feminist agent and more to do with her explicitly linking her deficiencies with her body and in doing so attributing her paternally inherited clumsiness to her genetic makeup: "I didn't get my balance problems from my mother."[18] Bella effectively displaces the association of helplessness from her femininity, from socialized learned behavior, and onto a more amorphous biological field that conflates biology with the patriarchal institution that both enables and limits her very agency. This displacement in turn points to latent anxieties of pro/creation in a saga that is rife with various forms of re/production. Analyzing the biological discourse in relation to the various forms of reproduction in Meyer's saga—vampire-human, vampire, and werewolf/shifter—illustrates how intertwining and competing sociopolitical positions destabilize the text's valorization of essentialist notions of sex.

Similar to the literary allusions to *Romeo and Juliet, Pride and Prejudice,* and *Wuthering Heights* that serve as backdrop for Bella and Edward's romance, so too do references to biology peppered throughout the saga contextualize discussions of bodily transformation. As Caitlin Flanagan astutely points out in her review of the saga, Bella and Edward first meet in biology (not English) class, where they "are both crackerjack biology students (Bella because she took an AP course back in Phoenix, and Edward because he has taken the class God knows how many times)."[19] Their first discursive exchange and flirtation is over an in-class assignment on cellular mitosis. Seemingly inconsequential, the assignment takes on a different meaning when, in *Breaking Dawn,* Carlisle speculates on the physiological differences between human, werewolf/shifter, vampire, and human-vampire hybrid bodies that are based on their respective number of chromosomal pairs: 23 in most human bodies, 24 in the werewolf/shifter and human-vampire hybrid bodies, and 25 in vampire bodies.[20] As mitosis marks the process of DNA and chromosome replication and division, it forms the cornerstone of Carlisle's theory.

The importance of chromosome replication also points to anxieties over human reproduction since the extra pair of chromosomes in human bodies is usually detected as a condition of Down's Syndrome or else a birth abnormality. The abnormality of the hybrid and werewolf/shifter bodies, however, triggers rapid physical growth and accelerated cell regeneration, which is paralleled in the vampires' bodies, which when dismembered have the capacity to reassemble themselves. Emphasizing the cellular difference between the two types of bodies is skin, a racial marker, which in the vampire's case scars permanently: as a newborn vampire, Bella notes that "scars were Jasper's most dominant feature."[21] Accelerated cell regeneration in the werewolf/shifter bodies is more suggestive of stem cells, "the body's building blocks or 'master cells' . . . that can develop or differentiate into any type of tissue or organ . . . and be used to repair damage . . . and minimize and/or potentially cure diseases."[22] Since the mid-1990s, banking the umbilical cord of newborns to cryogenically preserve the cord stem cells has been encouraged by cord blood banks, which emphasize the potential use of these cells by the child as well as his or her "siblings, parents, grandparents and other members of [the] extended family."[23] Implicit in Meyer's saga, this rhetoric promotes ideological constructions of the biological nuclear family at the same time that it naturalizes scientific intervention, legitimizing the latter insofar as it promotes a seemingly natural reproductive and social order with the capacity for healing and saving lives.

The extra pair of chromosomes in the hybrid and nonhuman bodies also points to the function of plasmids, the "self-replicating *extra-chromosomal* circular DNA molecules" used to "generate multiple copies of the same gene"[24] in cloning experiments. While the popular understanding of cloning characterizes the clone as an identical replication of the original, a June 1999 report prepared by the Council on Ethical and Judicial Affairs of the American Medical Association stipulates, "Human clones would be identical insofar as they would have the same nuclear genes as the donor . . . Since environment has a profound influence on development, human clones likely would be different in terms of personality and other characteristics."[25] Reading the werewolf/shifter as a metaphor for cloning in Meyer's texts is best illustrated by the Quileute's oral stories that retell the origins of what Edward refers to as the "genetic quirk which allowed the transmutation."[26] The legends trace the clones back to an original donor, Taha Aki, who "had the idea that changed

[them] all"[27]: he "was more than either wolf or man. They called him Taha Aki the Great Wolf, or Taha Aki the Spirit Man. He led the tribe for many, many years, for he did not age . . . Taha Aki fathered many sons, and some of these found that, after they had reached the age of manhood, they, too, could transform into wolves."[28] The patrilineal inherited genetic mutations of the werewolf/shifter support the notion of an original nuclear gene, identified in the stories as an idea, from one donor, Taha Aki. When triggered, the clones of the nuclear gene produce the same change or effect in the various host bodies, Taha Aki's descendants, allowing them to shapeshift into wolves, all of which physically differ from one another: "The wolves were all different, because they were spirit wolves and reflected the man they were inside."[29]

When applied to vampiric reproduction, however, the metaphor of cloning raises different issues. Bella's transformation from human to vampire in *Breaking Dawn* is more suggestive of organ transplant operations: she describes adjusting to "[t]he eyes . . . unwilling to say *my eyes*,"[30] "my new face, my new skin,"[31] "this new body."[32] Her description of her transformation implicitly alludes to the Human Genome Project proposal of cloning as a suitable and ethical substitute for organ donorship, as well as a vehicle for repairing degenerative diseases at the cellular level: in its most benign form, the "goal of this process is not to create cloned human beings, but rather to harvest stem cells that can be used to study human development and to treat disease."[33] Similarly in Meyer's texts, the re/production of good vampires is proposed as a means of saving human lives—Edward, Esme, Rosalie, Emmett, Alice, and Bella—and their transformation into an altered biological being is the debatable byproduct. As Bella puts it, Carlisle "doesn't end lives, he saves them."[34] However, not all human lives are to be saved, and Meyer's texts are quick to privilege the exceptional individual over the mediocre, the original over the mass-produced. In *Breaking Dawn*, for instance, when Jacob tries to convince Bella to terminate her pregnancy and opt for a second pregnancy with a different sperm donor, Bella responds, "I should kill my baby and replace it with some *generic substitute*? Artificial insemination? . . . *Any* baby will do?"[35] Bella's response not only affirms an essentialist bias in her objection to clinical fertilization but, more importantly, points to class anxieties that intertwine with issues of sex and reproduction. The "generic substitute" points to a pharmaceutical-driven capitalist economy whereby the brand name competes with the generic alternative that has a lower price. Privileging the brand name as it were, Bella further affirms her social aspirations by insisting she has the Cullen brand, and, although she rejects clinical fertilization, the text undermines her objection by valorizing other medical interventions that rely on equally contrived, clinical procedures.

The privileging of the original (or brand name) over the copy (or generic) is furthered in the introduction of the armies of newborn vampires in *Eclipse*, which are reminiscent of popular representations of artificial-life clones. The newborns are, for the most part, indistinguishable from one another, and the threat lies in the faceless mass of sameness they present and in their misuse by their creators. Jasper describes the newborns as "volatile, wild, and almost impossible to control" as well as "incredibly powerful physically."[36] Enslaved by "their instincts and thus predictable," they "turn on each other as easily as on the army you point them at"; and while one is manageable, "fifteen, together are a nightmare": their threat lies in their "overwhelming numbers" and cohesiveness.[37] The newborns in Victoria's army are represented as expendable, disposable weapons void of subjectivity and civic rights. In this vein, the newborns are reminiscent of popular characterizations of artificial lifeforms proposed to be ethical replacements for humans in less desirable or morally objectionable professions. While the good vampires denounce the creation of newborn armies, disposing of the newborns does not raise ethical questions unless the newborns demonstrate individualist traits, as Bree does in *Eclipse*. Hence, Meyer's texts accept and do not question the utilitarian function of the clone; what is at stake here is not the clone's purpose or rights, but its creation.

Alluding to Mary Shelley's *Frankenstein*, Meyer terms her vampires as creators and presumes them to be male. In *Twilight*, for instance, when telling Bella Alice's story, Edward refers to "him" before the text confirms that James was the anonymous creator who made and subsequently abandoned her: "she doesn't know who *created* her. She woke alone. Whoever *made* her walked away, and none of us understand why, or how, *he* could. If she hadn't had that other sense, if she hadn't seen Jasper and Carlisle and known that she would someday become *one of us*, she probably would have turned into a total savage."[38] Edward assumes an uninstructed female vampire without proper indoctrination by a male patriarchal figure is bound to become an uncivilized monster, which is how Bella perceives Victoria, repeatedly using the term "wild" to describe her,[39] her gaze,[40] and her "chaotic" hair.[41] Upon first seeing Victoria, Bella notices the "woman was wilder" with "brilliant orange hair . . . filled with leaves and debris from the woods."[42] Linking Victoria to nature, Bella states, "Victoria had always seemed like a force of nature to me—like a hurricane moving toward the coast in a straight line—unavoidable, implacable, but predictable," and it is not until Victoria and Edward's final confrontation that Bella concedes (but does not question) her limiting Victoria's capabilities.[43] Although Alice, as part of the Cullen family, is presented as civilized, as are Esme and Rosalie, in his explanation of her civility

Edward chooses to focus only on Jasper and Carlisle, Alice's future mate and father-figure, thereby highlighting the imbalance of power along gender lines that is characteristic of the vampire family. In order to belong, to be "one of us," the civilized female vampire, like Alice, must willingly submit to the law of the father and take on a subservient role.

Yet female vampires repeatedly demonstrate a capacity for self-control, a prized quality in a responsible, civilized creator. Rosalie demonstrates her self-restraint when she resists feeding on Emmett in order to bring him to Carlisle to transform, and Edward assumes her fear of failure is why she was unable to create him herself.[44] Similarly, the newborn Bree in *Eclipse*, although unschooled, privileges self-preservation and restrains herself from attacking Bella after surrendering to the Cullens and the Volturi, only to be executed by the latter for having been created by an irresponsible creator.[45] Most illustrative, however, is Bella's self-restraint as a newborn in *Breaking Dawn*, which leads Edward to characterize her feats as exceptional, uncharacteristic anomalies. Read in tandem, however, a pattern is discernible and suggestive of a different ontological trajectory than the accepted patriarchal version Edward uses to indoctrinate Bella into "good" vampirehood or immortality.

Naturalizing the roles of male vampires as creators, the description of vampire saliva as a form of semen or "lubricant"[46] further supports the notion that creation is a biological male act. Reinforcing the ideal of the patrilineal, in the case of the vampire-human hybrids the venom is inherited only by the male progeny, as Nahuel, in *Breaking Dawn* states: "My sisters are not venomous, but whether that's due to gender or a random chance . . . who knows?"[47] Who indeed? Reminiscent of a newborn's latching at the breast, Renesmee first bites Bella's maternal human body. It is not her bite but Edward's venom that "heals" and "saves" Bella, thereby allowing her to fulfill her roles as wife and mother. Without Edward's venom, Bella would not have been transformed; without his venom-as-semen, Bella would not have been re/born as a vampire. The issue of linking the venom to a sex thus raises significant issues. If the hybrid fetus breaks or kills the human maternal body at birth, and the hybrid newborn's instinct is to bite the body from which it has emerged, an assumption can be made that the newborn hybrid bites the maternal body not to feed (as the nursing analogy suggests) but to heal the wounds inflicted by its birth, to transform the body to function as its caregiver. In *Breaking Dawn*, Hulien recalls that Pire (Nahuel's mother) "died quickly" and she was unable to "save her" sister; Nahuel then "bit" Hulien when she "tried to lift him from her [mother's] body" and "struggled through the underbrush" to curl up next to her and wait for her to transform into a vampire.[48] Without the venom in their bite, the female hybrid newborns do not have the capacity to heal/transform the maternal or surrogate mothers' bodies, thereby reiterating that the maternal body exists primarily to support the male offspring, which in turn creates her. In these cases, the male creator, an infant, is the maker of the female vampire; he symbolically creates the mother.

This is not to say that female vampires are incapable of re/producing. Alice is well-versed in the theory of vampire reproduction, as she tells Bella "the mechanics" of becoming a vampire.[49] Alice explains that when vampire venom enters the bloodstream it begins the transformation: "As long as the heart keeps beating, the poison spreads, healing, changing the body as it moves through it. Eventually the heart stops, and the conversion is finished."[50] While "venom" and "poison" have negative connotations, describing these compounds as "healing" and "changing the body" from within suggests the venom is akin to a benign pharmaceutical product with considerable side-effects, which contextualizes Meyer's texts in a capitalist age largely driven by a pharmaceutical economy. The shift from blood to saliva points to contemporary scientific advancements whereby saliva is used for DNA testing,[51] thereby reinforcing the anxieties over a pharmaceutically driven economy and genetic manipulation already at play. Also present is a discourse reminiscent of evangelical religions, as the transformation from human to vampire is described as a "conversion" necessary to "save" a human life by "healing" the body from within. Vampirism is portrayed, in part, as a play on born again Christianity. The "newborn" must abandon his or her former life, family, and friends, and, in the case of the good vampires, live a life of self-restraint and service.

While it is possible for female vampires to become creators in theory, the resistance in the texts to any of them actually doing so raise flags. For instance, when en route to Voltaria to rescue Edward, Bella presses Alice to "change" her: "Oh Alice, do it now! Bite me!"[52] After the Cullen vote to accept her into the family passes, Bella turns to Alice again: "Well, Alice . . . Where do you want to do this?"[53] Alice's response, however, implies homosexual panic that further distances women from the fields of creation as determined in the texts: "'Uh, Bella,' Alice interjected in an anxious voice. 'I don't think I'm *ready* for that.'"[54] If physically capable of creating vampires, why do Rosalie and Alice refuse to do so? Why does Bella, as a newborn vampire, resolve to alert Carlisle of the ramifications of using morphine during the conversion process in case "*he* ever needed to create another vampire?"[55] These questions can be addressed by examining the policing of reproduction more closely.

From the outset, the valorization of patrilineal heritage is established. Bella privileges Charlie's genes over her mother's when she describes herself as physically resembling her mother, but she undermines that connection by asserting, "She looks a lot like me, but she's prettier . . . I have too much Charlie in me."[56] She equally privileges Edward's genes over her own when she first imagines her "little nudger"[57] as male: "I don't know he's a boy . . . he's a little mystery. But I always see a boy in my head,"[58] "a tiny Edward"[59] with "Edward's eyes—green as his had been when he was human."[60] When seeing Renesmee, she marvels that "Edward *was* there in her features" and notes that "Charlie had a place in her thick curls, though their color matched Edward's."[61] Although she concedes that, as Edward tells her, Renesmee "has exactly [her human] color eyes,"[62] she later undermines her own resemblance when she thinks that Charlie recognizes her "eyes—*his eyes*—copied exactly into [Renesmee's] perfect face" when he first meets her.[63] The fertile female body (Bella's, her mother's) thus functions primarily as an incubator for the reproduction of male genes. As the female human is distanced from her labor, from the product her body produces, she operates merely as the means to re-produce the modes of production physically (her body as machinery capable of producing another body) and ideologically (participating in, accepting, and instilling patriarchal ideology).

Female subservience is further implied as the male creators, again remi-niscent of Victor Frankenstein, are charged with taking responsibility over their creations, whereas the female creators are more severely treated; by the conclusion of the saga, the female creators have been eradicated and none of them are given a voice. For instance, Nahuel rejects his biological father Joham who, although he comes back to resume his paternal duties, first aban-dons a pregnant Pire and her newborn. Nahuel has been raised to repudiate Joham as a monster, and his rejection of him lies in his characterization of him as a Nazi-like invader conducting experiments on indigenous peoples of the Amazon: "Joham . . . considers himself a scientist. He thinks he's creating a new super-race."[64] By the conclusion of the saga, Joham, the "immortal so fond of experimentation," is presumed to be stopped because the Volturi will "speak" with him,[65] but the text is inconclusive as to what exactly will be the outcome of the Volturi's intervention.

In contrast, female vampires who usurp their constricting supportive roles by taking on the role of creator are demonized and punished directly. In *Eclipse*, Maria's initial strategizing for regaining her territory in Mexico at first marks her as a careful and conscientious creator; as Jasper recalls, "She wanted a superior army, so she sought out specific humans who had poten-tial. Then she gave us much more attention, more training than anyone else had bothered with. She taught us to fight, and she taught us to be invisible to humans."[66] However, the newborns "meant little . . . they were pawns, they were disposable," and when Jasper recognizes a newborn male as "civilized,"[67] he hails him as a subject, questions Maria's dominance, and eventually deserts her. Maria's power is then fractured by her greed to acquire more territory, which in turn leads to her becoming an irresponsible creator and to her downfall. Maria serves as a parallel for Victoria, who creates a newborn army to carry out her vendetta, and it is presumed (for she is never actually given a voice) that she cares little for her newborns because she does not take proper responsibility from the get-go: "she doesn't know what she's doing, so the newborns are all out of control."[68] Jasper's comment "[W]hoever made them just set them loose"[69] undermines Victoria's parental and intellectual capabilities. Unlike as with James, Victoria's mate who is introduced in *Twilight* and destroyed in the background of Bella's consciousness, Victoria's destruction in *Eclipse* is brutally explicit as her dismemberment takes place literally in front of Bella. Even the more civilized and responsible female creator, Carlisle's female counterpart (Tanya's mother), who, like Carlisle, fulfills her desire for companionship by creating daughters over a spouse, steps outside the bounds of acceptable procreation when she creates and protects an outlawed being, an immortal child.[70] Tanya's mother is punished literally and symbolically by the Volturi, by the law, for taking motherhood into her own hands. Siding with the law, her legal daughters refute their mother's actions and participate in the policing of her transgression and its aftermath.

In contrast, Carlisle, a curious blend of Frankensteinian creator and monster, is offered as a positive example of a conscientious creator. His desire for a companion is resolved when he fulfills Elizabeth's dying request and saves her son, Edward; unlike Shelley's monster's desire for a spousal companion, which horrifies Victor as he thinks of the possibility of their biological reproduction,[71] Carlisle's ideal companion is not a spouse but a perfect child, a son. Although Carlisle's behavior and actions are legitimized and praised throughout the saga, there is an unnerving slip that suggests otherwise. In *Breaking Dawn*, when Jacob "randomly" wonders "what [his] chromosomes are like," Carlisle reveals he satisfied his scientific curiosity while Jacob was unconscious. Looking embarrassed, he tells Jacob, "I'm sorry. I should have asked . . . I promise you that I did *not* mean you any harm. It's just that . . . I find your species fascinating. I suppose that the elements of vampiric nature have come to seem commonplace to me over the centuries. Your family's divergence from humanity is much more interesting. Magical, almost."[72] Although Carlisle's unethical behavior is rapidly dismissed, his revelation takes on more ominous overtones when we consider the history of Carlisle's and Jacob's connection. Carlisle, a 16th-century-born Englishman, is a settler-invader in the New World who enters into a treaty with the Quileutes upon arrival in the early 20th century. The saga didactically polarizes the vampires and the werewolf/shapeshifters along postcolonial binaries like caucasian/native, wealthy/underprivileged, and technological/natural. Whereas the discourse used to describe vampiric reproduction includes words like "theory" and "mechanics," and the process is clinically described, the genetic mutation in the werewolf/shifter's transformation is described as part of an oral, living history as well as "magical." Carlisle has evolved into a modern physician who nevertheless finds Jacob's body and his people "fascinating" specimens for scientific study. "Magical," in a postcolonial context, thus implies a civilized/ primitive binary distinction.

Carlisle's use of Jacob's body while he is an unconscious subject who has not given consent is suggestive of the use of Native Americans for scientific experimentation in the 20th century. Maureen Lux, for instance, confronts the use of the Qu'Appelle as test subjects for the tuberculosis vaccine in 1933 in southern Saskatchewan. As she notes, it "was a rather easy matter to gain access to boarding school students, where school principals, not parents, consented to have students examined (sic) and tested."[73] Simi- larly, Jane Lawrence discusses the routine sterilization of Native American women in the 1960s and 1970s. This "common occurrence" is described by Bertha Medicine Bull as follows: two fifteen year-old girls "were having appendectomies when the doctors sterilized them without their knowledge or consent."[74] Although Carlisle does not sterilize or use Jacob's body for medical testing, his indiscretion is nevertheless a violation that, when con- textualized historically, reconciles his monstrosity with his racial, socioeco- nomic, and sexual subject positions.

Alienating vampire women from the sphere of pro/creation then, from their (potential) labor, Meyer's saga further marks them as being in a state of Lacanian lack. Most of the female characters who experience transformations link their changes to their unfulfilled desires of motherhood, like Esme and Rosalie. It is Leah's experiences as a werewolf/shifter in *Breaking Dawn*, how- ever, that best illustrate this point. Leah's horror at joining Sam's pack has less to do with being subjected to a homosocial world that antagonizes her and more to do with *why* her body has changed; as she tells Jacob, "There's some- thing wrong with me. I don't have the ability to pass on the gene, apparently, despite my stellar bloodlines. So I become a freak—the girlie-wolf—good for nothing else. I'm a genetic dead end and we both know it."[75] Leah's alien- ation within the pack is largely a result of being a different-gendered being, a non-woman/non-man in a world of men. Of interest, in the film adaptation *Breaking Dawn, Part I*,[76] the exchange between Leah (Julia Jones) and Jacob (Taylor Lautner) is significantly shortened and changed; Leah states she wishes she could "imprint on someone" as a means of escaping her position as the rejected ex-girlfriend of the werewolf/shifter pack leader, Sam (Chaske Spencer), thereby bypassing the issue of reproduction altogether. In omitting from the dialogue Leah's concerns over her fertility, the film narrative shifts to demean her as a simple, jilted lover: a jealous woman.

While Edward is repeatedly described as being "frozen" throughout the saga, in part because of his body temperature and solid mass and in part because that is his reaction to unforeseen developments or being in a state of momentary shock, Bella takes this a step further in *Breaking Dawn* when she echoes Jacob and Meyer in her speculation as to why female vampires cannot carry out a pregnancy. Meyer explains she avoided addressing the issue of male vampire fertility directly and concentrated instead on "the female half of the equation—female vampires cannot have children because their bodies no longer change in any aspect. There is no changing cycle to begin with, and their bodies couldn't expand to fit a growing child, either."[77] Bella, parroting Meyer, is at odds with what an advanced biology student should know about biological reproduction, and with what she has already learned in scrutinizing the Volturi's bodies. Upon meeting the Volturi, Bella notes the color of Aro's eyes is "clouded, milky"; his skin is "translucently white, like onionskin, and it looked just as delicate"; and his cheek seems "powdery, like chalk."[78] His skin is "hard, but . . . brittle—shale rather than granite."[79] Since the bodies of the ancient vampires mark the ageing process, it stands to reason that their bodies do change, albeit at a much slower pace than those of humans.

It thus falls to human women to play a role in the biological process of reproduction, and it is within these limits that the value of a fertile human woman is determined. As Bella strives to assert her right to her body, to choose between a human or vampire existence, Edward and Jacob strive to assert their control over her body by insisting that she remain human, or rather, fertile. By *Eclipse*, the debate is explicitly hinged on a single human experience: procreative heterosexual intercourse. Conflicted between a future with Edward and a future with Jacob, Bella envisions "the bobbing heads of two small, black-haired children, running away from [her] into the familiar forest" when she realizes she is in love with Jacob and fast-forwards to what their future could be.[80] Even in her vision, her presumed children are more closely associated with Jacob's dominant genes and the forest she associates with La Push; the children are running *from* rather than *to* her. In *Breaking Dawn*, Edward and Jacob both envision *their* (and in keeping with the erotic triangle each others') offspring growing inside Bella's body, effectively alienating the human woman from her body and reproductive labor. When Jacob first sees Bella's pregnant body, he thinks, "I didn't want to imagine him inside her. I didn't want to know that something I hated so much had taken root *in the body I loved*."[81] For Jacob, Bella's body is "distorted,"[82] and when Edward proposes an alternative—"If it's a child she wants, she can have it. She can have half a dozen babies . . . She can have puppies"[83]—Jacob has an image of Bella pregnant "in a more natural way. Round with *my* child."[84] In their exchange, neither Edward nor Jacob recognizes Bella's offspring as hers; while Edward is willing to let her have a child with another man, his reference to "puppies" (stemming from the Cullens' derogatory term, "dog," for the werewolf/shifter) reveals his acknowledgement of the parental claim on the offspring. Thus Bella can have *Jacob's* child if she wants, but neither his nor Edward's is to be regarded as *Bella's*. The dehumanization of Bella is further underscored by Edward's and Jacob's exclusive focus on her body rather than on her person, which reiterates the value of her function rather than that of her subjectivity.

Drawing on pro-choice rhetoric, the representation of Bella's pregnancy and delivery furthers the public debate over abortion. The female characters (Bella, Rosalie, Esme, and to a lesser extent Leah) band together in affirming Bella's right to choose—to choose to carry out her pregnancy that is, regardless of the consequences to her own bodily health—and keep the male characters (Edward, Carlisle, and Jacob) from exerting control over her body/fetus. When Jacob first confronts Edward about Bella's pregnancy, he wonders why Edward has allowed the pregnancy to continue: "'She won't *let* you.' The sarcasm was acid on my tongue. 'Did you ever notice that she's exactly as strong as a normal hundred-and-ten pound human girl? How stupid are you vamps? Hold her down and knock her out with drugs.'"[85] Edward's response, "I wanted to" and "Carlisle would have,"[86] makes it clear that they seek to assert their dominance and control over Bella's body (what is best for Bella), deeming her mentally and emotionally incapable and easily manipulated by Rosalie's presumed selfish agenda. The power struggle splits the Cullen household into supporting either Rosalie or Edward, but significantly leaving Bella, the latest addition to the Cullen clan, outside the decision-making process altogether.[87] Interestingly, in the film adaptation, the gender conflict is eliminated as two Cullen female characters take on the debate: while Rosalie takes on the pro-life rhetoric by insisting Alice refer to the "baby," Alice counters with pro-choice rhetoric by consistently referring to "the fetus." As in the book, however, Bella is left outside the debate.

Bella's home-birth emergency cesarean effectively bridges various contemporary and contentious approaches to childbirth, reconciling by necessity the homeopathic and medicalized alternatives. In doing so, the description of the procedure further displaces the abject body by focusing on the monstrous hybrid it produces. As Valerius notes, "[A]bortion remains a contested issue. In response to its legalization, an anti-abortion movement has emerged and reframed the debate, asserting the legal and political rights of the unborn in opposition to the rights of women."[88] Conservative readings of Meyer's saga describe *Breaking Dawn* as "a piece of anti-abortion rhetoric."[89] Such readings are supported by Edward's acceptance of carrying out the pregnancy once he identifies the fetus as a sentient being with "remarkably developed mental facilities"[90] and the capacity to love: "He . . . *loves* her,"[91] "absolutely *adores* [her]."[92] Once on board, he takes over and establishes his role as Bella's physician, savior, and creator, displacing Rosalie, who has protected the pro-life position, as she fails in the delivery (she loses control), literally leaving the actual birth to Edward and Jacob and excluding the women from the birth scene. Once Edward adopts the pro-life line, he is naturalized as a proper father-figure and legitimized as a conscientious creator. It is his foresight and ingenuity—extracting and saving his venom to inject into Bella's heart after performing a caesarian with his teeth—that "saves" Bella and child, making good on the text's promise that he is Carlisle's prodigal son.

Similarly, Bella's pregnancy works to reposition Jacob in his proper patrilineal place. Jacob accepts his patrilineal inheritance, being an Alpha leader, when he challenges Sam's decisions to protect Bella's body and offspring from the pack. His genetic desire goes so far as to remap onto the body of the newborn hybrid when Bella's body is no longer fertile. First he voices his fear over Bella's pregnant (abject) body: "How many times had I imagined her naked? Now I couldn't look. I was afraid to have these memories in my head."[93] Describing Bella's body as a "broken, bled-out, mangled corpse," Jacob notes, "[T]his body has no more draw for me. The senseless need to be near her had vanished. Or maybe *moved* was a better word."[94] Disturbingly, Jacob transfers his desire onto that of another future fertile female, Renesmee, thereby ensuring the potential for passing on his inherited genetic quirk: "It was the baby girl in the blond vampire's arms that held me here now."[95] Pregnancy, labor and delivery, and debates about abortion, then, have little to do with female bodies. The abject female body is used to enable male characters to take on more prominent social roles, thereby suggesting that class is biologically, rather than socially, determined.

Bella's abject body thus emphasizes the function of the fertile woman to support and enhance the subjectivity of men and reconciles the natural/medical tension at play. The rupture of Bella's body coincides with the rupture of her placenta, yet another inadequacy that preempts the emergency cesarean over the planned one that Jacob finds repulsive. As in *Rosemary's Baby*, Bella is caught in the midst of two competing narratives: woman-centered midwifery versus institutionalized, male-centered medicine. Like Rosemary, Bella's "traumatic home delivery is not the positive experience proposed by a homeopathic health movement as a corrective to the over-medicalization of childbirth in hospitals,"[96] as Carlisle's library/office has been turned into a makeshift hospital delivery room, and she, like Rosemary, is largely "unconscious for the delivery of her baby and entirely alienated from the experience of childbirth."[97] In Meyer's text, this experience is doubled as Bella's alienation also coincides with her own birth as a vampire, her taking on a different abject body. Symbolically, Bella's human life ends when she births Renesmee, when she completes her biological function.

The abortion debate is then reconfigured into an ethical debate over genetic experimentation when Renesmee's right to exist is brought into question. Although Renesmee's birth is the result of ignorance rather than premeditated scientific experimentation like that of Johan's offspring, and her existence is therefore said to be natural rather than contrived, her right to be recognized as a proper subject—determined by the Volturi as one who can be subjugated by the law—is contested because she is a categorical unknown: "[W]e know nothing of what she will become!"[98] Edward's argument in her defense supports essentialist notions of sex as he differentiates his role as her "*biological father*" rather than as her "creator," as he is Bella's.[99] It is with this issue that the contradictions in the text are tangible, thereby implicitly questioning the ethics and science of vampiric reproduction.

Serving a utilitarian function (companionship or soldiering territory), Meyer's texts further draw on religious metaphors in an attempt to define vampire reproduction as an accepted method of "saving" humans. The idea that death means "too much waste," a concept that is introduced in Carlisle's thoughts to justify "saving" Rosalie, for instance,[100] points to socioscientific perspectives that see the human body in its capacity for saving or enhancing human life, like transplanting organs or banking blood and plasma for transfusions. Taken further, cryogenically preserving harvested organs, banking umbilical cords to preserve the stem-cells, and cloning cells are portrayed as benign, quasi-natural methods that help sustain, prolong, enhance, and possibly cure multiple, biologically related human bodies. Yet the contentious debates over the subjectivity of hybrid bodies privilege the natural over the scientific (or experimental), which call into question the very experimentation associated with such scientific advancements. Hence, although Meyer's text explicitly champions biological reproduction and fetal subjectivity, concessions that challenge natural or biological notions of sex seem plausible. Seemingly outside this contradictory stance lies the abject female body of the seemingly unchanging vampire and werewolf/shifter woman which is frozen, in stasis, waiting for new societal and ideological developments to allow it to fulfill its potential beyond the reproductive capabilities and restrictions of its human counterpart.

Notes

1. Stephenie Meyer, *Twilight* (New York: Little, Brown and Company, 2006), 19.
2. Meyer, *Twilight*, 50.
3. Meyer, *Twilight*, 62.

4. Meyer, *Twilight*, 260.

5. Meyer, *Twilight*, 463.

6. Meyer, *Twilight*, 206, 340.

7. Stephenie Meyer, *New Moon* (New York: Little, Brown and Company, 2008), 478.

8. Stephenie Meyer, *Breaking Dawn* (New York: Little, Brown and Company, 2008), 466.

9. Meyer, *Twilight*, 199.

10. Meyer, *Twilight*, 204.

11. This sentiment was raised during the discussion of the panel All that Glitters II, where a version of this paper was presented as part of the Vampires: Myths of the Past, Present and Future conference held at the University of London, November 3, 2011.

12. *Nosferatu, eine Symphonie des Grauens*, dir. F. W. Murnau, 1922.

13. Nina Auerbach, *Our Vampires, Ourselves* (Chicago: University of Chicago Press, 1995).

14. Judith E. Johnson, "Women and Vampires: Nightmare or Utopia?" *Kenyon Review New Series* 15 (1993): 75.

15. Melissa Ames, "Vamping Up Sex: Audience, Age, & Portrayals of Sexuality in Vampire Narratives," *Journal of Dracula Studies* 12 (2010): 83.

16. Ames, "Vamping Up Sex," 87.

17. Meyer, *New Moon*, 474. Bella's ambition, evident here in her desire to become a superhero in her own right, is upward mobility. Although she continuously denies her interest in Edward's (or the Cullens') money, her desire for immortality is not only a desire for eternity with her love interest but, symbolically, for eternity as a super-being and, more specifically, as a Cullen (with all the monetary privileges that being a member of that powerful and influential family entails).

18. Meyer, *Twilight*, 81.

19. Caitlin Flanagan, "What Girls Want," *Atlantic*, December 2008, www.theatlantic.com/magazine/archive/2008/12/what-girls-want/7161/.

20. Meyer, *Breaking Dawn*, 237.

21. Meyer, *Breaking Dawn*, 402.

22. Cord Blood Bank of Canada (CBBC), www.cordbloodbankofcanada.com/whybank.html.

23. Cord Blood Bank.

24. Human Genome Project (HGM), www.ornl.gov/sci/techresources/Human_Genome/elsi/cloning.shtml; my emphasis.

25. American Medical Association, "The Ethics of Human Cloning," www.ama-assn.org/resources/doc/ethics/report98.pdf.

26. Stephenie Meyer, *Eclipse* (New York: Little, Brown and Company, 2007), 31.

27. Meyer, *Eclipse*, 249.

28. Meyer, *Eclipse*, 251.

29. Meyer, *Eclipse*, 251.

30. Meyer, *Breaking Dawn*, 403.

31. Meyer, *Breaking Dawn*, 467.

32. Meyer, *Breaking Dawn*, 474.

33. Human Genome Project.

34. Meyer, *Breaking Dawn*, 191.

35. Meyer, *Breaking Dawn*, 195; my emphasis.

36. Meyer, *Eclipse*, 290.

37. Meyer, *Eclipse*, 290.

38. Meyer, *Twilight*, 291; my emphasis.

39. Meyer, *Eclipse*, 544.

40. Meyer, *Eclipse*, 542.

41. Meyer, *Twilight*, 376.

42. Meyer, *Twilight*, 376.

43. Meyer, *Eclipse*, 387.

44. Meyer, *Twilight*, 289.

45. Meyer, *Eclipse*, 578.

46. Stephenie Meyer, "Frequently Asked Questions," The Official Website of Stephanie Meyer, www.stepheniemeyer.com/bd_faq.html.

47. Meyer, *Breaking Dawn*, 737.

48. Meyer, *Breaking Dawn*, 735–36.

49. Meyer, *Twilight*, 413.

50. Meyer, *Twilight*, 414.

51. Shohini Chaudhuri, "Visit of the Body Snatchers: Alien Invasion Themes in Vampire Narratives," *Camera Obscura* 40–41 (1997): 181–98.

52. Meyer, *New Moon*, 436.

53. Meyer, *New Moon*, 535.

54. Meyer, *New Moon*, 535.

55. Meyer, *Breaking Dawn*, 397 (my emphasis).

56. Meyer, *Twilight*, 105.

57. Meyer, *Breaking Dawn*, 133.

58. Meyer, *Breaking Dawn*, 192.

59. Meyer, *Breaking Dawn*, 128.

60. Meyer, *Breaking Dawn*, 132.

61. Meyer, *Breaking Dawn*, 439.

62. Meyer, *Breaking Dawn*, 429.

63. Meyer, *Breaking Dawn*, 509 (my emphasis).

64. Meyer, *Breaking Dawn*, 737.

65. Meyer, *Breaking Dawn*, 738.

66. Meyer, *Eclipse*, 295–96.

67. Meyer, *Eclipse*, 298.

68. Meyer, *Eclipse*, 388.

69. Meyer, *Eclipse*, 303.

70. Interestingly, both choose same-sex child companions, but the immortal child in question is male.

71. His horror also leads him to destroy the second body he assembled prior to animating it, which in turn leads his creature to vengeance, beginning by depriving Victor of his spousal companion, Elizabeth.

72. Meyer, *Breaking Dawn*, 237.

73. Maureen Lux, "Perfect Subjects: Race, Tuberculosis, and the Qu'Appelle BCG Vaccine Trial," *Canadian Bulletin of Medical History* 15 (1998): 284–85.

74. Jane Lawrence, "The Indian Health Service and the Sterilization of Native American Women," *American Indian Quarterly* 24 (2000): 400.

75. Meyer, *Breaking Dawn*, 318.

76. *Breaking Dawn, Part I*, dir. Bill Condon, 2011.

77. Meyer, "Frequently Asked Questions."

78. Meyer, *New Moon*, 467.

79. Meyer, *New Moon*, 473.

80. Meyer, *Eclipse*, 529.

81. Meyer, *Breaking Dawn*, 174; my emphasis.

82. Meyer, *Breaking Dawn*, 182.

83. Meyer, *Breaking Dawn*, 180.

84. Meyer, *Breaking Dawn*, 182.

85. Meyer, *Breaking Dawn*, 178.

86. Meyer, *Breaking Dawn*, 178.

87. Meyer, *Breaking Dawn*, 178.

88. Karyn Valerius, "'Rosemary's Baby,' Gothic Pregnancy, and Fetal Subjects," *College Literature* 32 (2005): 129.

89. Ames, "Vamping Up Sex," 89.

90. Meyer, *Breaking Dawn*, 339.

91. Meyer, *Breaking Dawn*, 339.

92. Meyer, *Breaking Dawn*, 327.

93. Meyer, *Breaking Dawn*, 349.

94. Meyer, *Breaking Dawn*, 355.

95. Meyer, *Breaking Dawn*, 360.

96. Valerius, "'Rosemary's Baby,'" 127.

97. Valerius, "'Rosemary's Baby,'" 127.

98. Meyer, *Breaking Dawn*, 715–16.

99. Meyer, *Breaking Dawn*, 586.

100. Meyer, *Eclipse*, 161.

15

The Vampire from an Evolutionary Perspective in Japanese Animation: *Blood+*

Burcu Genç

FROM EARLIEST HISTORY, the human mind conceived of vampires. "One of the earliest pieces of writing that archaeologists have discovered was not a love poem, recipe, or religious text but rather a magical spell written around 4000 B.C. . . . by a mother in an attempt to keep her child safe from the attack of the EKIMMOU, a type of vampiric spirit."[1] This mythical creature, the vampire, whose origin has remained a mystery throughout the centuries, continues to haunt our minds today. Like an organic being that is continuously evolving, the vampire also has never ceased to change in response to the altering conditions of life. In each book or film, it has gained a new ability or quality and has become stronger. However, nothing inspires discussion of what the vampire really is and where it comes from as much as the bodily form it takes. Vampires have appeared as monsters, bats, and wolves. Although none of these forms has stayed as popular as the human form, the vampire has been widely accepted to be beastly and monstrous due to its savage nature and lust for blood. Yet "monsters have a double function . . . simultaneously marking the boundaries between the normal and the pathological but also exposing the fragility of the very taken-for-grantedness of such categories."[2] Similarly, a quest for the origins of the vampire consolidates the fragility of accepted boundaries:

> It is the monster that used to be human; it is the undead that used to be alive; it is the monster that *looks like us*. We look into the mirror it provides and we see a version of ourselves. Or, more accurately, keeping in mind the orthodoxy that vampires cast no mirror reflections, we look into the mirror and see nothing *but* ourselves.[3]

Accordingly, this chapter intends to investigate the ways in which boundaries are constructed between humans and vampires by employing contemporary evolutionary discourse and examining how these boundaries are transcended in *Blood+*, a popular Japanese anime series. Partly based on a discourse of evolution and genetics, *Blood+* paves the way for a change in our perception of the vampire by blurring the differences between us and them, attributing to vampires a scientific reality rather than a place in fantasy. The blurring of boundaries between humans and vampires by means of evolutionary discourse and genetics leads to a change in the positions of the villain and the victim. In *Blood+*, for example, Amshel Goldsmith, a human willingly turned vampire and Diva's chevalier, abuses her out of his desire for knowledge.

A blood feud between two twin vampire sisters, Saya and Diva, creates the main story in the *Blood+* series. They are discovered within the womb of a dead chiropteran by biologists Amshel and George, who bring up the twins under different conditions. While George raises Saya just like an ordinary human child, Diva is kept in prison. It is when Saya releases her that Diva fights furiously, killing George while turning Amshel into a vampire. After this incident, Saya swears to avenge the death of George and destroy all chiropterans who bring disaster to humanity, so she, with her chevalier, Haji, sets out with this aim. We learn about these incidents dating back to the mid-19th century through flashbacks, as Saya remembers her past. In the present day, Diva has five chevaliers: Amshel, Solomon, Nathan, Karl, and James, in addition to the Cinq Flèches group led by them. Saya has only one chevalier and a human group called the Red Shield, led by descendants of George, the biologist. The Red Shield group suspects that Cinq Flèches is creating artificial vampires with a substance called Delta-67. With the aim of stopping Cinq Flèches, Red Shield both seeks Saya as support and supports her in return.

Chiropterans are different from vampires in various respects. These creatures are not affected by sunlight nor do they sleep during the day. More importantly, they have a strict class hierarchy in terms of their power and status. Ordinary chiropterans generally confront us as humans-turned-vampires in the series. They cannot hold their former human bodily forms and are not necessarily intelligent beings. They usually cannot talk or express any sentiments. They cannot be killed with ordinary guns or by humans due to their high level of healing powers. Only chiropterans have the power to kill one another. In their three-part hierarchy, chevaliers occupy the second order with their massive power and ability to move very quickly. Unlike ordinary chiropterans, they can hold their former human bodily forms and are charged with a duty to protect the queen or mother chiropteran. The chevaliers' strength and difference from an ordinary chiropteran stems from the fact that they become chevaliers by drinking the blood of the queen.

The only and most important mystery about chiropterans is how the queen first came into being. At the time when Amshel and George found both babies, Diva and Saya, in the womb of a dead chiropteran, the twins were in human form. More importantly, during the entire series, we do not see a single scene where either of them assumes another bodily appearance. As a matter of fact, during the times when Saya suffers from memory loss, forgetting that she is a chiropteran, she still keeps her human bodily form. These images contribute to the further blurring of boundaries between human and vampires. However, none of these images provides us with scientific information on the issue as much as crucial research made on humans newly turned into chiropterans, including Saya's little brother, Riku, from her adoptive family. After Diva kills Saya's little brother by sucking his blood, Saya gives a second life to him with her own blood. Up to this point, the birth of a new chiropteran is the same as the birth of a vampire. But the rest of the story does not go quite the same way. Riku stays unconscious for days. During that time, he is kept in a laboratory to be observed and examined. As a result of various tests, it is discovered that vampires and humans are almost the same genetically. The whole difference between the two stems from one genetic nucleotide that hides itself in the process of transformation. Julia, a Red Shield researcher, and professor Collins talk about the possibility of an unknown element in Riku's blood as an answer to the difference between humans and chiropterans:

> Julia: It [The nucleotide] was isolated from blood cell DNA taken from Riku. Clearly, it does not match with any of the four nucleotides, adenine, guanine, cytosine and thymine.
>
> Professor Collins: The Fifth nucleotide?
>
> Julia: I've never heard anything like this. It seems that we're very close to the answer. ("The Red Shield" 12:14–36)

The story is a familiar one. In fact, it immediately evokes a news article from the late 1990s concerning the genetic similarity between humans and chimpanzees. Beneath the headline "It's official. He is almost human,"[4] Elain L. Graham goes on to explain the significance of this genetic similarity when she states,

> The gene is a potent object of desire, and carries multiple associations. It serves as a convenient and tangible element that comes to stand vicariously for the complex mixture of environment, sociability, natural selection and biology which separates "human" from "almost human." The gene . . . thereby comes to represent what it means to be human . . . where it is a tiny configuration of genetic material, DNA, that plays the decisive role in negotiating the mixture

of curiosity and anxiety engendered by a blurring of the boundaries between "us" and "them."[5]

As Charles Darwin himself explained in *On the Origin of Species*, "[N]o one definition has as yet satisfied all naturalists; yet every naturalist knows vaguely what he means when he speaks of a species."[6] What is defined as a species might well be called "variety." The distinction between the two terms is quite vague and arbitrary. In any case, whether distinct species or related varieties, it has been difficult to draw a conclusion about the relationship between humans and vampires because vampirism has never been conceived as a biological condition until the rise of purebloods or investigations from a scientific perspective of literary works and films.[7] Vampires have always remained within the borders of fancy. As *Blood+* draws our attention to the difference between humans and vampires on a genetic level, it is no longer hard to distinguish between them as two species. However, this analysis on a genetic level with regard to the relation between humans and vampires does not refute the blurring of the boundaries within which the vampire could be established as a distinct species because, in Darwinian terms, a species is a "strongly-marked and well-defined" variety.[8] He describes the transition from variety to species with an emphasis on the origin from a common parent: "[A]llied species have descended from a common parent; and during the process of modification [one] has become adapted to the conditions of life . . . and exterminated its original parent and all the transitional varieties between its past and present states."[9]

Darwin's suggestion of allied species through a common parent can be one of the explanations for the mysterious existence of the queen chiropteran. It suggests that the queen, the strongest of all chiropterans and most unique, came into being under natural variation over a long time period by diverging from human beings. However, even without a common parent, variation and genetic shifts are possible. As Juengst notes, species are not "static collections of organisms that can be 'preserved' against change like a can of fruit; they wax and wane with every birth and death and their genetic complexions shift across time and space."[10] Therefore, in addition to diverging from her allied species, humanity, the queen might have come into being as a result of genetic shifts over time.

On the other hand, Darwin's allied species through a common parent does not bring any light to bear on chevaliers and their relationship to human beings. It would be more accurate to define chevaliers from a transhumanist point of view. Within transhumanist borders, vampires can be identified as a future form or evolved form of human beings. Julian Savulescu, in his article "The Human Prejudice and Moral Status of Enhanced Beings," defines transhumans as "humans who have been so significantly modified and enhanced that there are significant non-human characteristics, e.g., chimeras, cyborgs."[11] Genetic enhancement of human beings is possible through a process called "transgenesis." "Transgenesis could be used to introduce gene coding for superior physical abilities from other animals. For example, humans could have the hearing of dogs, the visual acuity of hawks, the night vision of owls, or even be able to navigate by sonar employed from bats."[12] All this may sound fanciful and unreal. Yet "it has been possible since about the 1980s to transfer genes taken from one species to another . . . There is no reason why genes from other species could not be transferred to human beings, creating transgenic humans."[13] The act of drinking the blood of the queen and as a result gaining longevity, physical strength and agility as well as massive supernatural powers conjures up in our minds the notion of *Blood+* as a symbol of transgenesis. Amshel Goldsmith is the first chevalier who willingly becomes a vampire, not only out of a curiosity to discover the truth about chiropterans but most importantly to become an enhanced human being. His own words while talking to Saya in the guise of a woman called Lisa implies this:

> Lisa: Why do the Chiroptera exist? Have you thought of what that means?
>
> Saya: What it means?
>
> Lisa: Chiroptera and humans . . .Why are they both allowed to exist? Where did we come from and where are we going? What do you think? ("Broken Heart," 8:58–9.18)

Vampires are created and depicted in *Blood+* in a unique way. Perhaps it would not be wrong to claim that *Blood+* is among the few depictions that take a novel approach to vampires. After Bram Stoker's *Dracula*, it is possible to see many different vampires with different levels of powers. Yet the uniqueness of *Blood+* is not rooted in how powerful its vampires are or what kind of supernatural powers they are armored with. Instead, the series derives its originality from the domestication of the supernatural by breaking the boundaries between humans and vampires. Rosemary Jackson argues in "Fantasies of Absence" that "[modern fantasy] does not invent supernatural regions, but presents a natural world inverted into something strange, something 'other.' It becomes 'domesticated,' humanized, turning from transcendental explorations to transcriptions of a human condition."[14] In the postmodern age, the vampire—with its physical strength, supernatural powers and longevity—"has been converted into a metaphor to hold up the mirror to our own human desires and anxieties."[15]

The fight between Cinq Flèche and Red Shield is a reflection of these human desires and anxieties. In fact, both Cinq Flèche and Red Shield can be argued to replace, to a certain extent, real-life transhumanists and bioconservatives. "Transhumanists on one side . . . believe that a wide range of enhancements should be developed and that people should be free to use them to transform themselves in quite radical ways; and bioconservatives on the other . . . believe that we should not substantially alter human biology or the human condition."[16] In line with the transhumanists, Amshel Goldsmith's motive behind his Delta-67 project is not free from the idea of human modification and enhancement. On the other hand, Red Shield is against this project. When Saya's adoptive father turns into a chiropteran after being caught by the men of the Cinq Flèche group, Red Shield reaffirms its commitment to fight and stop them. Red Shield considers this project destructive of humanity because, as most bioconservatives conclude regarding drastic alteration of the current human condition, "[t]he first victim of transhumanism might be equality . . . If we start transforming ourselves into something superior, what rights will these enhanced creatures claim, and what rights will they possess when compared to those left behind? If some move ahead, can anyone afford not to follow?"[17]

The concerns of Red Shield are justifiable. Amshel appears in the series as exactly the kind of twisted transhumanist that bioconservatives oppose. His conversation with Saya towards the end of the series shows this clearly:

> Saya: You turned humans into chiroptera with those drugs of yours and created tools of warfare like the Schiff . . .
>
> Amshel: Because that is what humans want. Do you know what runs through the battlefield?
>
> Saya: What runs through?
>
> Amshel: Blood, sweat, tears and money. To a greater or a lesser extent, humans, even now, are continuing with their foolish wars. Everything is for the sake of what runs through there. I am simply approaching humans who set up conflicts and supplying them with what they want. ("Skyscraper Opera," 19:01–36)

Although Amshel Goldsmith prides himself on being a chiropteran with massive powers, in his Delta-67 project he creates with Diva's blood chiropterans that are disposable. He does not aim for equality for all. These disposable chiropterans are called "Schiff." They are created to be used as weapons, so they are not supposed to have intelligence or emotions. In the first trial, Amshel Goldsmith cannot achieve his aim and the Schiffs turn out to have intelligence and emotions. Their characteristics are actually closer to the characteristics of vampires, with which we are familiar. They cannot walk in the sun, and the weakness of their bodies require that they drink blood often. Further, in a short time, their bodies become crystallized and they die despite their efforts to stay alive. Schiffs are the first group that suffers from Amshel

Goldsmith's ambitions for power. In his second trial, Amshel manages to create artificial chiropterans/vampires that are agile and powerful yet without emotions, like robots. To test them, he organizes a concert for Diva and has food containing the substance Delta-67 distributed to people in the concert area. People who eat the food turn into an ordinary kind of chiropteran upon hearing the singing of Diva. The reason why Delta-67 can turn people into chiropterans is that Delta-67 is "made from the unique blood type . . . of a beautiful girl [Diva]," as one of the researchers who works on the project in Vietnam says ("Moon over Ekaterinburg," 17:13–21). However, as soon as these people turn into chiropterans, Amshel orders his artificial vampires to kill the newly born chiropterans. He does this because he has it in mind to sell these artificial vampires to governments as weaponry. These concert-goers become chiropterans without their consent and suffer death as test subjects of Amshel's master plan.

The third and the most important death that comes as a result of Amshel's ambition is Diva's. After Saya's younger brother becomes a chevalier, Diva catches him and sucks all of his blood. At the beginning of the second season, we learn that Diva is pregnant. How she manages this remains a mystery be-cause the scene is cut as soon as she starts to drink Riku's blood. Whether it is through a sexual union or a different kind of ritual that belongs to chirop-terans is not possible to tell. However, this pregnancy costs Diva dearly in her final battle against her sister, Saya, because, due to the pregnancy, the power of her blood decreases. When both sisters thrust their swords covered with their blood into one another, nothing happens to Saya but Diva dies. From the very beginning of the series, we have known that their blood is poisonous to one another. However, at the end, this proves to be wrong. Diva is weaker due to her pregnancy, and for that reason she dies. One of Diva's chevaliers, Nathan, confesses at the end that Diva wanted to have a family but Amshel pushed the limits of her body for his own ambition. Although Amshel does not intentionally harm the queen because, like all chevaliers, he is emotionally attached to her, his ambition makes him blind: "I want to find out everything about Diva, to search thoroughly, to know thoroughly. This is supreme love" ("Skyscraper Opera," 13:29–37).

Amshel Goldsmith's "desire for mastery motivates enhancement."[18] His actions end in the death of a chiropteran who, in addition to being the strongest of its kind, is his life-giver. It would not be wrong, then, to claim that *Blood+* also shines a fresh light on vampires in terms of villains and victims. From a physically weak human being, Amshel willingly turns into a chiropteran to satisfy his ambition for strength and power, as well as his desire for knowledge. More importantly, after turning into a chiropteran, Amshel does not change his mind, and he continues with his scheme. In other words, he still acts with his human mind as opposed to other human-turned-vampire examples both in literature and film. As a result, *Blood+* creates a character who abuses both human beings and chiropterans around him—intentionally or not.

By availing itself of the contemporary scientific debates of our age, *Blood+* blurs the boundaries between humans and vampires. Boundaries are deconstructed through Darwin's idea of allied species and transhumanist points of view. Use of the scientific discourse of the day by *Blood+* creators domesticates the vampire in its own unique way with a passage from the world of fancy to that of science fiction. Although all of the main characters have the same bodily form—except in times of battle when chevaliers assume a chiropteran form—who is human and who is not is complicated. This complexity is also reflected in the position of villain and victim. Amshel Goldsmith is a hybrid. It is not possible to define him as essentially human or chiropteran. He is the embodiment of both. As a natural result of this, he is the enemy of both species. As Nathan says to Amshel, "[T]here is no need for the world and Diva to exist for the sake of your worthless experiments" ("Skyscraper Opera" 4:24).

We'll never know how natural selection works this out, as the *Blood+* saga has ended . . . for now.

Notes

1. Theresa Bane, *Encyclopedia of Vampire Mythology* (Jefferson, NC: McFarland & Company, 1969), 7.

2. Elain L. Graham, *Representations of the Post/Human: Monsters, Aliens and Others in Popular Culture* (Manchester, UK: Manchester University Press, 2002), 39.

3. Veronica Hollinger, "Fantasies of Absence: The Postmodern Vampire," in *Blood Read: The Vampire as a Metaphor in Contemporary Culture*, ed. Joan Gordon and Veronica Hollinger (Philadelphia: University of Pennsylvania Press, 1997), 201.

4. Graham, *Representations*, 23.

5. Graham, *Representations*, 24.

6. Charles Darwin, *On the Origin of Species*, ed. Gillian Beer (New York: Oxford University Press, 1996), 37.

7. See Barbara Brodman and James E. Doan, eds., *The Universal Vampire: Origins and Evolution of a Legend* (Teaneck, NJ: Fairleigh Dickinson University Press, 2013).

8. Darwin, *On the Origin*, 45.

9. Darwin, *On the Origin*, 131.

10. Nick Bostrom and Julian Savulescu, "Introduction," in *Human Enhancement*, ed. Nick Bostrom and Julian Savulescu (Oxford: Oxford University Press, 2009), 5.

11. Julian Savulescu, "The Human Prejudice and the Moral Status of Enhanced Beings: What Do We Owe the Gods?" in Bostrom and Savulescu, *Human Enhancement*, 214.

12. Savulescu, "The Human Prejudice," 213–14.
13. Savulescu, "The Human Prejudice," 211–12.
14. Quoted in Hollinger, "Fantasies of Absence," 199.
15. Hollinger, "Fantasies of Absence," 199.
16. Bostrom and Savulescu, "Introduction," 1.
17. Savulescu, "The Human Prejudice," 211.
18. Bostrom and Savulescu, "Introduction," 7.

Filmography

"Broken Heart," *Blood+: Volume Two*, writ. Asuka Katsura, dir. Junichi Fujisaku, prod. Katsuji Morishita (Sony Pictures Home Entertainment, 2008), DVD.

"Moon over Ekaterinburg," *Blood+:Volume Two*, writ. Asuka Katsura, dir. Junichi Fujisaku, prod. Katsuji Morishita (Sony Pictures Home Entertainment, 2008), DVD.

"The Red Shield," *Blood+: Volume Two*, writ. Asuka Katsura, dir. Junichi Fujisaku, prod. Katsuji Morishita (Sony Pictures Home Entertainment, 2008), DVD.

"Skyscraper Opera," *Blood+: Volume Four*, writ. Asuka Katsura, dir. Junichi Fujisaku, prod. Katsuji Morishita (Sony Pictures Home Entertainment, 2009), DVD.

16

Adapting *Dracula* to an Irish Context: Reconfiguring the Universal Vampire

James E. Doan and Barbara Brodman

A Play Is Born

WHILE WORKING ON THE FIRST VOLUME in our vampire project, *The Universal Vampire: Origins and Evolution of a Legend*,[1] James decided to try his hand at adapting the novel *Dracula* to a more literal Irish context. Set in London and County Sligo in 1888, it constitutes a prequel to the novel. The play, titled *The Irish Dracula: A Melodrama in Five Acts*, received two initial readings: the first with the Irish Theatre of Florida in August 2012 and the second at the American Conference for Irish Studies (ACIS) West meeting in Park City, Utah, in October 2012, "Ireland and Adaptation." Both of us were involved in the readings, along with actors, theatre professors and graduate students. James later received a mini-grant from Farquhar College (Nova Southeastern University) to do workshops and a staged dramatic reading of the play with Nova Southeastern University students, alumni, faculty members and community actors in March and April 2013.

The play fills a niche in the overall discourse on Bram Stoker's 1897 novel. Though many scholars have noted the Irish origins of themes and authorship of the novel, no one has yet successfully adapted the novel to an Irish (or Anglo-Irish) context. James also decided that melodrama (literally "music" + "drama") was the appropriate genre to use for an adaptation of *Dracula* to a theatrical form, insofar as it involves an exaggerated plot and characters to appeal to the audience's emotions. He hit upon the idea of a prequel that would introduce the real-life author of the novel, Bram Stoker, and the legendary English actor/director Henry Irving, for whom Stoker worked as a

stage and business manager for 27 years, and whom many consider a proto-
type for the title character in the novel.[2] He then added characters based on
those found in the novel, though translated into their respective Irish, English
and Anglo-Irish counterparts, highlighting the hybrid nature of the political
and cultural reality of late-19th-century Britain and Ireland.[3] In addition, he
used real places, such as the Lyceum Theatre in London and Markree Castle
in County Sligo, Ireland, residence of the Cooper family, who have lived there
since the 17th century.[4]

   Even though many view the novel *Dracula* as reveling in heterosexual perversity, a sizable body of scholarship deals with its repressed homoeroticism.[5]
Some scholars have linked it to Stoker's homosexual panic after the arrest and
conviction of Oscar Wilde for "gross indecency" in 1895. Certainly Wilde and
Stoker were intimately connected. In 1878 Stoker married Florence Balcombe,
a Dublin-born beauty who had earlier dated Oscar Wilde. The two writers
remained friends for at least twenty years in Dublin and London until Oscar's
arrest.[6] One view of the novel holds that "*Dracula* explores Stoker's fear and
anxiety as a closeted homosexual man during Wilde's trial."[7] Stoker suppressed
the first chapter of the novel, generally viewed as the most homoerotic in terms
of the relationship between Dracula and Jonathan Harker, and it was only published, as "Dracula's Guest," after his death.[8] Furthermore, Stoker's working
notes for *Dracula*, preserved in the Rosenbach Library, Philadelphia, and dating
from 1890, clearly show his obsession from the beginning of the writing project
with the sentence "This man belongs to me"[9] in the very first outline. Sir Christopher Frayling recently emphasized this during his keynote address on Stoker
and *Dracula* at the conference "Vampire: Myths of the Past and the Future,"
held at the University of London, November 3, 2011, implying that Stoker was
fixated on domination or control of one male by another. This emerges in the
play with two sets of master/servant relationships, Irving and Stoker on one
hand, and Lord Cooper and Tadhg on the other.

   Bram Stoker spent much of his youth in County Sligo, where he would
have heard stories of the 1845–1850 famine, which may have had a subconscious influence on him in later years. James tried to capture a sense of the
horror which the famine (called "The Great Hunger" in Ireland) undoubtedly produced even years later, using true anecdotes such as the drowning
of famine victims in Black Lake, County Mayo, following their unsuccessful
foray to secure food at the Delphi Lodge. *Dearg fhola* ("red of blood") is one
of the possible Irish etymologies for the name "Dracula," though we both
suspect Stoker was thinking of Vlad Dracula, the Romanian prince, when he
constructed his Count.[10] However, the Anglo-Irish landlords he had seen in
his native country weren't far behind the Count in terms of their indifference
to the suffering of their tenantry. Not all the landlords were equally complicit

in the tragedy, however, and some, like the fictional Lord Cooper in the play, did kill the game on their estates to make large cauldrons of soup to feed the starving tenants.

As noted in several of the critical studies of the novel, *Dracula* is filled with various types of gender and political reversals and inversions, including "the return of the repressed." James has maintained these in this play, with Mina Murray, initially depicted as an innocuous typist but later taking on a more masculine role and saving her fiancé, the Gaelicized Seán Haircéar, from Lord Cooper. This also approximates the gender shifts in Oscar Wilde's plays (e.g., in the character of Lady Bracknell in *The Importance of Being Earnest*) and it may, in fact, have deep roots in Irish folklore and mythology.[11] Another reference to Irish myth and ritual occurs in the use of the Béaltaine celebration (April 30–May 1). Though there are no references to human sacrifice or blood-letting in honor of the goddess on this date in modern Irish history, there is certainly clear evidence of prehistoric ritual killing by strangling, stabbing, bludgeoning or hanging and burial in bogs in the British Isles and on the continent.[12] Lucan, Julius Caesar, Suetonius and Cicero all mention the Celtic practice of human sacrifice, which they view as barbaric,[13] with Caesar's reference to Celtic sacrifice of war captives by burning them alive in giant wicker figures, which forms the basis of modern treatments such as *The Wicker Man*.[14] Stoker may have been aware of the Celtic origins of the feast in Ireland, though he substitutes in the novel the parallel Northern and Central European observance Walpurgisnacht (usually April 30–May 1), or specifically St. George's Eve and Day (April 22–23), which he associates with various supernatural phenomena.[15]

This leads to our decision to de-literalize the vampires in the play. After much discussion between us, James chose to present the two villains (namely Irving and Lord Cooper) as metaphorical vampires: the former psychologically and materially manipulating Stoker, and the latter draining the blood of Haircéar, though with a sacrificial knife rather than fangs. This also reflects an earlier tradition of the vampire killing his victim with a knife as found in Polidori's "The Vampyre" from 1819, with which our project began.[16]

The Play

The Irish Dracula: A Melodrama in Five Acts by James E. Doan

Dramatis Personae

Henry Irving, actor/director of the Lyceum Theatre, Wellington Street, Westminster, London—50, tall, slender, with an aristocratic bearing.

Abraham (Bram) Stoker, former Dublin civil servant, now business manager for the Lyceum and part-time novelist—40, greying hair and full, trimmed beard.

Lucilla Desmond, actress of the Lyceum and friend of Stoker—mid-40s, though tries to look younger, an accomplished woman of the world, with dyed blonde hair—a Sarah Bernhardt type.

Mina Murray, an English typist, though of Irish descent, working for Stoker and engaged to Seán Haircéar—early 20s, medium brown hair, rather unassuming.

Seán Haircéar (pronounced "har-ker"), a young solicitor from County Longford working in London—mid-20s, dark-haired, Gaelic type—good-looking, muscular.

Lord Edward Cooper, Anglo-Irish owner of Markree Castle, County Sligo, and would-be part-time resident of London—also appears to be in his late 50s or early 60s, could be played by the same actor as Henry Irving.

Dr. John Seward, physician/amateur psychiatrist, with a clinic in London—late 30s/early 40s, sporting a goatee and moustache, considers himself quite debonair; an admirer of Lucilla.

A messenger—early 20s, Cockney speaker; he later plays a servant (*Tadhg*) at Markree Castle.

The Play Is Set in London and in County Sligo during the Months of April and May, 1888.

Scenes of the Play

Act I, Scene 1—Henry Irving's dressing room, Lyceum Theatre—afternoon, April 26

Act I, Scene 2—Public house, Wellington Street, London—early evening, April 26

Act I, Scene 3—Dressing room, Lyceum Theatre—late that evening

Act II, Scene 1—Drawing room, Markree Castle, County Sligo—early evening, April 30

Act II, Scene 2—Drawing room, Markree Castle—about two hours later

Act II, Scene 3—Mina Murray's bedsit, Notting Hill Gate, London; Seán Haircéar's room, Markree Caste (split stage)—late evening, April 30

Act II, Scene 4—Drawing room, Markree Castle—11:50 p.m. that night

Act III, Scene 1—Stoker's office at the Lyceum Theatre—10:00 a.m., May 2

Act III, Scene 2—Dr. Seward's surgery, near Piccadilly Circus—about 2:00 p.m. that afternoon

Act III, Scene 3—Dr. Seward's surgery—about 5:00 p.m. that day

Act III, Scene 4—Stoker's office—about 1 hour later

Act III, Scene 5—Seán Haircéar's room in Markree Castle—at the same time

Act III, Scene 6—Irving's dressing room at the Lyceum Theatre—about one-half hour later

Act IV, Scene 1—Village inn, Toberbride, County Sligo—early evening, May 5

Act IV, Scene 2—Front of Markree Castle, County Sligo—about 9:00 p.m. that night

Act IV, Scene 3—Drawing room, Markree Castle—2 hours later

Act IV, Scene 4—Seán Haircéar's room, as in Act II, Scene 3—10 minutes later

Act V, Scene 1—Public house, Wellington Street, London, as in Act I, Scene 2—late afternoon, May 25

Act I, Scene 1

Mid-afternoon in Henry Irving's dressing room in the Lyceum Theatre, London. On his table are a script for Macbeth, *make-up jars, a wig, etc. Irving is wearing a dark green tartan kilt and sash over a long-sleeved white shirt. He is charging back and forth holding a claymore (a large, two-edged sword) aimed at an invisible foe and reciting his lines from Act V, Scene 8 of* Macbeth.

IRVING. "Of all men else I have avoided thee. / But get thee back! My soul is too much charged / With blood of thine already."

STOKER (*coming into the dressing room rather sheepishly*). Mr. Irving, there's a problem with tonight's box office returns . . .

IRVING (*putting down the sword*). What is it man? Can't you see I'm trying to rehearse?

STOKER. Sorry, sir, but we seem to have misplaced a good share of the receipts.

IRVING. How much? Speak up!

STOKER. About two hundred pounds, I'm afraid.

IRVING. How could you have misplaced that much!

STOKER. I was distracted when a group of actors burst into the office. They were arguing over whether Macduff should hold your head above his own after decapitating you, or thrust it towards the audience. I thought I put the money in the central desk drawer, but when I looked later I couldn't find it.

IRVING. Well, then, if you can't find it I shall merely dock it from your salary!

STOKER. I'll look, sir.

IRVING (*peremptorily*). Then make sure you do.

IRVING *exits.*

STOKER. How many years have I slaved for that man and never got a word of thanks!

LUCILLA *enters.*

LUCILLA. Bram, darling, what has happened? You look as though you've lost your last, best friend.

STOKER. I'm afraid I've lost a bit of tonight's takings and Irving wants to take it out of my hide.

LUCILLA. He always says those things and never does them.

STOKER. Yes, but this time he seems to be serious.

LUCILLA. Why don't I help you look for it?

STOKER. Would you really?

LUCILLA. Of course, darling: aren't we in this boat together?

STOKER. You're right: and sometimes I think it's rapidly sinking.

LUCILLA *and* STOKER *exchange glances and then exit. End of scene.*

ACT I, Scene 2

Early that evening (about 6:00 p.m.) in a public house adjacent to the theatre, Stoker is sitting at a table drinking a pint of bitters, when in walk Seán Hair-céar and his fiancée, Mina. They are holding hands, obviously in love with each other. They see Stoker and walk over to his table.

STOKER. Good evening, friends. How are you both doing?

SEÁN. Very well, Mr. Stoker.

STOKER. Please call me Bram (*extending his right hand*).

SEÁN. Very well, then, "Bram" (*shaking the proffered hand*).

STOKER. What brings you out to Westminster on a Thursday evening?

MINA (*with a slight Cockney accent*). Seán has been arranging transportation to Sligo this coming Saturday. He's doing some conveyancing for Lord Cooper, who's buying a villa in Pimlico.

STOKER. Very fashionable area that and quite central.

SEÁN. Yes, that appears to be his idea: he wants to be able to come to the theatre, but still be able to go out into the country without much bother.

STOKER. Have you ever met Lord Cooper?

SEÁN. No, I can't say I have. He has only corresponded with my firm of solicitors.

STOKER. I heard in Dublin that he was rather reclusive: that no one sees him but a few servants.

SEÁN. I believe you're right, but now he suddenly wants to go out into the world.

MINA. That does seem rather odd, particularly at his age.

STOKER. Whatever do you mean, Miss Mina: you know a man can go out into the world and even marry whenever he chooses, even at the ripe old age of 60!

MINA. That's not what I meant: it's just that someone who's spent most of his life secluded in an Irish castle isn't likely to want to mingle with the masses in central London.

SEÁN. Well perhaps that explains it: he may have tired of all that countryside and want to see a bit of city life. At any rate, I'll be meeting him by next Monday evening in Sligo.

MINA. I am a bit concerned about your travelling across the Irish Sea and then overland without any chance of rest.

SEÁN. I'm well used to it, my love: remember I come from a village in the Irish Midlands and had to travel a good 20 miles just to get to a decent-sized town. Dublin was a metropolis for me and I can't even say what London's like in comparison to that.

MINA. Ah, for those of us who grew up in London, it's not such a great thing. Often I think I would love to move to Ireland and breathe some fresh Irish air.

SEÁN. You know that's what we plan to do, *a chara*, when I've gotten my solicitor's license and can practice on my own.

STOKER. That sounds a commendable idea to me. I've thought of returning to Dublin, but something . . . or someone . . . here has a strange hold over me . . .

Enter LUCILLA *on the arm of* DR. SEWARD.

LUCILLA (*coming up to the table*). Bram, have you met Dr. John Seward? John, this is my good friend and confidant, Abraham, or Bram, Stoker.

DR. SEWARD (*extending his hand*). Very nice to see you again, old chap. We met when Lucilla was performing last season. In the meanwhile, she has told me so much about you.

STOKER (*slightly taken aback*). Oh, has she now? (*also extending his hand to Seward*).

LUCILLA. Of course all of it extremely complimentary.

DR. SEWARD. She's said that you virtually hold the Lyceum together with little recognition for your efforts.

STOKER (*rather abashed*). Well, that's not entirely true . . .

LUCILLA. Oh darling, you know it is. Whatever would poor Henry do without you . . .

STOKER. I doubt he would like being called "poor."

LUCILLA. You know what I mean. He may be the greatest Shakespearean actor of his day, but he couldn't manage the theatre if his life depended on it.

STOKER. By the way, do you both know Mina Murray, my typist, and her fiancé, Seán Haircéar? Mina and Seán, these are my friends, the actrine Lucilla Desmond and her escort, Dr. John Seward.

DR. SEWARD and LUCILLA (*together*). No, but it's lovely to meet you (*the men shake hands while the women lightly embrace and separate*).

MINA. Miss Desmond, how long have you worked in the theatre?

LUCILLA. Mina, dear, it's been far too long. I was an ingénue when Henry brought his production of *Hamlet* to Dublin in '76 and I played Ophelia, I believe.

STOKER. Actually, my dear Lucilla, I think it was Gertrude.

LUCILLA. Well, either way I was one of the younger members of the company. Certainly Ophelia was one of my greatest roles, second only to Lady M. in the new production.

Enter MESSENGER, *crossing over to* STOKER.

MESSENGER. Beggin' your pardon, gov'nuh, but I have an urgent message from Mr. Irving. He requests your immediate return to sort out somefink or other.

STOKER (*to others, before chugging down the rest of his pint*). Then I guess duty calls and I must go back. Dr. Seward, John, will I see you at the dress rehearsal this evening?

DR. SEWARD. You may depend on it.

STOKER *exits as the others look at him rather bemusedly. End of scene.*

ACT I, Scene 3

Late that evening, in the dressing room, as in Act I, Scene 1. Irving is at his dressing table, removing his make-up, now just wearing the long shirt with ruffled sleeves, open at the neck, without the sash, and with dried fake blood around the neckline.

Enter STOKER.

STOKER. Mr. Irving, I thought the dress rehearsal went quite well, considering . . .

IRVING. What do you mean, "considering"?

STOKER. Well, sir, all the bad luck, with the light can falling from the track, Mr. Conrad toppling from the stage in Act III . . .

IRVING. I told you to mark the stage better.

STOKER. I did, sir, but someone erased the chalk lines.

IRVING. Stoker, how many times have I told you to check on these things before the show begins?

STOKER (*changing the topic*). Ahem, I thought Miss Desmond was in quite good form this evening.

IRVING. Passable, merely passable. She wasn't particularly convincing in her mad scene. All that wringing of her hands to no end.

STOKER. Mr. Irving, have you met her friend Dr. John Seward yet?

IRVING. I have, but what of it?

STOKER. They seem to get on quite well together.

IRVING. Other than the fact he's a bit of a quack, he seems a rather decent fellow.

STOKER. What do you mean by "quack," sir?

IRVING. He experiments with various drugs in the treatments at his clinic, and I hear he also uses a new therapy called hypnosis.

STOKER. And what, pray tell, is this hypnosis used for?

IRVING. Allegedly it's to help patients recover forgotten memories.

STOKER. And what might the purpose of that be?

IRVING. Well, if they've been sexually interfered with, for example, by an uncle or their father even, it would help them remember that.

STOKER. And what would the good of that be? (*then, slipping into Irish brogue*): sure, isn't it better to let the poor creatures forgot anything like that ever happened to them?

IRVING. You bloody Irish are all the same: wanting to pretend nothing evil has ever transpired in the hopes that things will soon get better.

STOKER. Do you mean like the . . . famine?

IRVING. I thought you lot never mentioned that.

STOKER. Normally we don't, only when you talk about evil . . .

IRVING. I hope you're not going to go rabbiting on about how we English were responsible for it!?

STOKER. No, sir, it's just that . . .

IRVING. What, man, speak up!

STOKER. Sir, this year marks the 40th anniversary of the worst of it and I was thinking of going back to the west of Ireland for some commemorations.

IRVING. Well, as long as it doesn't conflict with this production or the one planned for the fall, I really don't care.

STOKER. No, sir, I assumed you didn't which is why I planned to go in May, once this show is completed.

IRVING. Well, then, it's all settled.

End of scene and Act I.

Act II, Scene 1

Drawing room of Markree Castle, County Sligo. The room is appointed in rather old-fashioned, mid-19th-century furnishings which look as though they've seen better days. There's a sofa along the rear right wall, a fireplace against the left wall, and two armchairs with a small table near the sofa, holding an old, leather-bound book and a small bell. Through a window to the left of the chairs and table one can see the sunset over a distant landscape. A servant (Tadhg) in worn livery enters the room through a door on stage right, followed by Seán Haircéar who is carrying a large leather portfolio.

TADHG (*turning to* SEÁN). Mr. Haircéar, I will inform his lordship that you have arrived. I know he has been expecting you. Please sit down while you await his arrival (*leading* SEÁN *to one of the armchairs and looking out the window*) and note the beautiful sunset from this spot!

Exit TADHG.

SEÁN (*sitting down and stretching his legs out*). Well, he might at least have offered me something to drink . . . (*He picks up the book, begins turning the pages and then reads*): "In 1653 John Cooper, Cornet, married the widow, Máire Rua O'Brien, whose husband Conor O'Brien, head of the clan, had been defeated and killed by the Cromwellian army." (*At this point a rustling is heard in the hallway and* SEÁN *closes the book.*)

Enter LORD EDWARD COOPER.

LORD COOPER (*extending his hand towards* SEÁN, *who stands and hurriedly sets the book down*). Mr. Haircéar, I see you have been reading up on my family's history.

SEÁN (*shaking hands with* LORD COOPER). Yes, Sir Edward: I noticed that your ancestors include the famous Máire Rua O'Brien.

LORD COOPER. Yes, she was a formidable woman, forced by the vicissitudes of fate to marry one of her second husband's enemies in order to preserve the family fortune.

SEÁN. Those must have been difficult times: either one married into the new English gentry or faced deportation to Connacht.

LORD COOPER. Right you are, and she must not have been too particular about the Catholic religion, since she was willing to convert to Protestantism to preserve her O'Brien sons' estate and, in fact, they even took the name Cooper. Eventually, Cromwell's bequest included the land and castle you're in now.

SEÁN. Does that bother you at all, the fact that "Old Ironsides," the butcher of Drogheda, endowed your family with the land and wealth they have held ever since?

LORD COOPER. I try not to think about it much. My family has done much good for the peasantry in the intervening 250 years, including large cauldrons of soup during the time of the Great Hunger. I think that has righted any wrongs committed by my ancestors.

SEÁN (*changing the topic*). My lord, I have brought the deed for the villa in Pimlico as you directed my firm.

LORD COOPER. There is no need to get into that immediately. Won't you have a glass of wine or some other refreshments? (*Ringing the small bell*)

Enter TADHG.

TADHG. Yes, milord?

LORD COOPER. Tadhg, would you bring in some claret and a few glasses?

TADHG *bows and exits.*

LORD COOPER. It is so difficult to get good servants these days. Tadhg and his family have been with us since the . . . you know . . . calamity.

SEÁN. Yes, sir, I understand. Many families in this part of the country were forced to move during that period. My own family left Sligo for County Long-ford, hoping to find work. They were lucky, which is why I grew up in Ireland rather than in England or Americay.

LORD COOPER. And then you read law in Dublin?

SEÁN. Yes, I was fortunate enough to be admitted to the Catholic University and from there I moved on to London since there were very few firms hiring in Dublin at the time.

LORD COOPER. Yes, I see. But don't you enjoy the pleasures which London has to offer?

TADHG *enters with tray holding a decanter filled with red wine and two crystal glasses, which he sets on the table and then exits.*

LORD COOPER (*to* SEÁN). Mr. Haircéar, let me pour you some wine. I rarely drink . . . wine . . . but I will share some with you to be sociable. Please sit over here on the sofa, which is much more comfortable. (*He pours two glasses, handing one to* SEÁN *and taking the other for himself. They both sit down on the sofa. He holds the glass towards the setting sun and admires the color and clarity. Then he says, under his breath*) This is a fine wine, paid for by the blood and sweat of my tenants . . . (*next, changing the topic*): Mr. Haircéar, why don't you show me the deed for the property in Pimlico and tell me more about the neighborhood?

SEÁN. Certainly, my lord (*pulling a sheaf of papers from the portfolio*). As you know, much of the district was built during the '20s, though this house is rather newer, yet still in the Regency style. I think you will find it quite comfortable. The villa is large without being too pretentious, and the garden sweeps down to a wooded copse. A ruined abbey lies some small distance from the house, and I've heard it said that the ghosts of monks are occasionally heard reciting their offices.

LORD COOPER (*looking at the document*). How appropriate . . . I mean the fact that the landscape includes a ruined abbey.

SEÁN. Yes, Lord Edward. I gather you have already deposited the required funds, so the document only awaits your signature.

LORD COOPER (*taking the document and reading it over*). Mr. Haircéar, this all seems to be quite correctly executed (*and then signing it*). Now, we need to think about eating something . . .

SEÁN. Milord, I thought I would return to the village inn once we'd completed this transaction.

LORD COOPER. No, I insist: I rarely have company for dinner, especially someone so well appointed . . . I mean educated as yourself. I think a nice, juicy beefsteak would be perfect for the occasion (*summoning* TADHG, *who quickly enters*). Tadhg, please take Mr. Haircéar's bags upstairs to the guest room. He will be staying with us for a few days.

SEÁN. But . . .

LORD COOPER. Mr. Haircéar, I won't take no for an answer.

TADHG *exits and one hears the sound of bags being dragged upstairs.*

LORD COOPER. Now, let me show you the view looking out over our garden here (*standing, helping* SEÁN *to his feet, and leading him to the window*). We are noted throughout the county for the beauty of our roses . . .

End of scene.

Act II, Scene 2

Drawing room of Markree Castle, about two hours later. Seán is seated in one of the armchairs with a brandy snifter in his hand, while Lord Cooper is standing in front of him. He has been holding forth on the history of his family in County Sligo and their estates.

LORD COOPER. So, you see, Mr. Haircéar, we have vastly improved the condition of larger estates in these parts, even though this has meant knocking down a few dilapidated cottages here and there.

SEÁN. But how has this helped the tenants?

LORD COOPER. The peasants had begun leaving even before the Hunger, unable to earn enough to pay the rents. We merely removed the unsightly ruins they left to provide better views.

SEÁN (*setting the glass on a side table and rising to his feet*). What about stories of starving tenants who came to the gates of estates like yours hoping for even a crust of bread?

LORD COOPER. As I said to you before, we had done all we could, even killing off all the game in the forests to cook into giant soups. We couldn't help it that it still wasn't enough and they began dying in droves.

SEÁN. Like the poor souls in Louisburg, who walked twelve miles to Delphi Lodge while your people were at dinner, supping on choice meats, and who were told there was no food for them? And then, when they started walking back, a violent storm came up, which blew them into the Black Lake so that hundreds of them drowned?

LORD COOPER. How was that our fault? We never asked them to come to the lodge, and we certainly couldn't control the weather . . .

End of scene.

Act II, Scene 3

Mina Murray's bedsit in Notting Hill Gate, around 10:00 p.m. There is a small bed, a bedside table and chair and wardrobe. The furniture is respectable, but none of it is very new. A dressing gown has been thrown over the chair, and Mina Murray is lying in bed tossing her head from side to side.

MINA (*in her sleep*). Oh, Seán, my love, where are you? (*Awakening*) Oh, I had the most horrible nightmare that my Seán was wrapped in a giant spider-web with a large black spider spinning down a thread ready to devour him! (*Then she rises from the bed and puts on the dressing gown, while her room grows dark.*)

Then light comes up on the other side to reveal Seán Haircéar's room in Markree Castle. He's lying in a four-poster bed with a red valence and a dark red bedspread covering him. There is another armchair, similar to the ones seen earlier in the drawing room, with his clothes and a towel draped over it. We see him by moonlight coming through an open window.

SEÁN (*tossing in bed*). A Mina mo chroí, tá grá mór agam ort! [Mina of my heart, I love you so much!] (*He reaches his arms out from the bed and awakens.*

Knock at the door. SEÁN *rises from the bed and quickly wraps a towel around his waist.*)

SEÁN. *Tar isteach*, I mean, Come in.

TADHG (*bearing a tray with a glass of milk*). Mr. Haircéar, milord thought you might like something to help you sleep after your long journey.

SEÁN. I had been asleep, but just awoke after having a strange dream. I thought my fiancée, Mina, was endangered back in London.

TADHG. Mr. Haircéar, sir, I imagine that is just from the exhaustion caused by your travels. The milk will undoubtedly soothe you and you'll sleep as soundly as a babe in his mother's arms!

SEÁN. Thanks for that, Tadhg (*drinking the milk*). Oh, this is good: it has a rather sweet taste.

TADHG. Oh, his lordship always insists on adding a special ingredient.

SEÁN. What is it then, chamomile or ginger?

TADHG. I couldn't say, Mr. Haircéar.

SEÁN (*beginning to grow drowsy*). Ah, I think I will sleep better now (*crawling back in bed*). Please thank his lordship for me.

TADHG. I will, sir, oh most definitely.

TADHG *exits*.

Light returns to the other side of the stage, and we see Mina with her hands raised to her head in fear, pulling her hair, looking quite frantic. Lights out. End of scene.

Act II, Scene 4

Drawing room in Markree Castle, same as Act II, scenes 1 and 2, now with a silver chalice on the table. With low lighting, we see TADHG *dragging in a heavy object which, as the light comes up, we see is the semi-nude body of the unconscious* SEÁN. *Tadhg brings him over to the sofa and then props him up on it, with one arm hanging down to the floor.* LORD COOPER *walks over to the prostrate form and takes hold of the arm.*

LORD COOPER (*to* TADHG). The drug seems to have done the trick: he's totally out. It's almost midnight, so the ritual must soon begin. He appears to be a virgin, so the goddess should be pleased.

TADHG. Yes, milord, it will soon be Béaltaine (*pronounced "Bel'-ti-ne"*), the ancient festival of the fires of Béal, and we must have our sacrifice or once again famine will come upon the land.

LORD COOPER. Our Celtic ancestors ended the ritual in the 17th century in the hopes of being accepted by their English overlords and we see what that led to—Cromwell and his men ravaging the land—and in this century the priests once again interfered, wanting to end paganism, leading to the great disaster 40 years ago.

SEÁN *on the sofa begins to stir.*

TADHG (*pulling out a small, bone-handled knife*). We must hurry, Lord Edward, before the victim awakens. (*He hands the knife to* LORD COOPER.)

LORD COOPER. I will cut his vein, while you hold the silver chalice and catch the blood. (*He cuts deeply into* SEÁN's *arm, and we see the blood beginning to flow freely into the chalice.*) Perhaps he will survive—he appears to be a strong youth—but the goddess will have her due . . . .

End of scene and Act II.

Short Intermission

Act III, Scene 1

Stoker sitting at a desk piled with copies of scripts, books and miscellaneous papers. Opposite him (on the other side of the desk) is an old manual typewriter, with a stack of paper next to it.

Enter MINA *with dishevelled hair and clothes, and a distracted air about her.*

STOKER (*looking concerned*). My God, Mina, whatever's wrong?

MINA. I haven't heard from Seán since he left on Saturday morning and I'm terribly worried something has happened to him.

STOKER. Well, it's only been four days.

MINA. Yes, but he planned to be at Markree Castle by Monday evening and he was going to telegraph me after the deed transfer was completed to let me know when he'd be returning.

STOKER. Perhaps the telegraph lines are down.

MINA. No, I checked and they're fine. I even sent a telegram to the inn in the town nearby to see if he'd been there, and they said there was no sign of him.

STOKER. Have you tried getting through to Lord Cooper directly?

MINA. No, because I'm afraid of seeming desperate.

STOKER. Perhaps I could try on your behalf.

MINA. Would you be so good as to do so?

STOKER. Of course, my dear Mina: I would do anything to promote your happiness. You've helped me so much by typing all my manuscripts over the years. Without you I'd never have achieved even the limited success as an author I have now.

MINA. Bram, what you need is a real "pot-boiler," an adventure story where a group of courageous men defeats a force of evil and maybe in the process saves a woman in distress!

STOKER. Mina, that's an excellent idea. I'll start to think about it once we've finished this wretched play. Everyone in theatre always says "The Scottish Play" is cursed, and I'm beginning to believe them! I'll get on the horn this afternoon and try to ring Lord Edward. I'm sure he must have a phone.

MINA. Thank you so much, Bram. I don't know how I'll ever thank you properly. Oh poor Seán, I hope he's alright.

STOKER (*patting her arm*). I'm sure he's fine, my dear Mina: I'm sure he's fine.

End of scene.

Act III, Scene 2

Dr. Seward's surgery near Piccadilly Circus, London. It's well furnished, with a desk and two chairs, a reclining barber's chair with leather straps, an IV machine, a tray of hypodermic needles, etc.

Enter LUCILLA DESMOND.

LUCILLA. John, it was so good of you to see me on such short notice.

DR. SEWARD. Why, whatever is the matter, my dear Lucilla?

LUCILLA. I've had these terrible headaches ever since I was a young girl almost 40, I mean 30, years ago, and they've begun to grow worse.

DR. SEWARD. Well, then I shall examine you and we will try to figure out their cause. Why don't you sit down here? (*pointing to the chair; he begins to feel her temples*). Does it hurt here . . . or here?

LUCILLA. No, John, it is more behind my eyes.

DR. SEWARD. That sounds like a migraine to me.

LUCILLA. And what causes them?

DR. SEWARD. We don't really know, but it could be triggered by light sensitivity.

LUCILLA. I'll try to keep the lights lower at home and in my dressing room at the theatre, but it's very difficult to control the light strength on stage.

DR. SEWARD. I understand, but I'll speak to Mr. Irving about it: perhaps we can redirect the lights somewhat.

LUCILLA. That might be worth trying . . . By the way, I have something else I'd like to mention, but you must promise not to tell anyone.

DR. SEWARD. Whatever is that, my dear?

LUCILLA. Young Mina, Bram's typist, has been having fainting spells and while she's unconscious she speaks of horrors happening to her beloved Seán.

DR. SEWARD. What sort of things does she describe?

LUCILLA. That he's being attacked by some kind of monstrous being, seeking to devour his blood, that sort of thing . . .

DR. SEWARD. That sounds rather serious. Why don't you bring her around to the surgery later this afternoon?

LUCILLA. I'll see if she's free. She was going to do some typing on Mr. Stoker's new novel.

DR. SEWARD. Very well, ring me here if she's able to come in. I should be available by 5:00 or so.

End of scene.

Act III, Scene 3

The same as in the former scene: it is later in the day, so the light is lower. Dr. Seward is doing paperwork at his desk.

Enter LUCILLA *and* MINA.

MINA. Dr. Seward (*extending her hand*), it is so good of you to see me on such short notice.

DR. SEWARD. Not at all, my dear Miss Mina. Lucilla here is quite worried about you. Why don't you lie on this reclining chair: I'd like to hypnotize you.

MINA. Will this hurt? (*as she lies on the reclining chair. Meanwhile Lucilla is standing to one side.*)

DR. SEWARD. Not at all, Mina. You won't even remember a thing. (He then takes a pocket watch from his waistcoat, and begins using it as a pendulum). Now, I want you to begin counting back from 100 . . . 99 . . . 98 . . .

MINA (*chiming in*). 97 . . . 96 . . . 95 (*then is apparently unconscious*). NO, don't hurt him (*yelling and writhing in her chair*). Get away from him! You horrible old man, why do you want his blood?

LUCILLA (*looking on aghast*). There she goes again, about the blood!

MINA. *A dearg fhola, dearg fhola* [pronounced "jar'-go-la"].

LUCILLA (*to DR. SEWARD*). Whatever does that mean?

DR. SEWARD. It sounds like Gaelic, "red of blood": one of my professors taught me a bit of it. We'd better awaken her (*he then begins shaking her shoulder gently*). Miss Mina, you may awaken now.

MINA (*begins to rouse*). Dr. Seward, what happened while I was asleep?

DR. SEWARD. I think you are psychically empathic with Seán, so you are somehow intuiting what is happening to him. I fear he is in grave danger.

MINA. Why do you say that?

DR. SEWARD. While you were unconscious you spoke of an old man seeking Seán's blood? Do you have any idea why?

MINA. No, except that I also had a nightmare Monday night in which a giant creature was trying to devour my Seán: maybe it's related to that?

DR. SEWARD. I have no idea, but I think we should ask Mr. Stoker's advice. He has family from that part of Ireland and is well aware of the local superstitions. I think we should stop by his office and see if he has any idea what's going on.

MINA and LUCILLA. Yes, by all means (*looking at each other in surprise and then taking each other's hand*).

End of scene.

Act III, Scene 4

Stoker's office as before. It is now growing dark, and we see Stoker behind his desk with his feet up on it, smoking a cigar.

DR. SEWARD (*bursting in*). Good heavens, man, at last we find you here!

STOKER. John, whatever is the matter?

MINA *and* LUCILLA *enter more demurely and move to the opposite side of the desk.*

DR. SEWARD. While Mina was under hypnosis she revealed some very disturbing things, namely that Seán may be in dire straits in Ireland.

MINA. Bram, were you able to reach Lord Cooper in Sligo?

STOKER. No, damn and blast: it appears the man hasn't caught up with modern technology and refuses to get a 'phone. The village telegraph office won't deliver a message to him. I fear I will have to travel there myself to get to the bottom of this matter.

DR. SEWARD, LUCILLA and MINA. Then, we're all coming, too (*looking at each other in surprise*).

STOKER. Very well, then, I'd best tell Mr. Irving: he won't be best pleased, but there's nought I can do about it!

End of scene.

Act III, Scene 5

Seán Haircéar's room in Markree Castle as in Act II, Scene 3. He is lying semi-conscious on the bed, stirring occasionally and groaning softly. A shadowy, cloaked figure enters through the door and approaches the bed. When she removes the hood we realize that it is Mina, though in spirit form. She lifts Seán from the bed and holds him upright, though his body is limp. She then begins to dance slowly with him, crooning softly.

MINA. Seán, *a chara*, never fear: we are coming for you. My love for you will carry us.

End of scene.

Act III, Scene 6

Henry Irving's dressing room, as in Act I, Scene 1. Irving is sitting at his table, reading a script. There's a short knock at the door and Stoker enters.

IRVING. What are you doing here, man. I thought you'd left for the day.

STOKER. I planned to, Mr. Irving, but something has come up which requires my immediate attention.

IRVING. And what is that, if you don't mind.

STOKER. Young Mr. Haircéar, Mina's fiancé, has apparently disappeared in Ireland and no one seems to know where he is. Moreover, she's had some rather disturbing dreams about him and while under hypnosis with Dr. Seward revealed he may be in terrible jeopardy.

IRVING. There you go again about Seward and his voodoo medicine. You know I don't believe in those things.

STOKER. Well I do, and she does, and that's what matters here.

IRVING. You mean to just up and leave like that, in the middle of this production?

STOKER. Yes, that's exactly what I mean. I'm sure you'll manage in my absence.

IRVING. Then take a long holiday in Ireland, because you may not have a job when you return.

STOKER. Well, then, Mr. Irving, au revoir, or as they say in Ireland, "See ya."

End of scene and Act III.

Intermission

Act IV, Scene 1

Village inn, Toberbride, County Sligo (a few kilometers from Markree Castle), around sunset. The stage shows the exterior of the building, a whitewashed, thatched cottage with flower boxes filled with geraniums and petunias, as well as a bench along the front. Mina Murray and Lucilla Desmond are sitting on the bench. They are wearing travelling clothes and light boots.

LUCILLA (*rubbing one of her boots*). My God, Mina, aren't you exhausted after all the travelling?

MINA. I am, but I want to go up to Markree Castle as soon as we can to enquire about Seán.

LUCILLA. I'm sure Dr. Seward and Bram will soon be back after sorting out our rooms. It's fortunate the inn was able to put us up on such short notice.

MINA. Did you notice the strange look the innkeeper gave us when Bram said we planned to go up to the Castle?

LUCILLA. And did you also see the quick sign of the cross he made when Bram mentioned Lord Cooper's name?

MINA. Yes: I do have an uneasy feeling about this place.

STOKER *and* DR. SEWARD *enter from the interior of the inn. Both are wearing light travelling suits and boots.*

STOKER. Well, at least they were able to arrange three rooms for us. Dr. Seward and I can share one, and each of you ladies will have your own, though sharing a single bathroom. However, they do have indoor toilets unlike the tavern where we stopped for lunch!

MINA. Bram, thank you so much for arranging this and taking in our satchels.

STOKER. No problem at all, my dear Mina. We also obtained directions to the Castle from here: it's only about a mile or so.

DR. SEWARD. I suggest we have a bite to eat before walking there: one needs to keep up one's strength in these situations.

LUCILLA. I agree: I'm simply famished after journeying by train from Dublin, and then by coach from Athlone. I thought we'd never get here.

STOKER. I realize things are a bit more primitive than you're used to in London, dear Lucilla.

LUCILLA. Bram, I realize that. I don't see how the Irish manage with these rutted dirt roads. It felt as though the wheels on the coach would break from the constant vibration. I doubt my English ancestors would have put up with these inconveniences!

STOKER. Lucilla, darling, your English ancestors? Why, your antecedents are as Irish as your hair roots are dark! Where do you think the Desmonds come from?

LUCILLA. I have no idea, Bram: I always assumed they were Norman, "from the mounts," or something.

STOKER. No, Lucilla, though they may be descended from the Norman-Welsh sons of Gerald, they are as Irish as I am.

DR. SEWARD. At any rate, Bram, we need to get in to supper before the dining room closes.

STOKER. You are absolutely right, John.

End of scene.

Act IV, Scene 2

Front of Markree Castle, in the baronial style, with large blocks of masonry, sconces in the form of male torsos holding lit torches on either side of a heavy, oak door with iron bars and a circular iron knock, and a semicircular gravel driveway leading to the entrance.

Enter STOKER, DR. SEWARD, LUCILLA *and* MINA, *walking along the driveway up to the Castle entrance.*

DR. SEWARD. This is certainly a formidable entry way!

STOKER. Yes, and no one could ever break into this establishment.

MINA (*clutching her shoulders*). I get a chill just looking at it.

LUCILLA. Do you think we should just go up and knock on the door?

STOKER. Why not? (*He proceeds to take the circular knocker and bang heavily on the door, which resonates with the sound. Several seconds lapse and we then see the door slowly opening. TADHG comes forth.*)

TADHG. Good evening. May I ask what you are seeking? We get very few visitors to the Castle.

MINA. Good sir, we are looking for my fiancé, a solicitor named Seán Haircéar, who came here on a business matter this past Monday.

TADHG. I'm afraid no one of that name has been here.

STOKER. But he was scheduled to meet with Lord Edward Cooper to convey a deed for a property in London.

TADHG. You would need to speak with his lordship about that.

STOKER. Is his lordship at home?

TADHG. I'm afraid not: he was called out rather suddenly on a most urgent matter. His friend, Lord Bunbury, has taken ill and he's gone to provide some aid.

DR. SEWARD. And when do you expect him to return?

TADHG. I'm not at all sure: his lordship doesn't consult with me on his comings and goings.

DR. SEWARD. Well, if he does return, could you ask him to let us know if he's heard anything from Mr. Haircéar? We are staying at the inn in Toberbride [pronounced "to-ber-bree'-je"].

TADHG. If he returns . . .

STOKER. Well, then, good night! (TADHG *retreats into the Castle and closes the door.*)

LUCILLA. What a disagreeable man! I'm not at all certain that his lordship was not lurking behind the door listening to the whole conversation.

DR. SEWARD. You may be right: the servant seemed to be hiding something.

STOKER. I think we should come back later tonight and see if we can find another entrance. I have newfangled electric torches in my bag which we can bring back with us.

LUCILLA. Very good: if Seán is here, we will find him.

End of scene.

Act IV, Scene 3

Drawing room of Markree Castle, as in Act II, scenes 1 and 2. The room is set up as before, though the table is now bare. We see the window in the center slowly opening.

STOKER (*sticking his head through*). I don't see anyone here. (*He pulls himself through and drops to the floor and then lends a hand to* LUCILLA *who comes in next, followed by* MINA *and then* DR. SEWARD. *They are all holding flashlights.*)

DR. SEWARD (*looking around*). It does seem rather quiet here—I notice the fireplace isn't even lit.

LUCILLA (*walking across the room to the door*). I'll look into the hallway to see if there's any sign of life (*she opens the door and enters, returning a few moments later*). No, nothing at all, which seems very odd. Not even a mastiff or Irish wolfhound. (*They then hear a sound from the hallway as if something has crashed.*)

MINA. I'm going to go through every room in this castle if necessary until I find my Seán. (*She then exits through the door.*)

STOKER. I guess we have no recourse but to follow her lead. Let's break up so we can search the whole castle. Lucilla, you come with me, and John, why don't you go with Mina. (*Exeunt all.*)

End of scene.

Act IV, Scene 4

Seán Haircéar's room, as in Act II, scene 3. We see Seán's arms tied to the top posters of the bed. He appears to be unconscious, but still alive. Enter MINA, *followed by* DR. SEWARD.)

MINA (*shouting*). I see Seán and I think he's alive! (*She runs over to the bed.*) My God, what have they done to you!

DR. SEWARD (*coming up next to her, beginning to untie* SEÁN's *arms and then rubbing them*). He's lost a lot of blood (*and then putting his head on* SEÁN's *chest*), but he's still breathing.

Enter LUCILLA *and* STOKER.

STOKER. You've found him then.

DR. SEWARD. Yes, we have, but he's barely alive. It looks as though he's been drained of his blood.

LUCILLA. Those blood-sucking bastards!

Enter TADHG, *holding the bone-handled knife seen in Act II, Scene 4.*

TADHG. Get away from him: he belongs to the goddess.

STOKER. What do you mean, man?

TADHG: His blood was drained in a sacrificial rite on Béaltaine. And now none of you will ever leave this castle. (*He lunges with the knife towards* STOKER, *who quickly disarms him and pockets the knife.*)

TADHG: Damn!

STOKER: I bet you all didn't know I was a champion boxer while at Trinity! (*He holds* TADHG's *arms behind him. Just then* LORD COOPER *enters with a larger dagger drawn.*)

MINA (*shouting*). Look out, Bram: someone else is coming in with a dagger.

STOKER (*letting go of* TADHG, *who falls to the floor*). You must be Lord Cooper.

LORD COOPER. That is I, and you must be some of Seán's infernal friends. I knew I shouldn't have let him live.

DR. SEWARD. So, Lord Cooper, what do you mean to do with us?

LORD COOPER. Perhaps the goddess will have an even larger sacrifice than usual.

LUCILLA. You mean to kill us all?

LORD COOPER (*laughing*). I do, fair lady, unless you can think of another solution.

LUCILLA. We could always just take Seán and pretend none of this ever happened . . .

LORD COOPER. At least until you got back to London, you mean. (*While they've been speaking,* MINA *has come around behind* LORD COOPER. *She pounces on his back, at which time he drops the dagger.* STOKER *goes to grab it, and a fight ensues between the two men. They tussle over the dagger.* COO-PER *holds it over* STOKER's *head ready to stab him, when* STOKER *pulls out the bone-handled knife and stabs* COOPER *in the chest.* COOPER *falls and grabs the end of the knife.*) Well, you and your accursed friends have done it: you've ended the Béaltaine ritual forever. I guess *I* am the goddess's last victim. (*He dies.*)

TADHG. I can't believe it: you've killed the master. (*Fade out.*)

End of scene and Act IV.

Act V, Scene 1

Public house on Wellington Street, London, as in Act I, Scene 2. At a large round table are seated STOKER *and* DR. SEWARD *with* LUCILLA *next to him. The latter is drinking a glass of white wine, while the men are drinking pints of beer. It is the evening of May 25, about three weeks after the previous act. Everyone has been drinking and they are obviously all in a good mood. There is a buzz in the background, as if the public house is fairly crowded.*

DR. SEWARD (*to* STOKER). So, you say you heard from the constabulary in Sligo Town today that they don't plan to prosecute the death of Lord Cooper.

STOKER: No, apparently there had been reports of mysterious disappearances in connection with Markree Castle for quite some time, as well as complaints of odd behavior concerning Lord Cooper, so they decided his death may have been warranted.

DR. SEWARD: That must have been quite a relief for you.

STOKER: You have no idea, my good man.

DR. SEWARD: And how are things going with Mr. Irving?

STOKER: Better since we returned. He actually seems to appreciate what I do for him!

Enter SEÁN, *with his arm bandaged and looking rather frail, supported by* MINA.

SEÁN (*to the rest of the assembly*). So, it's been decided: Mina and I are to have a June wedding! (*General applause; then* SEÁN *takes* MINA's *hand.*) If it hadn't been for her, I don't know whether any of us would have survived . . .

MINA: It was nothing no other red-blooded, Irishwoman wouldn't have done.

LUCILLA: Yes, I guess we're all Irish under the skin.

DR. SEWARD: Well, perhaps not all of us . . . unless you want to count by marriage.

STOKER: You mean . . .

DR. SEWARD: Yes, Lucilla and I are to be married, too (*taking* LUCILLA'S *hand*).

STOKER: Well, then this is a time for celebration.

DR. SEWARD: I guess we could conclude that Lord Cooper actually brought us all together and showed us the vital importance of being . . .

LUCILLA: What, my darling?

DR. SEWARD: Earnestly, I can't recall what I was going to say.

End of scene and Act V.

Curtain.

Notes

1. Barbara Brodman and James E. Doan, eds., *The Universal Vampire: Origins and Evolution of a Legend* (Teaneck, NJ: Fairleigh Dickinson University Press), 2013.

2. Barbara Belford explores this in her biography *Bram Stoker and the Man Who Was Dracula* (Cambridge, MA: Perseus Books, 1996). Irving's imperious mannerisms and his penchant for playing villainous roles, such as Richard III and Macbeth, made him a natural to serve as a model for Count Dracula in the novel. Interestingly, Irving never agreed to play Dracula on stage. He was knighted by Queen Victoria in 1895.

3. The Irish cultural context for the novel has been suggested by numerous scholars, including most recently Paul E. H. Davis in "Dracula Anticipated: The 'Undead' in Anglo-Irish Literature," in Brodman and Doan, *The Universal Vampire*, 17–32. Joseph Valente explores this in *Dracula's Crypt: Bram Stoker, Irishness and the Question*

of Blood (Urbana: University of Illinois Press, 2002); as does Paul Murray in *From the Shadow of Dracula: A Life of Bram Stoker* (London: Jonathan Cape, 2004).

4. Of course, Lord Edward Cooper in the play is entirely fictional and meant to bear no resemblance to anyone living or dead.

5. For example, Christopher Craft, "'Kiss Me with Those Red Lips': Gender and Inversion in Bran Stoker's Dracula," *Representations* 8 (1984): 107–33; Marjorie Howes, "The Mediation of the Feminine: Bisexuality, Homoerotic Desire, and Self-Expression in Bran Stoker's *Dracula*," *Texas Studies in Literature and Language* 30 (1988): 104–19; and Elaine Showalter, *Sexual Anarchy: Gender and Culture at the Fin de Siècle* (New York: Viking Penguin, 1990).

6. However, Stoker apparently visited Wilde on the continent after his release from prison: see "Why Dracula Never Loses His Bite," *Irish Times*, January 4, 2009.

7. Talia Schaffer, "'A Wilde Desire Took Me': The Homoerotic History of *Dracula*," *English Literary History* 61 (1994): 381–425. James deliberately used numerous Wildean paraphrases, and even direct allusions to his plays, such as *The Importance of Being Earnest*, in this work to highlight the close connection between the two writers.

8. It was published in *Dracula's Guest and Other Weird Stories* (London: George Routledge and Sons, 1914).

9. The line, of course, occurs in the novel at the moment when Count Dracula discovers his vampire brides seducing Harker. Bram Stoker, *Dracula* (1897), ed. John Paul Riquelme (Boston and New York: Bedford/St. Martin's, 2002), 62. See also Joseph S. Bierman, "The Genesis and Dating of *Dracula* from Bram Stoker's Working Notes," *Notes and Queries* 24 (1977): 39–41.

10. This identification is seen as early as Bacil F. Kirtley's article "*Dracula*, the Monastic Chronicles and Slavic Folklore," *Midwest Folklore* 6 (1956), and it has since become a staple of Dracula scholarship. However, it has been challenged by such scholars as Elizabeth Miller, David Skal and Daniel Farson. See Elizabeth Miller, *Reflections on Dracula* (White Rock, BC: Transylvania Press), ch. 1.

11. See, for example, Michael Patrick Laponte, *Between Irishmen: Queering Irish Literary and Cultural Nationalisms* (dissertation, University of British Columbia, 2007) for a recent study of this in relation to numerous 19th- to 21st-century Irish writers.

12. See "Bog bodies of Northern Europe," Wikipedia, http://en.wikipedia.org/wiki/Bog_bodies_of_Northern_Europe, for a detailed list of occurrences.

13. See "Druid," Wikipedia, http://en.wikipedia.org/wiki/Druid, for further citations.

14. Based on David Pinner's novel *Ritual* (London: Hutchinson/Arrow, 1967), there have been two film versions of *The Wicker Man*, the first in 1973, written by Anthony Shaffer and directed by Robin Hardy and critically acclaimed, with a second, far less successful remake, directed by Neil LaBute in 2006.

15. Cristina Artenie deals with the confusion over the dates between the Western (Gregorian) and Eastern Orthodox calendars in "Dracula's Kitchen: A Glossary of Transylvanian Cuisine, Language and Ethnography," in Brodman and Doan, *The Universal Vampire*, 48–51.

16. John William Polidori, "The Vampyre," in *The New Monthly Magazine and Universal Register* 1 (1819).

Selected Bibliography

Auerbach, Nina. *Our Vampires, Ourselves*. Chicago: University of Chicago Press, 1995.

Backus, Margot. *The Gothic Family Romance*. Durham, NC: Duke University Press, 1999.

Bane, Theresa. *Encyclopedia of Vampire Mythology*. Jefferson, NC: McFarland & Company, 1969.

Barber, Paul. *Vampires, Burial and Death, Folklore and Reality*. New York: Yale University Press, 2010.

Barthes, Roland, *The Language of Fashion*. Oxford: Berg, 2006.

———. *Mythologies*. London: Vintage, 1993.

Beahm, George. *Bedazzled: Stephenie Meyer and the "Twilight" Phenomenon*. London: J. R. Books, 2009.

Belford, Barbara. *Bram Stoker and the Man Who Was Dracula*. Cambridge, MA: Perseus Books, 1996.

Botting, Fred. *Gothic*. London: Routledge, 1996.

Butler, Judith. *Gender Trouble: Feminism and the Subversity of Identity*. London: Routledge, 1990.

Carter, Margaret L. "The Vampire as Alien in Contemporary Fiction." In *Blood Read: The Vampire as Metaphor in Contemporary Culture*, edited by Joan Gordon and Veronica Hollinger. 27–44. Philadelphia: University of Pennsylvania Press, 1997.

Charnas, Suzy Mckee. "Meditations in Red: On Writing the "Vampire Tapestry,"" in *Blood Read: The Vampire as Metaphor in Contemporary Culture*. 59–68.

Chaudhuri, Shohini. "Visit of the Body Snatchers: Alien Invasion Themes in Vampire Narratives." *Camera Obscura: A Journal of Feminism, Culture, and Media Studies* 40–41 (1997): 181–98.

Craik, Jennifer. *The Face of Fashion: Cultural Studies in Fashion*. London: Routledge, 1993.

Douglas, Mary. *Purity and Danger: An Analysis of the Concepts of Pollution and Taboo*. New York: Routledge, 1966.

Dundes, Alan, ed. *The Vampire: A Casebook*. Madison: University of Wisconsin Press, 1998.

Enwistle, Joanne. *The Fashioned Body: Fashion Dress and Modern Social Theory*. Cambridge: Polity, 2002.

Graham, Elain L. *Representations of the Post/human: Monsters, Aliens and Others in Popular Culture*. Manchester, UK: Manchester University Press, 2002.

Heiland, Donna. *Gothic and Gender: An Introduction*. Oxford: Blackwell Publishing, 2004.

Hollinger, Veronica. "Fantasies of Absence: The Postmodern Vampire." In *Blood Read: the Vampire as Metaphor in Contemporary Culture*. 199–212.

Hoppenstand, Gary and Ray B. Browne, eds. *The Gothic World of Anne Rice*. Bowling Green, OH: Bowling Green State University Popular Press, 1996.

Jackson, Kevin. *Bite: A Vampire Handbook*. London: Portobello Books, 2009.

Kristeva, Julia. *Powers of Horror: An Essay on Abjection,* trans. Leon S. Roudiez. New York: Columbia University Press, 1982.

Levinas, Emmanuel. *Totality and Infinity: An Essay on Exteriority*. trans. Alphonso Lingis. Pittsburgh, PA: Duquesne University Press, 1969.

McClellend, Bruce. *Slayers and their Vampires: A Cultural History of Killing the Dead*. Ann Arbor: University of Michigan Press, 2006.

Murray, Paul. *From the Shadow of Dracula: A Life of Bram Stoker*. London: Jonathan Cape, 2004.

Parasecoli, Fabio. *Bite Me: Food in Popular Culture*. Oxford: Berg, 2008.

Polidori, J. W. *The Vampyre and Other Tales of the Macabre*. Oxford: Oxford World's Classics, 2008.

Rickels, Laurence. *The Vampire Lectures*. Minneapolis: University of Minnesota Press, 1999.

Sceats, Sarah. "Oral Sex: Vampiric Transgression and the Writing of Angela Carter." *Tulsa Studies in Women's Literature* 20 (2001): 107–121.

Schofield Clark, Lynn. *From Angels to Aliens: Teenagers, the Media, and the Supernatural*. Oxford: Oxford University Press, 2003.

Stoker, Bram. *Dracula*. London: Penguin Books, 2003.

——. *Dracula*, edited by John Paul Riquelme. New York: St. Martin's, 2002.

Summers, Montague. *The Vampire: His Kith and Kin*. New York: University Books, 1928.

Tomc, Sandra. "Dieting and Damnation: Anne Rice's *Interview with the Vampire*." In *Blood Read: The Vampire as Metaphor in Contemporary Culture*, 95–113.

Valente, Joseph. *Dracula's Crypt: Bram Stoker, Irishness and the Question of Blood*. Urbana: University of Illinois Press, 2002.

Williams, David. *Deformed Discourse: The Function of the Monster in Medieval Thought and Literature.* Exeter, UK: University of Exeter Press, 1996.

Williamson, Milly. *The Lure of the Vampire: Gender, Fiction and Fandom from Bram Stoker to Buffy.* London: Wallflower, 2005.

Wilson, Elizabeth, "Fashion and the Postmodern Body." In *Chic Thrills,* edited by Juliet Ash and Elizabeth Wilson, 3–15. London: Pandora, 1992.

———. "Feminism and Fashion." In *The Fashion Reader,* edited by Linda Welters and Abbey Lillethun, 323–31. Oxford: Berg, 2011.

Index

About the Editors and Contributors

Photo Credit: Bob Eighmie

Barbara Brodman is professor of humanities at Nova Southeastern University. She holds master and doctoral degrees in Hispanic languages and literature, Latin American studies, and international business, and she has published widely in international arts and affairs. She has collaborated with James Doan for the past seven years on a number of vampire projects, including a paper they coauthored on Don Juan and the romantic vampire and a book, *The Universal Vampire: Origins and Evolution of a Legend*. They are currently planning a conference on Ireland and the supernatural, to be held in Fort Lauderdale, Florida, in 2014.

James E. Doan is a professor of Humanities at Nova Southeastern University, where he teaches courses in literature, the arts, and folklore and mythology, including a course on the vampire, which he has taught for over twenty years. He holds an M.A. in folklore and mythology (University of Southern California), and an M.A. in Celtic languages and literature as well as a Ph.D. in folklore and Celtic studies from Harvard University. He authored the play, *The Irish Dracula: A Melodrama in Five Acts*, included in this volume, and coedited *The Universal Vampire: Origins and Evolution of a Legend* with his colleague Barbara Brodman.

About the Contributors

Zélie Asava is a faculty lecturer at University College Dublin and Institute of Art, Design and Technology (Dun Laoghaire). She is the author of many articles on the intersection between race, gender, and sexuality in Irish, French, African, and American cinema. She has published and taught on horror films, and she wrote her M.A. thesis on contemporary representations of black vampires in film. In 2009 she completed her Ph.D. on mixed-race representations in American and French cinema.

Simon Bacon is an independent scholar currently doing research for a project titled "The Vampire in Neverland: The Eternal Child in Film and Literature." He organized the conference Vampires: Myth of the Past and the Future, held at the University of London in November 2011, and he is editing the post-conference publication with a forward by Sir Christopher Frayling. He also edits the academic journal *Monsters and the Monstrous*, and he has published numerous essays dealing with the vampire through the ages.

Alaina Christensen earned an M.A. in English literature from Colorado State University. Her M.A. final project utilized the work of Jean Baudrillard to examine the phenomenon around vampires in contemporary pop culture, emphasizing the metaphorical identity construction that takes place in the relationship between female readers and vampire bodies. She is currently pursuing independent adventures in academia.

Burcu Genç is currently a Ph.D. candidate at the University of Kent and an English teacher at Istanbul Aydin University. Her publications include *Masochistic Men and Female Vampires: A New Approach to Rape Fantasy, An Exploration of Rape Fantasy through the Female Vampires of Romantic and Victorian Periods.*

Sarah Heaton is senior lecturer and deputy head of English at the University of Chester. She gained her Ph.D. at Keele University, and her main research focus is architecture, the rise of the department store, and fashion in literature. She is currently working on a monograph, *Fashioning the Transatlantic*, a chapter of which, "Consuming Clothes and Dressing Desire in the *Twilight* series," was published in *The Human Vampire*.

Karin Hirmer completed an M.A. at the University of Regensburg in 2003 with a thesis titled "Crying Men: Masculinity and Its Connection to Crying in 20th-century Literature." She is currently finishing her Ph.D. dissertation "Control in American Drama of the 1990s." In addition to gender studies, she specializes in media studies, in particular contemporary film and TV shows. A paper on *Smallville*'s Lois Lane will be published soon.

Hope Jennings is an assistant professor of English at Wright State University, Lake Campus. Her research examines the intersection of myth and gender in women's writing, with essays and criticism in the *Journal of Contemporary Literature*; *Margaret Atwood Studies*; and *Interdisciplinary Humanities*. She also has chapters on Angela Carter in two forthcoming anthologies.

Murray Leeder holds a Ph.D. from Carleton University and teaches at both Carleton and Algonquin College. He previously published an essay on the vampire film *Fright Night* (1985) in the *Journal of Popular Film and Television*, along with other articles in such journals as *Early Modern Visual Culture*; *Journal of Popular Culture, Popular Music and Society*; the *Irish Journal of Gothic and Horror Studies*; and the *Canadian Journal of Film Studies*.

Marie-Luise Loeffler earned her M.A. from the University of Leipzig in 2006, majoring in American studies and art history. She is currently working on her Ph.D. at the American Studies Department of the University of Leipzig and has researched extensively as a visiting scholar at the Center for Comparative Studies in Race and Ethnicity at Stanford University, focusing on the construction of interracial relationships in contemporary African American women's vampire fiction.

Cheyenne Mathews holds a B.A. in speech communication from the University of Louisiana, Monroe, and an M.A. in literature from Texas State University. She is an independent scholar who specializes in pop-culture studies through literary and cultural analysis. This is her first essay on vampire mythology.

Donna Mitchell is completing a Ph.D. in English literature at Mary Immaculate College, University of Limerick, Ireland. Her thesis is titled "How the Silent Female Found Her Voice," and it focuses on the evolution of the female figure in the Gothic literary genre. Her M.A. research and dissertation focused on the contemporary Gothic hero in Anne Rice's work. Her conference papers have been based specifically on the Gothic female.

Ben Murnane is completing his Ph.D. in the School of English, Trinity College, Dublin. He is the author of three books, including a memoir, *Two in a Million*, and a collection of poetry, *Feather Silence*. Ben has written for several newspapers and for Irish national radio. He is also writer/director, with Emma Eager, of an award-winning short film, *Two Suitcases*.

Melissa Olson has degrees in English literature and film studies from the University of Southern California, as well as an M.A. in creative writing from the University of Wisconsin, Milwaukee. Her work has been published in the *Chippewa Falls Herald Telegram* and the *International Journal of Comic Review* at the University of Wisconsin, Milwaukee. Her urban fantasy novel *Dead Spots* was published in 2012.

Batia Boe Stolar is an associate professor of English at Lakehead University, where she teaches Canadian and American literature, film studies, literary theory, and the Gothic. Her work has been published in collections such as *Downtown Canada* and *Image and Territory: Essays on Atom Egoyan*.

Victoria Williams received a Ph.D. at King's College, London, for a thesis examining the role of continental European fairytales in 19th-century British literature and art, and in film. Her research interests focus on fairytales, folklore, and the Gothic, particularly in relation to Victorian literature, and British and American film. She has contributed many entries to *Movies in*

American History: An Encyclopedia and written on Ingrid Bergman's female Gothic films for the *Directory of World Cinema: Sweden*.

Christine Wilson is an instructor at Wright State University, Lake Campus, where she teaches English. She received her Ph.D. from Michigan State University. Her essays and criticism have appeared in *Legacy, Popular Ghosts* and *Red Cedar Review*.